GOVERNANCE

FRAMEWORKS

GOVERNANCE FRAMEWORKS

For Public Project Development and Estimation

Ole Jonny Klakegg, MSc

Terry Williams, PhD, PMP

Ole Morten Magnussen, MSc

Project Management Institute

GOVERNANCE FRAMEWORKS for Public Project Development and Estimation

ISBN: 978-1-933890-78-4

Published by:

Project Management Institute, Inc.
14 Campus Boulevard
Newtown Square, Pennsylvania 19073-3299 USA.
Phone: +610-356-4600
Fax: +610-356-4647
E-mail: customercare@pmi.org
Internet: www.PMI.org/Marketplace

PMI Publications welcomes corrections and comments on its books. Please feel free to send comments on typographical, formatting, or other errors. Simply make a copy of the relevant page of the book, mark the error, and send it to: Book Editor, PMI Publications, 14 Campus Boulevard, Newtown Square, PA 19073-3299 USA.

To inquire about discounts for resale or educational purposes,
please contact the PMI Book Service Center.

PMI Book Service Center
P.O. Box 932683, Atlanta, GA 31193-2683 USA
Phone: 1-866-276-4764 (within the U.S. or Canada) or +1-770-280-4129 (globally)
Fax: +1-770-280-4113
E-mail: book.orders@pmi.org

Contents

Executive Summary

This report compares three different governance frameworks installed in the United Kingdom and Norway over the last decade. The frameworks are the Office of Government Commerce (OGC) Gateway Process in the United Kingdom, the Ministry of Defence (MoD) Acquisition Operating Framework in the United Kingdom, and the Quality Assurance Scheme by the Ministry of Finance in Norway.

The focus is on the governance of projects in the front-end phase. Our hypothesis is that the governance framework under which the investment project is planned and executed is important. In other words, the public governance framework under which an investment project is planned has a significant effect upon the project, particularly upon the effectiveness of cost estimation and time planning (in the front-end of major public projects). In turn, it is believed to influence the probability of success in a positive way.

The purpose of the report is to seek better understanding of how the governance framework and the projects interact and how the framework influences the project. We look for evidence that there is such an effect and how important this is. The governance frameworks have to be viewed against this background of the economic context in the United Kingdom and Norway. Corporate governance is based on the shareholder value model in the United Kingdom and a communitarian model in Norway. This influences the thinking about how to do business. The administrative traditions in the two countries are different and this difference influences the governance as well. In the United Kingdom, there is a strong individual responsibility, while in Norway the responsibility of the state is more evident.

Governance is an unclear concept. Thus, this report gives a thorough background on how governance has been interpreted in scientific literature, theoretical models, and the development trends, including recent new public management (NPM) and post-NPM reforms. Chapter 2 concludes with definitions on several important concepts used in this report and a new definition: *Governance framework—an organized structure established as authoritative within the institution, comprising processes and rules established to ensure projects meet their purpose.*

Governance frameworks may be characterized by describing their development process (the story), the embedded governance principles (the values), the structure of the framework (the content), and the detailed governance elements (adaptable to the purpose of analysis). This common structure is important in order to analyze them systematically.

Based on interviews with key people in the development of these frameworks and a large number of documents and reports, the governance frameworks are systematically analyzed and their purposes, structural characteristics, and important means and effects are described. The analysis compares the frameworks as they were mid-2007 and includes the latest developments (not yet fully implemented) in the beginning of 2008.

The development process behind the three frameworks includes both similarities and distinct differences. Similarities include high-level anchoring, motivation, and aims. Differences include scope, implementation of the frameworks, and support organization. All frameworks have achieved positive results. The main message is that the frameworks have to be closely adapted to the administrative culture and system in which it is working.

On the surface, the governance principles show some distinctive features. The Norwegian framework shows mandatory control measures in a robust, simple structure, while the MoD (UK) framework reveals a mandatory complete quality system for the defense acquisition process. The OGC (UK) is a complex system working by the force of influential recommendations by senior experts. Below these apparent main features, all the frameworks include similar principles about how to do business. These are closely connected to Western economic thinking.

The structures of the three frameworks are obviously very different, although some similarities were also found. The Norwegian and MoD frameworks both have two critical gateways, whereas the OGC framework has six "friendly" gateways, meaning the project gets good advice on further development but is not stopped by control intervention. The frameworks all use very different means for vertical and horizontal coordination. The Norwegian framework uses only resources external to the state. The OGC framework is mainly external, but may use internal resources in some cases. The MoD framework uses mainly internal assessors.

This study has focused cost and time on a more detailed level. The most important differences are found in the different ways cost and time are focused in the different frameworks. The Norwegian framework has a clear control focus and looks almost exclusively on cost. The MoD framework focuses on the life cycle and the OGC concentrates on the business case. The Norwegian and MoD frameworks include accuracy and detailed recommendations, whereas the OGC has comments that are more general. The Norwegian framework does not offer answers to how the project should meet the governance demands. The two UK frameworks both link to toolboxes with necessary methods and tools to manage the job.

The most notable observation from the four cases in this report is arguably the flexibility in implementation found in all cases. The cases show interesting differences in decision-making processes and illustrate the conflict between political decision making and the rational foundation of the governance frameworks. All cases illustrate the importance of having a governance framework. The main achieved value seems to be reassurance for the decision makers and legitimization for the project organization. None of the cases in this small sample show any major influence from the framework gateway on the project. All cases show projects performing to current plans, but none of them were finished at the time of completion of this report.

The report includes a thorough investigation into theoretical perspectives and theories, mainly from economy and social sciences. Thirty-two aspects of theory are assessed, and it is indicated whether each framework design seems to have put weak or strong emphasis on each of these aspects. This report gives a purely theoretical analysis and does not document the actual reasoning behind the governance frameworks described in this report. Chapter 4 is useful as a reference for theoretical perspectives on governance frameworks. Chapter 4 may also be further developed into an analytical framework for supporting design of governance frameworks in other contexts than the ones documented in this report. Findings in the cases include indications supporting the theoretical explanations.

The main impression in this study is that there are many ways to design a good governance framework for public investment projects. The three examples in this report are good frameworks and illustrate many important aspects that should be taken into consideration to strengthen governance of projects. Although these frameworks are different they do share several similarities. They continuously or stepwise develop further, and the latest transitions, implemented in 2008, seem to make them come closer to each other. This development indicates the empirical part of this kind of study may have the properties of "fresh produce."

This report offers a wide range of different perspectives on governance of projects in general and governance frameworks for public investment projects in particular. We believe this report gives useful insights and some tools for the design and implementation of governance frameworks.

1 Introduction

1.1 BACKGROUND

The increased use of projects as a way to organize and perform various tasks, not only in the business or industry environment but in all sectors of society, is challenged by a current focus on problems associated with the major projects. Despite the emphasis placed on improved methods to analyze and manage projects, the track record of projects reveals fundamental problems such as inadequate needs assessments, initial poor designs, tactical budgeting by authorities, inadequate cost estimation and risk assessment, etc. Classic examples documenting some of these problems are the Sydney Opera House in Australia (Hall, 1981), the Boston Artery/Tunnel in the United States (Altshuler & Luberoff, 2003), the Channel Tunnel in the United Kingdom and France (Morris & Hough, 1987; Anguera, 2006), and the Åsgard oil and gas field development in Norway (Norwegian Official Reports [NOU], 1999). These are spectacular cases well known in the project and program management world. The challenges for large investment projects are not unique for these megaprojects. Smaller projects fail but they do not get the same attention, since they are not as visible as the examples mentioned. This literature has identified two major problem areas:

- The issue of choosing and evaluating the right concept or alternative.
- The problems in executing large, complex projects.

Both of these areas are important. In this study, we focus on the decision-making problem in the front-end of projects. Project management literature has traditionally focused on the operational perspective of management. This study examines the strategic perspective of the project owner. The focus area is illustrated in Figure 1-1. We will look at the framework under which the project concept is chosen and evaluated, continuing through the governance of the planning and execution. Governance frameworks that help to improve the initial and fundamental design of projects and to avoid some of the common problems related to the implementation of projects represent a potential for considerable savings and added value.

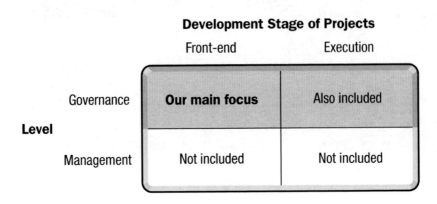

FIGURE 1-1.   THE FOCUS AREA OF THIS STUDY

This study focuses on public investment projects. We look at less known projects that are complex and challenging, but of a more modest dimension and certainly less exposed than the previously mentioned projects. Our cases have not been chosen as examples showing signs of problems in projects, but because they have been identified to have potential for highlighting some of the effects of governance frameworks. Our study object is governance frameworks established by the government in the United Kingdom and Norway to improve the performance of major public projects.

1.2   DEVELOPMENT IN THE PROJECT LITERATURE AND PROJECT MANAGEMENT PROFESSION

From the beginning, the primary focus of project and program management (PPM) has been closely linked to the methods and tools perspective. This focus is still evident in 2007. In the earlier days of public projects, it is clear that insufficient attention was paid to the early phases of a project (in the United Kingdom, this pattern started to change with the influential Downey Report (Downey et al., 1969), which laid down the policy that early project definition should take up 15% of the cost and 25% of the time of the project. Results from an extensive international study by the IMEC Research Program published in Miller and Lessard (2000) clearly illustrated the importance of focusing on the early phases of major investment projects. A similar focus on front-end management has been carried out in Norway where the government has introduced a quality-at-entry regime and a research program to support it (Klakegg, Samset, & Magnussen, 2005).

We now understand that this early phase is vital, although there has been debate for much of that time (Slevin & Pinto, 1989) about the extent to which detailed planning should be carried out. However, it is not clear what the effects of the various governance frameworks set up by different governments have on the choice of concept and the development of project plans and estimates. Such frameworks are set up as self-evidently appropriate, but we know that apparently self-evident correctness does not apply to complex projects (Lundin, 1995; Packendorff, 1995; Williams, 2005.

One clear driver is the desire to develop plans within an environment that is changing all the time. Malgrati and Damiani describe this action as "the Cartesian clarity of inner structures clashes with the increasing porosity of projects to complex contexts that they seek to deny" (Ulri & Ulri, 2000, as cited in Malgrati & Damiani, 2002, p. 372). The risk, in short, is that the idealistic "island of order" may suddenly turn into a more realistic, very classic, "iron cage." This is particularly the case in trying to define the project goals (Engwall, 2002), since "projects are complex, ambiguous, confusing phenomena wherein the idea of a single, clear goal is at odds with the reality" (Linehan & Kavanagh, 2004, p. 56). The response must look towards a governance framework that will comprehend such changes; the key is particularly the development of flexibility within the front-end of projects, a vital part of the thinking within the Norwegian University of Science and Technology (NTNU) (Olsson & Samset, 2006).

A second clear driver is the effect of bias on the estimates. There has also been well-known and well-documented work by Flyvbjerg, Bruzelius, and Rothengatter (2003) describing the effects of optimism bias and strategic under-estimation (both underestimating costs and overestimating revenue and other benefits), which are also known problems in the private sector (Condon, 2006). However, it is not clear what the effects of the various governance frameworks set up by different governments have in exacerbating or ameliorating these effects, which is crucial to understanding how to tackle this problem, rather than the sledgehammer of simply adding factors onto estimates as is currently the UK guidance (HM Treasury, 2003) based on Flyvbjerg's work (note in particular Flyvbjerg et al. 2003) (which of course will embed such features into the process).

In the world of project and program management, there still are a lot of discussions concerning the influence of the early phase/front-end planning in projects. In recent years, this influence has developed to include the important aspect of governance throughout the project life cycle. This development is described as a growing awareness of the importance of governance regimes (Klakegg, 2006). Miller and Hobbs (2005) described the new trend of project governance, and Turner (2006) defined the nature of project governance. Darshana Patel (2007) even goes so far as to call it "the project governance movement" (p. 1) connecting the phenomenon to the increasing use of project management offices (PMO) (Aubry, Hobbs, & Thuillier, 2007).

Turner (1999) showed how organizations can undertake projects and programs in order to help achieve their strategic objectives. Artto and Dietrich (2004) showed how program/project strategy can be developed from corporate and business strategies, and Artto, Kujala, Dietrich, and Martinsuo (2007) further investigated the implementation of strategy through projects. Morris and Jamieson (2004) carried out a major study into how organizations can realize their corporate strategy through projects and programs, including a number of case studies of organizations actually moving strategy into projects.

Other aspects of this have already been studied by some authors: Brunetto and Farr-Wharton (2002) showed that government reforms have improved the efficiency of processes undertaken during the life of a project, but have failed to address the issues arising from a lack of policy clarity relating to "what should be developed." Winch (2006) looked at contracts as a governance instrument. Youker and Brown (2001) have described the hierarchy of objectives. Eskerod, Blickfeldt, and Toft (2004) questioned the underlying assumption of rationality in decision making within portfolio management.

The Association for Project Management (APM) (2002, 2007) has established guidelines for the governance of project management in single- and multi-owned projects, thereby marking one of the most important contributions to the issues in the field studied in this report. We will come back to some of these contributions later in this report. Current bodies of knowledge in project management, however, hardly even mention this issue (such as *A Guide to the Project Management Body of Knowledge (PMBOK Guide®) – Third Edition* (Project Management Institute [PMI], 2004), the body of knowledge developed by the Association for Project Management (APM), the *APM Body of Knowledge* (APM, 2006), and the *Project Management Pathways* (Stevens, 2002).

The overall impression from investigating the state of the art in the project management literature in fields related to, or with an interface to governance, is that most contributions look at the continuing failure of projects as a project management problem. We take a different approach by looking at this lack of success as a governance problem. The project management literature (with a few exceptions) does not seem to have a firm grip on the concept of governance. We, therefore, think there is a need to take a closer look at this field.

1.3   PUBLIC PROJECTS: A GOVERNMENT PERSPECTIVE

The project management literature has not fully taken in the aspect of governance, but what about the real executors of governance in public projects: Governments. How are they handling this issue? In the United Kingdom, the National Audit Office (NAO) and the Office of Government Commerce (OGC) have agreed on a list of common failures in projects, after assessing results in a large number of public projects (OGC, 2005). See Chapter 5.3.1 for the complete list. It includes governance aspects like a lack of a clear link between the project and the organization's key strategic priorities, including agreed measures of success, lack of clear senior management and ministerial ownership and leadership, evaluation of proposals driven by initial price rather than long-term value for money, and lack of understanding of and contact with the supply industry at senior levels in the organization. These findings are believed to be relevant to other countries and to the private sector, too. The potential for improvement should not be underestimated.

In order to meet the demand for better management and control of public projects, the Norwegian Ministry of Finance established a mandatory external Quality Assurance Scheme for all large public investment projects with an expected budget above 500 million (NOK)/$83 million (US) in the year 2000 (Magnussen & Olsson, 2006). Its equivalents in the United Kingdom are stage-gated frameworks imposed by bodies such as the OGC based on the OGC Gateway™ Process (OGC, 2004a) and the PRINCE2™ project management method (OGC, 2002a) and the new governance framework implemented by Ministry of Defence (MoD) in the United Kingdom. It seems governments—at least in these two countries—are trying to do something with the problems in question. This action motivates us to look closer at these initiatives.

The frameworks approach the problems of major public investment projects in very different ways. This comparative study will give the necessary background to understand the strength of the underlying hypothesis. It will also enlighten several problem areas and policy instruments (Bemelmans-Videc, Rist, & Vedung, 1998) available to improve the performance of projects. We return to this topic later.

Primarily, we examine how the governance regimes for major investment projects in different countries determine or affect project performance. In this report, we will also compare this with the intended effect of these frameworks.

The study is limited. While we will take a broad view and look at the overall effect of the frameworks, we cannot look into all possible aspects of project planning and management. We will focus somewhat upon the planning of time and cost, because they are very important factors in determining a project's future success. In any framework, the basic problem of under/overestimation will exist. In this study we will, if possible, question to what degree the two frameworks in this study have the potential to reduce the problem; the consequences of the different approaches to the cost estimation process in terms of review or control of estimates are important targets for investigation, because they reveal examples of practical steps to reduce cost overruns.

1.4 UNDERLYING HYPOTHESIS AND RESEARCH QUESTIONS

The governance framework, including government roles, policies, regulations, etc., is documented to have vital importance to the planning process and management of projects (Morris & Hough, 1987; Collingridge, 1992; Berg et al., 1999; Miller & Lessard, 2000; APM, 2002; Flyvbjerg et al., 2003). These authors and several others have also discussed the effect of the governance framework on projects, but often focused on a superior aspect (i.e., the decision-making process) and without revealing the specific way these frameworks interact with the actual planning and management of the projects. This study is designed to go into this field.

Our hypothesis is that the governance framework under which the investment project is planned and executed is important. In other words, the public governance framework under which an investment project is planned has a significant effect upon the project, particularly upon the effectiveness of cost estimation and time planning (in the front-end of major public projects). In turn, this is believed to influence the probability of success in a positive way.

Our study seeks a better understanding of how the governance framework and the projects interact and how the framework influences the project. We look for evidence that there is such an effect and its importance.

The initial research questions are as follows:

- What fundamentally characterizes an institutional framework and how do frameworks differ?
- How do the frameworks work out in practice? What effect does the framework have on a project? How well does that agree with the intended effects? And does this suggest any improvements to the frameworks?
- To what extent does the framework guard against underestimation in time and cost; and does it allow overrun to be exposed and/or reduced and for cost control to be effective?

In order to be able to come closer to answers to these and similar questions, it is necessary first to look more closely at the concept of governance and what it means in the world of projects. We will address that in the next chapter. The rest of this chapter looks at the specific context of the frameworks studied in this report.

1.5 ECONOMIC CONTEXT IN THE UNITED KINGDOM AND NORWAY

The study compares frameworks for front-end appraisal of major public projects (Samset, Berg, & Klakegg, 2006). Specifically, we analyze the background for and describe the current status of the frameworks implemented in the United Kingdom and Norway. These two countries were chosen for a few reasons: (a) they represent interesting and different approaches to the issue and (b) other countries tend to look to these two sources for impulses on how to improve their own governance frameworks. These two frameworks were well documented and easily available to the authors.

Comparing the frameworks for public investment projects in different countries should include taking into consideration some aspects of the national economics of the countries in question. By choosing the United Kingdom and Norway for comparison, it is important to remember that these are both western European democracies and highly developed countries. They have many things in common.

Initially, let us look at some of the characteristic economic data from Britain (UK) and Norway. This information tells us something about the context in which decisions of major public investment projects are made.

Figure 1-2 shows characteristic differences between Britain and Norway. Norway clearly has a higher gross domestic product (GDP) per capita than Britain. This statistic is probably best explained with the combination of high oil- and gas-related income and a small population in Norway. The statistic has a clear tendency to show small countries having higher GDP per capita than populous countries. Britain (which also has oil revenues) is also well above the European Union (EU) average. Looking at relative price levels, the picture is pretty much the same. Norway is among the countries with the highest price level together with the other Nordic countries; only Switzerland is at the same level as the Nordic region. Britain is again above the EU average, but in this case moderately.

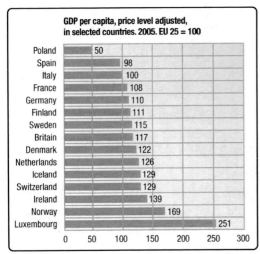
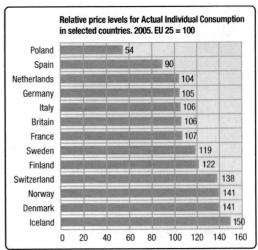

FIGURE 1-2.   **GDP PER CAPITA AND RELATIVE PRICE LEVELS IN OECD COUNTRIES COMPARED TO THE EU AVERAGE. Source: 2007 © Statistics Norway (with further reference to OECD)**

These calculations do not tell us a lot about the frameworks for major public investment projects as such, but they do reveal something about the context within which they work. The statistics put Norway in a position as a high-income/low-population country with high-level cost. This puts Norway among the small, rich, western, developed economies. This group of countries can be characterized as relatively homogeneous and can potentially have great benefit from transferring this experience. Britain is more representative of larger countries in the developed world. In this group of countries, we will find many of the economically leading countries of the world. Each of these has the economic weight and position to influence the development. This puts a special responsibility on these countries to be careful when transferring experience from other countries, but it still has great potential when done with appropriate consideration. The two groups of countries represented here cover an economically significant part of the world. Therefore, we would argue that these are important cases for potential role models when designing governance frameworks for major public investment projects. However, a more detailed discussion about how these experiences may be transferred to other countries follows towards the end of the report.

The rest of this section gives a few more details about the economy in the two countries. These details might help us explain some effects later in the report, as well as being relevant to the discussion about generalization of the findings in this report. All OECD member countries except for Turkey follow the international 1993 *System of National Accounts*, so there is good comparability between countries for most of the relevant economic key figures (as long as OECD is the source). In some cases we had to go directly into the national budgets of the United Kingdom and Norway to get data. In these cases we comment on the comparability of the figures. The precision of these figures cannot be better than the limited search for data, and the results derived may also be affected by the knowledge of the authors. None of them are experts in the field of economics.

Norway and the United Kingdom have different economies. One of the differences is the scale of the public sector. The size of the public sector relative to the whole of the economy is one factor which can explain some effects in public governance. Several measures could be used to characterize this—we have chosen the number of employees in the state administration (excluding state-owned businesses/corporations) as a percentage of the total active workforce. This is chosen because it is available and tells us something about the people involved in governing the projects we study in this report. The numbers in 2005 are Norway 10.7% (Statistics Norway 2007) and the UK 18.9% (Heap et al. 2005). This means that the relative size of the public sector is much larger in the United Kingdom than in Norway. This could indicate that in the United Kingdom more activities are performed by civil servants, and that in United Kingdom more functions are kept at a state level.

Economically, the size (in number of employees) is not the main point, although it does tell something about the importance of the public sector as an employer and driving force in the economy. Looking at the effect of this employment is more important in finding out how the economy is working. A fragment of this is shown in Figure 1-3.

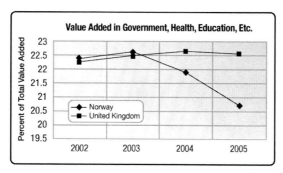

FIGURE 1-3.   **VALUE ADDED IN GOVERNMENT. (Source: OECD Factbook 2007: Economic, Environmental, and Social Statistics - ISBN 92-64-02946-X © OECD 2007. The numbers in Figure 3 cover government and personal services like health, education etc. provided by the government.)**

Gross value added is defined as output minus intermediate consumption and equals the sum of employee compensation, gross operating surplus, and taxes less subsidies on production and imports, except for next taxes on products. The shares of each sector are calculated by dividing the value added in each sector by total value added. Total gross value added is less than GDP because it excludes value-added tax (VAT) and similar product taxes. The government includes public administration, law and order, and defense.

Figure 1-2 gives the impression that the public sector in the United Kingdom is approaching a limit and that Norway already may have crossed this limit with a sharp decline in value added. Over the last years, the value added in this sector has been reduced. OECD comments on the long-term trends in value added for different sectors:

> *The share of agriculture has been declining throughout the period in almost all countries and, towards the end of the period, makes a significant contribution only in Iceland (fishing), New Zealand and Turkey. Shares in industry have also been falling throughout the period. Manufacturing is the most important activity within industry except in **Norway**, where oil and gas production are more important.*
>
> *All service activities account for around 70% of total gross value added for the OECD countries as a whole, with very high shares in Denmark, France, Greece, Luxembourg and the **United Kingdom** and rather low shares in the Czech Republic, Korea, **Norway** and Turkey. It should be noted, however, that, in most countries, the largest part of service value added is goods-related and consists of trade, transport, and business services purchased by industry. A high share of service value added does not necessarily mean that a country has become a service economy; the production, transport and distribution of goods remain the predominant activities in most OECD countries in terms of employment and value added.*

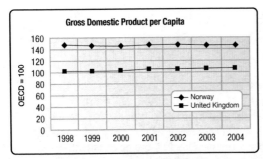
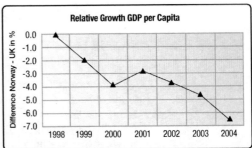

FIGURE 1-4.   **COMPARISON OF GROSS DOMESTIC PRODUCT IN THE UNITED KINGDOM AND NORWAY. (Source: http://lysander.sourceoecd.org/vl=475071/ cl=12/nw=1/rpsv/factbook/02-04-01.htm)**

Figure 1-4 gives a comparison of GDP in the UK and Norway. On the left, Gross domestic product per capita, adjusted for differences in price levels. Selected countries OECD=100. The calculations are based on the price levels and purchasing power parities in 2000. (Source: National Accounts of OECD Countries, volume 1, 2006. More information: http://www.oecd.org/ and http://www.ssb.no/ppp_en/). On the right: The difference Norway–UK adjusted to diff. 1998=0, difference shown in %. Norway seems to be losing position, relatively speaking. The UK has a significantly better development than Norway up to 2004. More recent figures have not been available.

As the left side of Figure 1-4 shows, the two countries compared in this study are very stable in economic terms. There is no dramatic change in the economy explaining the focus on major investment projects at the end of the 1990s and beginning of 21st century. By looking at the difference between the two countries (right hand side of Figure 1-4), the difference is surprisingly clear. Norway's position seems to be weakening.

Figure 1-5 shows one of the important differences between the two countries quite clearly. The United Kingdom has a large economy, but it also has a great deficit. Great deficits normally mean money is a limiting resource in society, especially in the public sector. Norway is in an opposite position with a small economy, but with great surplus. In Norway, money is plentiful. One should expect this to influence heavily on the thinking among decision makers. Figure 1-6 presents investments in the United Kingdom and Norway.

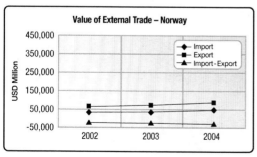
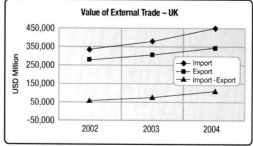

FIGURE 1-5.   COMPARISON OF EXTERNAL TRADE IN THE UNITED KINGDOM AND NORWAY

Figure 1-5 gives a comparison of external trade in the UK and Norway On the left: Big economy, great deficit for the UK. On the right: Small economy, great surplus for Norway. Source: National Accounts of OECD Countries, Volume 1, 2006.

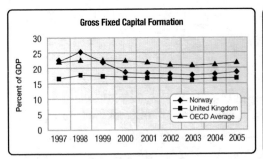 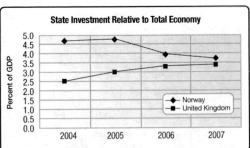

FIGURE 1-6.   **COMPARISON OF STATE INVESTMENTS OVER TIME IN UK AND NORWAY.**

Figure 1-6 gives a comparison of state investments over time in UK and Norway. On the left, the overall picture—Gross fixed capital formation (GFCF) is the acquisition, less disposal of fixed assets, i.e., products which are expected to be used in production for several years for the whole economy (OECD Factbook 2007 - Economic, Environmental, and Social Statistics, available at http://titania.sourceoecd. org.) On the right, the differences in current trends[1] in investment level for the major projects focused in this report. (National Budget for 2004–2007 [Norwegian Ministry of Finance] and the Budget 2007 Report [HM Treasury 2007a]).

The trends in Figure 1-6[2] show that the Norwegian government has spent relatively less money on investments over the last years, especially after a "boom" in the late 1990s. This may seem counter-intuitive to the picture given in Figure 1-5 where a large surplus is shown. In Norway, money is plentiful, but still there seems to be reluctance to invest. The UK is gradually investing more, but the level seems to be flattening out at approximately the same level as Norway.

A brief look at the official explanations for the economic policy in the two countries:

In Norway: "The Norwegian economy is experiencing its strongest expansion in thirty years, with annual growth in Mainland-GDP averaging more than 4.5 % over the past four years. Employment has increased substantially and the unemployment rate has fallen to a historically low level. Real wage growth is high, due to low consumer price inflation, while producer costs have picked up only moderately so far."(from; Fiscal Budget 2008: Underpinning Macroeconomic Stability. Press release 60/2007 [5.10.2007] from the Ministry of Finance). Although the United Kingdom may seem to have had an even stronger boom in the relevant period of time, Norway

---

1. The UK government has chosen 1April–30 March as their budget year. In Norway 1 January–31 December is used. It is assumed commensurable enough for this brief comparison.
2. Please note that Figures 1-5 and -6 and the text do not refer to the same period of time. Figures from the same period of time were not available.

has a "high pressure" economy. This calls for moderation and careful considerations about public spending both in service and investment. Fear of increasing inflation, level of interest rent, and a too strong value of the Norwegian currency are factors to be considered.

What about the UK? The UK economy is currently experiencing its longest unbroken expansion on record, with GDP now having grown for 58 consecutive quarters. Over the past 10 years, the Government's macroeconomic framework has delivered more stability in terms of GDP growth and inflation rates than in any decade since the war. This historically low volatility puts the UK in a strong position to respond to the global economic challenges of the next decade (HM Treasury 2007a). Long-term economic stability is the goal of the treasury as well.

Comparison of these two quotations shows two ministries that describe the economic situation in their countries almost identically. Of course, these are political statements and describe economic realities, but they add to the understanding of the background for the issues discussed in this report. We believe that explanations of differences in governance of public projects are not easily found in the economic situation.

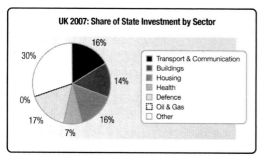
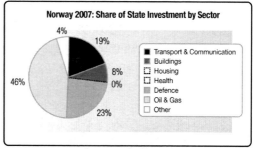

FIGURE 1-7.   **COMPARISON OF STATE INVESTMENT PROFILES IN UK AND NORWAY. SHARE OF INVESTMENTS IN DIFFERENT SECTORS. Sources: National Budget for 2007 (Norwegian Ministry of Finance) and the Budget 2007 Report (Her Majesty's Treasury).**

Figure 1-7 needs an explanation. We have used the same division in sectors for both countries. Some care should be taken in the interpretation of the data presented here, because there are differences in definition of sectors in the two countries. It is, however, assumed to be commensurable enough for this brief comparison. The United Kingdom officially uses the term *department*. Norway uses the term *ministry*. The terms are not precisely comparable. It is easy to define the defense, oil and gas, and health sectors. These are basically defined equally in the two countries. They simply correspond with the department in question. Transport and communication is not quite as simple, because in Norway some large basic ICT investments are included here, along with the dominating road projects and a few railway projects. Transport dominates, however, in both countries, so a comparison is assumed to be justified. Other ICT investments (systems) are placed in the budgets of other departments in both countries. The building sector is more difficult to define and compare. In Norway, university buildings and a few large projects in the culture sector are found here, as well as some office buildings. In the United Kingdom, only investments in the education department are included here. Housing is a significant state sector in the United Kingdom, but not in Norway where this sorts under local authorities. The "other" sector comprises all other investments (not included in the above-mentioned). Further difficulties are caused by the heavy use of private finance initiative (PFI) in the United Kingdom, and also the partially devolved budgets to Scotland, Wales, and Ireland, each of which differs in the position of the state (e.g., in Scotland, water is publicly owned, in England it is privately owned).

There is reason to believe that the two countries have different limits to what size an investment should have to be identified in this budget process. The impression is that in Norway, large investments are identified individually and accounted for in the budgets, whereas the small ones are incorporated in the large service budgets (frame budgets for each department). This means that not all investment projects are actually in the figures used to make Figure 1-7 (see also Figure 1-6). In the United Kingdom, it seems that the budgets for each department are frame budgets for service (resource) and investments (capital), respectively. This may give interesting guidance on the way investments are focused in the two countries. It could possibly lead to a generally higher awareness and focus on the large investment projects on a high level in Norway. On the other hand, if a single investment project makes its way up to the table of the Prime Minister, the Cabinet, or Parliament in the United Kingdom, it probably has a larger impact on the specific project.

Another major difference not identified in Figure 1-6 is the extensive use of Private-Public Partnerships (PPPs) in the United Kingdom (such as the PFI). These projects do not appear in the budgets as capital investments but as long-term contracts for delivery of a service. In Norway, this approach is not widely used. Three road projects are currently performed as PPP-projects in Norway, and an evaluation of this experiment is currently under way.

As Figure 1-7 shows, there is a different relative size of all sectors. Transport has approximately the same level of investment in both countries, but it is larger in Norway. The defense sector is significantly larger in the United Kingdom. The building sector is also significantly larger in the United Kingdom than in Norway, despite the fact that three ministries are covered in the Norwegian figures and only one department in the United Kingdom. A practical explanation may be that all building projects are smaller in Norway due to the smaller population and number of users accordingly. The significant differences are made up of elements following clearly different policies in the two countries. The oil and gas sector in the United Kingdom is a private sector, whereas it is the dominating public sector in Norway. In the United Kingdom, the health sector is large, whereas in Norway this sector was made self-financing by owner reform in 2001. Housing follows the same pattern, as it is not responsibility of the state in Norway. The "other" category is dominating in the United Kingdom with 30% of the investment, among other reasons because of the special budgetary provisions for the more or less autonomous governments in Wales and Northern Ireland. A significant amount of the investments are also channeled through local authorities. There will probably be some investments within the category "other" in the UK that would actually belong in transport, building, etc. However, we do not have more detailed knowledge of these figures, and we assume this would not change the overall picture.

In the case of Norway, Figure 1-7 helps explain why the oil and gas sector is the excluded sector not subject to the general governance framework described in this report. This sector is of a different scale (46% of the total investments), a different political level (completely decisive of the Norwegian economy), and of a different nature (international actors and networks are dominating the business in this sector). The decision-making processes are different in this sector. In the United Kingdom, the defense sector is excluded and given its own governance framework. The explanation for this is not found in Figure 1-7 or any of the other economic figures above. In this case, it is a choice founded on other reasons. We will get back to these reasons when the UK MoD governance framework is studied.

In the continuing discussions of this report, more details of economics and the political situation in the two chosen countries may be added, as far as it is relevant to explain differences or effects, or if this kind of information may shed light on other possible explanations. We have included this introduction as a reminder that applying the conclusions of this study has to be done carefully. One should expect the governance frameworks to be influenced by this background. Thus, if elements of a governance framework are copied to another setting, other effects than intended may be the result.

1.6 THE STARTING POINT OF THIS JOURNEY

To sum up the introduction before heading into the real study, we have found that:

- The major public investment projects have problems in two main areas:
  - ○ evaluating alternatives and choosing the right concept, and
  - ○ executing large, complex projects well.
- The governments in some countries have initiated governance frameworks in order to deal with both problems.
- The project literature has, to some extent, acknowledged this too, but still not taken in the essence of governance. There is still confusion about what the concept "governance" means.
- The main focus in the project management world is on executing projects well (delivering outputs on cost, time, and quality, and increasing efficiency in the project management processes), not on the front-end challenges.
- We have chosen to compare two countries; both are western developed countries with good economies and well-developed governments. We hope to find explanations for and new insight into why and how these initiatives should give success in future public projects. The economic context in the two countries can explain why there is an urge to secure against wasting public funds, but does not reveal the details about why the frameworks are so different in the two countries.
- Three frameworks cover most of the large public projects in these countries. Knowledge about these frameworks is available. Some cases are available too. We will try to increase the knowledge about the frameworks and their effect.

Our journey from this starting point goes through theory on governance and projects, practice on governance frameworks, and deeper insight through actual cases towards an analysis as we seek to look at the impact of the framework under which the investment project is planned and executed.

2 Governance

2.1 INTRODUCTION

The word "governance" is associated with words like government, governing, and control. Government is a governing body (see Figure 2-1). Governing is using one's position or ability to influence or direct development. For example, the governing party is the political party in power in a country. Control is a matter of being able to decide over, define limitations for, delegate authority to, or withdraw from someone. The classical means of governance are regulations (proscriptions/injunctions or prescriptions/orders), economic means (sanctions or incentives), and information (advice or warnings) (Bemelmans-Videc et al., 1998). The concept of governance is the essence of management on a superior level.

Governance, from a management perspective, is the complex process of steering multiple firms, agencies, and organizations that are both operationally autonomous and structurally coupled in projects through various forms of reciprocal interdependencies (Jessop, 1997). The rise of the term "governance" to prominence stems from the difficulties of hierarchical coordination, either by firms or by the state. (Miller & Floricel, 2000, p. 135).

There are also a lot of derivatives of the concept of governance. Examples are public governance, corporate governance, project governance, transaction governance, supply-chain governance, etc. (some of these will be discussed later). There is much confusion in presentations and discussions on the matter of project governance and governance in general. This paper will try to make the concept of governance clearer for the purposes of this study.

Wikipedia says: "Governance is that separate process or certain part of management or leadership processes that makes decisions that define expectations, grant power, or verify performance. Frequently a government is established to administer these processes and systems. Governance (in business) is the action of developing and managing consistent, cohesive policies, processes and decision rights for a given area of responsibility. For example, managing at a corporate level: privacy, internal investment, the use of data."

This definition gives a general idea about the concept of governance. There are still several problems and ambiguities attached to the word. Therefore, we have to look closely into some of its aspects. One problem is understanding where governance stops and management begins. This topic is discussed later.

Government

From Wikipedia, the free encyclopedia

A **government** is a body that has the authority to make and the power to enforce rules and laws within a civil, corporate, religious, academic, or other organization or group. In its broadest sense, "to govern" means to administer or supervise, whether over a state, a set group of people, or a collection of assets.

The word government is derived from the Greek κυβερναν (kybernan), which means "to steer" or "to control".

Typically, "the government" refers to the executive function of the state. In many countries (particularly those having parliamentary systems), the **government** refers to the executive branch of government or a specifically named executive, such as the Blair government (compare to the **administration** as in the Bush administration in U.S. usage). In countries using the Westminster system, the party in government will also usually control the legislature.

FIGURE 2-1.   GOVERNMENT—A GENERAL INTRODUCTION

Rhodes (1997) defined governance as a "non-hierarchical form of steering, where state and nonstate actors participate in the formulation and implementation of public policy." This definition contradicts the traditional hierarchical model of government. The consequence of this kind of thinking is discussed later in this chapter. Driessen (2005) makes a distinction between "multilevel" governance (highlighting the various tiers of government: local, regional, national, or supranational) and "multiactor" governance (reflecting the involvement of both public and private actors). Multiactor governance is in the same direction as Rhodes is heading, but we chose to start with the other direction.

2.2   THE TOP OF THE PYRAMID?

From looking at the words used to describe governance, there is obviously a set of levels on which you can define a specific form of governance. In the world of organizational theory, the pyramid is often used as a symbol, indicating that on top of any system there is someone governing over all the lower levels by the help of controlling the next level, which controls the next level, etc.

The international level is governed by several institutions established to settle matters where the interests of several nations, peoples, or regions are involved. The United Nations, World Bank, OECD, World Trade Organization, and European Union are examples. All of these represent governance on a superior level within their defined areas of interest/responsibility.

Many people would argue that these superior governing institutions are weakening and that the real governance is represented by other forces, like the United States on the political arena and the multinational corporations on the economic arena. These discussions are very interesting as such, but in this setting, they are just mentioned as a background for the following discussion of governance relevant to our project. The point here is that **the governing party of public investment projects is not the top of the pyramid**. In this perspective, there is always a more superior purpose above the project, program, or portfolio.

Abbott and Snidal (2001) discussed the use of standards as a mechanism of international governance and showed how these can play different roles under different circumstances. They look at different government arrangements, varying combinations of private and public governance, and varying levels of governance (national, regional, and global) in light of scope of the problem and the capacity of institutions. They define international governance as "the formal and informal bundles of rules, roles and relationships that define and regulate the social practices of state and non-state actors in international affairs" (p. 346). The diversity of governance arrangements naturally stems from the diversity of problems that states, firms, and other actors are attempting to resolve. Among other things, they point out that no "pure" governance form can handle all problems effectively, and no single governance blend (combination of private and public arrangements) is always best. This may be used to raise the question of governance to international levels.

Flyvbjerg et al. (2003), investigating several megaprojects across borders (international projects), observed the same: governance is relative—the same formula will not work everywhere. Another illustration of this conclusion is the evaluation of the Channel Tunnel linking the United Kingdom and France (Anguera, 2006), where differences between the two countries are shown.

Miller and Floricel (2000) showed that "The institutionalist approach aims to identify the various governance modes that enable coordination of major actors in society (North 1990). Each society develops its own architecture, and optimal solutions are hard to identify" (Coriat, 1998; Hollingsworth & Boyer, 1997, p. 137). The international aspect is not pursued further here. We will, however, come back to the parallel discussion of differences in governance structure architecture within a country later in this report.

2.3   PUBLIC SECTOR GOVERNANCE

Since this study involves public investment projects on the national level, clearly public governance is one of the main issues in our work. Public sector governance has two parallel subsystems: the political and the administrative (Klakegg, n.d.). The political governance is implemented through making decisions and giving priority. The decision makers in this subsystem are the politicians. The administrative governance includes developing the basis for decisions made in the political subsystem and implements the political decisions. Civil servants work in this subsystem as decision makers, planners, etc. The political subsystem is not discussed further here. We will focus on the administrative subsystem with its administrative governing parties and systems, often called "the administration."

Wikipedia (2007) says "Public administration can be broadly described as the study and implementation of policy. As a moral endeavor, public administration is linked to pursuing the public good through the creation of civil society and social justice. The adjective 'public' often denotes 'government,' though it increasingly encompasses Non-Governmental Organizations (NGOs) such as those of civil society or any entity and its management not specifically acting in self-interest."

Public governance is a wide area of interest that cannot be given full justice in a document of this length. Authors like Professors Lægreid (2006), Christensen (2007) and Peters and Pierre (1998) describe (public) governance as a concept which is unclear, ambiguous, and disputed. Different authors define (public) governance differently and use it in a wide variety of ways, both descriptive and explanatory. Stoker (1998) describes governance as "a change in the meaning of government" (p. 17).

There appears to be a mix of governance and operational management in the public governance literature. This mix may add to the confusion about what governance is. It makes a deeper study of governance important in order to have a nuanced picture of what it is, and what makes governance different from management and good practice.

Christensen says: "Governance has become a rather fashionable term that is used to describe almost any aspect of the work of the political-administrative apparatus, so its content is pretty ambiguous. In most cases, government would be a better and more precise term. Some authors say that government is decision-making, control and planning systems inside the political-administrative apparatus, while governance extends this system to non-public actors, like the 'joined-up' system created by Tony Blair in the United Kingdom" (Christensen, 2007, p. 7).

Stoker (1998) says "government is characterized by its ability to make decisions and its capacity to enforce them. In particular government is understood to refer to the formal and institutional processes which operate at the level of the nation state to maintain public order and facilitate collective action" (p. 17).

Governance on the highest level is a very general concept including "all" aspects of governing and control. The World Bank defined governance in 1992: "Governance is the manner in which power is exercised in the management of a country's economic and social resources for development" (Kaufmann & Kray, 2007, p. 4). In 2007 this definition was reformulated to "...the manner in which public officials and institutions acquire and exercise the authority to shape public policy and provide public goods and services" (World Bank, 2007, p. 1). Kaufmann and Kraay extend this definition to say that it is "...the traditions and institutions by which authority in a country is exercised. This includes the process by which governments are selected, monitored and replaced; the capacity of the government to effectively formulate and implement sound policies; and the respect of citizens and the state for the institutions that govern economic and social interactions among them" (p. 4).

These World Bank definitions paint a stable picture over the last decade, and Kaufmann and Kraay observe that "while the many existing definitions of governance cover a broad range of issues, one should not conclude that there is a total lack of definitional consensus in this area. Most definitions of governance agree on the importance of a capable state operating under the rule of law" (p. 6).

Kooiman and Van Vliet (1993) challenge the notion that the government can impose governance alone when they say, "The governance concept points to the creation of a structure or an order which cannot be externally imposed but is the result of the interaction of a multiplicity of governing and each other influencing actors" (p. 64). Rhodes (1996) describes governance as a "change in the meaning of government, referring to a new process of governing; or a changed condition of ordered rule; or the new method by which society is governed" (pp. 652–653).

For the purpose of this report, it seems more appropriate to choose a more neutral and open definition that is not connected closely to a political context. We will use this alternate definition (given uncited in Wikipedia) that describes **governance** as: "The use of institutions, structures of authority and even collaboration to allocate resources and coordinate or control activity in society or the economy."

The roots of governance lie very close to government, so it is only natural to find this point towards the public sector: governance implies the use of civic institutions and networks to create the policies and programs that citizens want (Peters & Pierre, 1998; Putnam, 1993). Government cannot do this alone. The citizens have to be involved, either through individual participation, voluntary associations, religious institutions, etc. (Berger & Neuhaus 1977; Sager 2006). As the world is changing faster and nongovernmental organizations become more and more important, the public context is getting more and more complex.

Traditionally, the area in mind is called public administration (PA). Some authors refer to the "old public administration" in order to distinguish between this starting point and the later developments. In the Western democracies, PA was based on a set of norms and values, which allows for trade-offs and prioritizing between different and often competing values and goals (Christensen & Lægreid, 2001; Olsen, 1997). It was a multifunctional and complex civil service model which has been strongly challenged in recent years (Christensen, 2007, p. 28).

Even if an updated, new PA concept is introduced, new public management (NPM) took over the arena (Bush, Johnsen, Klausen, & Vanebo, 2005). NPM has introduced many of the same ways of thinking and designing systems in the public sector as is traditionally used in private sector in Europe (Pollitt & Bouckaert, 2000) and Scandinavia (Bush et al., 2005). NPM is the postmodern version of governance in public sector inspired by economic and rational thinking. The development has often been associated with the governments of President Ronald Reagan in the United States and Prime Minister Maggie Thatcher in the United Kingdom during the 1980s.

Christensen describes the new public management reforms as follows (Christensen, 2007): "Most NPM reform efforts have had similar goals: to improve the effectiveness and efficiency of the public sector, enhance the responsiveness of public agencies to their clients and customers, reduce public expenditure, and improve managerial accountability" (Wright, 1994, p. 28). This is certainly a very broad set of goals, making NPM a broad reform of government. Of course, the practical implementation of the reform and the focus in each country vary, but in general, it seems evident that public governance was coming closer to corporate (private sector) governance in this period. Pollitt (2003) has studied this phenomenon in the public reforms in New Zealand, illustrating the tensions created by this development.

The public sector is increasingly organized through independent public entities, strategic leadership, and contracts. The means used is strong vertical and horizontal specialization of administrative systems, competitive tendering, customer choice, etc. In addition, NPM prescribes cultural changes aimed at making the government apparatus more user-friendly and market-oriented (Christensen & Lægreid, 2001).

This development also increases the importance of projects in public sector. The parallel of the government agency (public sector) is the corporation (private sector). Therefore, we need to look at both these two directions to get a "complete" picture of governance. There is a lot of critical literature (Christensen & Lægreid, 2001) and others referred to by Klausen in Bush et al. (2005) pointing out that NPM (and also corporate governance) do not fully take into consideration the specific context of public sector. Some authors regard it as somewhat naive. Christensen (2006) shows that NPM reforms failed to deliver increased efficiency, "both in a micro and particularly macro way" (p. 32), and may have been followed by a tendency of decrease in quality of public services.

A basic idea of NPM was to "let the managers manage," increasing their freedom to act within their area of responsibility and to measure their effort by results. This freedom, based on a contract to deliver results, has to be balanced by control efforts. This contradictory tendency has over time grown more visible and is the core of the next wave of development in public governance: the post-NPM reforms. Schmidtlein (2004) investigates the new control measurements used in higher education discussing the appropriateness of underlying assumptions.

Because of NPM failing to deliver efficiency, the increased fragmentation and what has been described as "the fear factor" (terrorism, tsunami, pandemics, etc.), there is a growing tendency toward (and obvious arguments for) reinstating a more central political and administrative control (Christensen, 2007, p. 32). Different terms are used to describe this tendency: "joined-up government" in the United Kingdom and "whole-of-government" in Australia. The Scandinavian countries (and the rest of Europe), still lagging behind the Anglo-American NPM pioneers, follow more or less the same patterns.

Compared to the NPM reforms, the post-NPM reforms are generally more about cultural than structural features (Christensen, 2007, p. 37). Now the mantra is to think about the collectivity and to find ways to collaborate with other public entities to find good solutions (see Bardach, 1998), and to focus on public ethos and standards is now more important than before (Brunsson & Jacobsson, 2002).

We have established that the topic of this report naturally has to link to the public sector and its governance. We are studying public governance frameworks established in a period of time, which can be called the post-NPM era in the Western developed countries.

We will in the following use this definition of **public governance** (OECD, 2005, p. 16):

> *Governance refers to the formal and informal arrangements that determine how public decisions are made and how public actions are carried out, from the perspective of maintaining a country's constitutional values in the face of changing problems, actors and environments.*

2.4 CORPORATE GOVERNANCE

The most common governance field or subject in literature on governance is "corporate governance." We need to study this field to put projects in the right perspective. What is corporate governance?

A definition of corporate governance is "a system [that] shapes who makes investment decisions in corporations, what types of investments they make, and how returns from investments are distributed" (O'Sullivan, 2000, as cited in Detomasi, 2006, p. 227; O'Sullivan, 2003, p. 24).

Corporate governance systems are composed of (Monks & Minow, 2004, as cited in Detomasi, 2006):

- Internal governance processes (structure, composition, and authority of the company's board of directors, the relationship between board and management and the internal financial and auditing controls to monitor performance).
- The quality of the independent auditing functions present in the national economy (normally fulfilled by an accredited accounting profession based on rigorous standards).
- The nature and quality of the corporate law and regulatory mechanisms existing within a national economy that are designed to shape corporate activity.

Detomasi (2006) emphasized that despite these common elements, corporate governance systems differ dramatically between nations with regards to purpose, structure, and function. Corporate governance systems reflect social, political, and economic purposes.

In 1983, Burgelman introduced the term *structural context*. He used this to place administrative mechanisms enabling top management to govern the effort of middle and operative level management to ensure that their actions are in line with the current concept of strategy and support coherent strategic behavior and strategy implementation. Examples of such mechanisms include strategic control systems, reward systems, and project screening criteria among others (Burgelman, 1983, as cited in Artto, Dietrich, & Nurminen, 2004). The management literature on strategy focuses two different types of top-down systems: value systems and performance measurement systems. Value systems describe the corporation's strategic mission, purpose, and vision. Performance systems are used to motivate, monitor, and reward achievement of specific goals (Artto et al., 2004).

Simons (1995) summarizes the management systems needed to exercise adequate control in organizations that demand flexibility, innovation, and creativity—the modern era of corporate business:

- Diagnostic control systems to help managers track the progress of individuals, departments, or production facilities toward strategically important goals.

- Belief systems to articulate the values and direction that senior managers want their employees to embrace.
- Boundary systems embedded in standards of ethical behavior and codes of conduct are invariably written in terms of activities that are off-limits.
- Interactive control systems, new formal systems created to share emerging information and to harness the creativity that often leads to new products, line extensions, processes, and even markets.

The balance between control and empowerment is vital to the efficiency and success in business. Empowerment to create value and new opportunities through freedom and motivation on one hand, and control on the other hand, are used to avoid economical losses and damaged reputation caused by subordinates and employees stretching the freedom too far.

Corporate Governance and Society

Jacoby (2005) gives a historic overview of the relations between corporate governance and society based on a similar understanding of the corporate governance system on a national level. His description of corporate governance is "it comprises the laws and practices by which managers are held accountable to those who have a legitimate stake in the corporation" (p. 69).

Authors like Detomasi (2006), Jacoby (2005), O'Sullivan (2000, 2003), and Abbott and Snidal (2001) all discuss differences between countries and the governance systems found in different countries. There seems to be two important categories of corporate governance systems:

- Shareholder-value systems (U.S., UK, Canada, etc.)
- Communitarian systems (Central and northern Europe, Japan, etc.)

The main difference seems to be who should be regarded as legitimate stakeholders. The shareholder-value system only regards shareholders as legitimate stakeholders. An example is the corporate governance in the United States: policy governance model, a new, rational paradigm for directors. Put simply, the policy governance model as applied in business answers one question: How can a group of peers, on behalf of shareholders, see to it that a business achieves what it should (normally in terms of shareholder value) and avoids unacceptable situations and actions? The model does not prescribe a certain structure, but a set of principles. These principles are universally applicable and sufficiently integrated to be called a "model" or, indeed, a *theory* of governance (Carver, 2001).

Communitarian systems also hold nonshareholder constituencies such as employees, banks, and the community in general as legitimate stakeholders. These practices occur in some countries by law (Germany, Norway, etc.), and in other countries with no legal requirement to do so (e.g., Japan).

Today, the shareholder-value system seems to be dominating international governance trends, influencing countries like France and Japan to phase out their systems of cross-shareholding to make way for international and institutional investors. Academics discuss whether the development seen will end in convergence to a common model or stay different. O'Sullivan (2003) compares and points out weaknesses in theories used to explain the development. She also documents systems changing significantly over time.

Clarke (2004) looked at different systems: an "outsider" system of market-based corporate governance predominant in the United States and the United Kingdom, characterized by dispersed ownership and primacy of shareholder value, is the current dominant force; but in Europe a "relationship-based system … has prevailed, reflecting the rich cultural diversity of the continent, and different corporate history and values" (p. 8). Then there are family-based systems as in Asia Pacific.

Jacoby (2005) gives an interesting overview of the development (especially the U.S. corporate governance system from the 1930s and up till today. The changing nature of governance systems are one of his main points. He says that "corporate governance is politically constructed and historically mutable" (p. 71). He points out several developments documenting that there are several interesting developments, here mentioned more or less chronologically up till today:

- Separation of ownership and control
- Welfare capitalism, New Deal
- Corporate social responsibility
- Institutional investors, speculating (raiding and stripping)
- Lean and mean companies, options, development of shareholder-value model.

In general terms, governance deals with the processes and systems by which an organization or society operates. The terms *good governance* and *governance* can be used in the same meaning (Grunfeldt & Jakobsen, 2006). Kaufmann and Vicente (2005) relate governance to the traditions and institutions by which authority is exercised for the common good.

Jacoby (2005, p. 79) quotes the Russel Sage study: "The share-holder value model is fundamentally about the distribution of resources and risk." This is one statement that points out a strong link to the subject of public investment projects. It is also about distribution of resources and risk.

The wide spectre of considerations necessary in decisions about public investment projects looks more like a parallel to the communitarian model. When designing public investment projects, there is no doubt decision makers have to consider the welfare of all relevant stakeholders (users, neighbors, interest groups, etc.) and the people/society in general. Distribution of welfare and resources are the fundamental reason why we have a public sector.

Our chosen definition is useful because it allows both shareholder-value and communitarian models; it also points to structures supporting setting and achieving goals. Understanding corporate governance is helpful to understand governance of public investment projects, or governance through projects (since projects are the means to achieve something), and we consider both governance *of* and governance *through* (public investment) projects.

Corporate governance is defined thus:

> *Corporate governance involves a set of relationships between a company's management, its board, its shareholders and other stakeholders. Corporate governance also provides the structure through which the objectives of the company are set, and the means of attaining those objectives and monitoring performance are determined (OECD, 2004, pp. 11).*

2.5   THEORETICAL PERSPECTIVES

Chelimsky (1997) writes, "We still don't seem to understand political processes very well, and especially their dynamic nature" (p. 56). Among authors trying to improve this state is Evert Vedung. His work includes several important contributions. Through evaluation, defined as the "careful retrospective assessment of the merit, worth, and value of administration, output, and outcome of government interventions, which is intended to play a role in future, practical action situations" (Vedung, 2000, p. 3), Vedung increases our knowledge of these processes. He uses a systems model (a general governance model) as context and verifies to which extent the processes and outcomes of government interventions are sufficient to meet citizen/legislative demands. Vedung questions the use of a hierarchical approach to public management, critiquing the rational model in which planners attempt to reduce the role of politics in government decision making.

Another author contributing to the understanding of these processes is Tore Sager (2006). In his article on critical communicative planning based on the theory of transaction cost economics, Sager shows how a critical planner can counteract distorted communication by augmenting the transaction costs of those trying to influence the decision. These are examples of contributions based on specific theoretical directions. Having such a theory basis is important. Hence, we need to look closer at the theories available to explain observations we make when analyzing the frameworks and cases later in this report.

What fields of theory may help us in our study? Clarke (2004) gives the basics of what corporate governance is about. He refers to **agency theory** (see Eisenhardt, 1989), in which each agent acts with self-interest in a "nexus of contracts," in particular, the separation of management (managers make decisions) and finance (financiers take the risks); **stewardship theory**, which allows for other than self-interest in the managers, giving them lots of other motives and says that you can have cooperative control of the firm; **networking theories** (see Jones, Heserly, & Borgatti, 1997) that look at the connections within an environment; and **stakeholder theory**, which looks at all stakeholders but particularly brings in employees. Each one of these theories is relevant to explain aspects of governance. Therefore, we include a brief description of each:

> *Principal-agent theory has especially focused on formal institutional design of structural devolution and delegation and when and why political executives create agencies and transfer formal power to them. Agencies are supposed to deal with informational asymmetries, handling blame, and increasing credibility and efficiency. Agencies can act contrary to the preferences of their political bosses (agency loss) by following their own preferences (shrinking) or because the agency has incentives to behave contrary to the wishes of the political executives (slippage). … This theory has also formed the basis for marketization and privatization and has inspired contract systems that use incentives and performance-enhancing structures.* (Christensen 2007, p. 11).

> *Contracts and delegated authority are control measures derived from principal-agent theory, according to Christensen, Lægreid, Roness, and Røvik (2007, p. 128).*

> *Public choice theory … presupposes that politicians and bureaucrats are motivated by self-interest. This theory, which is skeptical towards collective interests and ethical-institutional considerations, is part of a conservative or neo-liberal agenda advocating a small state and extensive personal freedom. It has inspired vertical structural specialization, where policy advice, regulation and implementation are divided, and it is also behind calls for larger central political staffs and alternative external policy advice to counteract the influence*

of bureaucrats. The theory also underlines the need for increased transparency and insight into vested interests and competition bias, clearer definition in contracts of rights and duties for public and private actors, and a reduction in the scope of influence of political executives in order to make some policy areas more autonomous" (Christensen, 2007, p. 11–12).

Specialized organization structures are a control measure derived from the public choice theory, according to Christensen et al. (2007, p. 128).

The **theory of transaction cost economics** (Williamson, 1979, 1981) is a theoretical foundation on which quite a few have based their analysis. It is an analytical tool mostly used to explain economic problems where asset specificity plays the key role (Encycogov, 2007). Transaction cost economics rely on competition to sort out the inefficient modes of organization (Williamson, 1985, p. 23). Contracts are able to support and facilitate transactions in a way that reduces the transaction costs, but in real life transaction technology is always imperfect. An often-mentioned reason is that it is impossible to allow for all contingencies in a contract because they are costly to monitor and enforce. A good reference on this topic is Williamson (1985). The main transaction technology in corporate governance is as follows: (1) decision systems, (2) performance monitoring systems, (3) incentive-based compensation systems, (4) bankruptcy systems, (5) ownership structures, (6) creditor structures, (7) capital structures, (8) market for corporate control, (9) market for management services, and (10) product market competition (Encycogov, 2007).

According to organization theorists, it is primarily preoccupied with decreasing insecurity and costs in transactions and focuses on the best way to organize production and the exchange of goods and services. The theory compares transaction costs and the use of hierarchies or markets. "The main idea is that a hierarchy should be used where there is a high level of insecurity, specialized activities and little competition. Critics point out that this theory takes little account of social, cultural and moral constraints. … the relevance of this theory for the design of the public apparatus is questioned" (Christensen, 2007, p 12). Turner and Keegan (2001) looked at various roles for project governance and used transaction costs to show that two roles are needed: the broker and the steward in multiproject organizations (Mitchell, Carew, & Clift, 2004). Winch (2001) also based his approach to developing a conceptual framework for project governance on transaction cost analysis and has some really interesting ways of approaching things. Müller and Turner (2005) looked at the use of transaction cost in minimizing costs for governing projects. Market, as an alternative to hierarchy, is a control measure derived from the theory of transaction cost economics, according to Christensen et al. (2007, p 128).

Another theoretical perspective is formed by combining **economic analysis** and **analysis of political behavior** (Peltzman, 1998): "... it asserts that special interests and interest groups will try to pursue their own goals and influence the outcome of public decision-making processes. A main competition for scarce resources...another option, sometimes called a **bureau-shaping perspective** (Dunleavy, 1985; James, 2003), expects bureaucrats and their institutions to benefit from the decisions made and the structures designed (Majone, 1996). One outcome might be, for example, that autonomous public units, like regulatory agencies, begin to set their own standards rather than those formulated by the legislature and the political executive (Pollitt & Bouckaert, 2004)" (Christensen, 2007, p. 12).

It is important to bear in mind that all of these four theoretical directions (principal-agent, public choice, transaction cost, and political behavior) are all versions of the **economic-rational perspective**.

The **instrumental-structural perspective** also looks at the analytical aspect as an important part of public decision-making processes. (March & Simon, 1958). Like the economic-rational perspective, it is preoccupied with examining the logic of consequence. "The rational perspective demands full rationality, the instrumental one talks about bounded rationality and satisfying solutions. The latter logic proceeds from the view that the world is rather complex and that public decision makers have to select certain decision-making premises because they have attention and capacity problems" (Simon, 1957). "What is important for that selection is the formal structure, i.e., the position and tasks the individual actors have will preselect most of the decision-making premises, in other words, one's structural position governs how one thinks and acts. This means that the structural design or structure of public organizations is important for the main content of the decision-making processes" (Christensen, 2007, p. 15). The instrumental perspective focuses more on the decision-making structure and the actor aspect than the rational perspective. The instrumental perspective focuses more on the reasons behind problems of control. This perspective is closely related to the topic of this report.

The **network perspective** looks at the organization and its environment as webs of relationships. These relationships decide how individuals, groups, and entities cooperate and interact. There are five reasons to take a network perspective (Nohria & Eccles, 1992):

> *All organizations are social networks and therefore need to be addressed and analysed in terms of a set of nodes linked by social relationships. The environment in which an organization operates might be viewed as a network of other organizations. Organizations are suspended in multiple, complex, overlapping webs of relationships and we are unlikely to see the overall pattern from the point of view of one organization. Actions, as*

well as attitudes and behaviour of actors in organizations, can best be
explained in terms of their position within networks of relationships.
The comparative analysis of organizations must take into account their
network characteristics (p. 4).

Authors like Pryke (2005) and Larson and Wikstrøm (2007) use the network
perspective to study governance and projects.

There are other ways of looking at things. An alternative is **the cultural-
institutional perspective**. According to this perspective, public organizations
develop gradually and are not possible to design and control. Norms and values are
supposed to be more important for the thoughts and actions of public actors than
formal norms, and they influence the development of formal structures. When people
act inside public institutions, they act according to a logic of appropriateness, not
according to a logic of consequence, which is typical for the rational and instrumental
perspectives (March & Olsen, 1989). Christensen et al. (2007) distinguishes between
a **cultural perspective**, where the main notion is of institutionalized organizations
with a unique internal organizational culture and traditions, and a **myth perspective**
that embraces the idea of institutionalized environments, where the focus is on the
significance of values and norms found in an organization's environment. Whereas
the cultural perspective leads to uniqueness, the myth perspective will lead towards
uniform solutions when many organizations buy into the same myths.

With reference to Christensen (2007, p. 21), two other perspectives are mentioned.
In **the environmental perspective**, the system (organization) is dependent on its
technical and institutional environment (Meyer & Rowan, 1978). It is quite close to
the instrumental perspective, but it focuses on how the environment influences the
organization, and how the organization adapts to its environment. In **the garbage can
perspective,** the collective rationality and instrumentality is rather low (Christensen,
2007, p. 26). The garbage can is a metaphor describing the decision-making process
as ambiguous, shifting, and unpredictable (like the contents of a garbage can), and
the decision-making situation is flexible and subject to change (March & Olsen,
1976). March and Olsen also point out that in the garbage can perspective, solutions
may end up seeking problems to solve, rather than the opposite, as is the case in the
instrumental perspective (Christensen et al. 2007, p. 58).

For readers interested in the more political side of the decision-making problems
touched upon in this chapter, we recommend Altschuler and Luberoff (2003) book
Mega-projects: The Changing Politics of Urban Public Investment. In this book, the authors
analyze the decision-making processes behind a wide range of megaprojects, explaining
the important sides of urban development over the last six decades or so, at least in
American cities. They define urban politics to include all levels of governance relevant

to the actual development (p. 46). They analyze the development in light of five broad theoretical categories (the first three are parts of the theory of urban politics):

- Elite-reputational (p. 50) argues that corporate elites dominate local politics. Government is their servant.
- Pluralist (p. 51) argues that influence is widely distributed. Government is influential together with many other individuals, groups, and entities.
- Elite-structural (p. 62) argues that elites tend to dominate, and that this is a function of the broader structures within which local politics occur.
- Public choice (p. 53) argues that politics are best explained as the expression of rational choice by actors within frameworks of incentives.
- Historic-institutional (p. 72) argues that collective choices are strongly influenced by institutional arrangements, which in turn largely reflects long-past decisions.

These theories of urban politics are not used in our analysis, but in the perspective of this report, they do point to the importance of the structures put in place by government to secure a fair and rational choice on behalf of the society. The latter perspectives are relevant for explaining aspects and effects of the public and corporate governance and decision making, but are less important in explaining the structural side of the issue. Therefore, let us return to the instrumental perspective and go deeper into regimes, frameworks, and systems.

2.6   REGIMES, FRAMEWORKS, AND SYSTEMS

In describing the Norwegian Quality Assurance Scheme, words like regime, system, and framework have been used (Magnussen & Samset, 2005; Klakegg, 2005). In international literature on megaprojects, the words used are governance regime (Miller & Hobbs, 2005), institutional arrangements and regulatory regime (Flyvbjerg et al., 2002), and institutional framework (Michaud & Lessard, 2000). These are words frequently used to describe elements or aspects of governance. How are they related?

Systems are the core of a whole set of theories and worldviews. Systems engineering is a well-known field with roots going back to cybernetics (Wiener, 1948, as cited in Klakegg, 2004). It has proved useful in many aspects of organizations and technical arrangements, based on its powerful tool of process modeling. A traditional understanding of systems (e.g., within quality management) is a defined, explicit set of arrangements in the form of procedures and tools (elements) and the structure in which they interact. Their terminology (ISO 9000, 2005) gives the following definition: "system: set of interrelated or interacting elements." Systems, by this definition, are important within management in the public sector and the investment projects that we are studying.

Shenhar, Dvir, Lehler, and Poli (2002) looked at frameworks for project management. They said, "We realized it is time to develop a universal, context-free, and simple-to-use framework that will help managers and organizations start a project by assessing the project type and selecting an appropriate management style" (p. 99). This statement is quite parallel to our use of the word framework, but in a more limited context. They start with the notion that different stakeholders have different needs for classifications of projects and conclude the frameworks cannot be one-size-fits-all. In this report the framework is not intended to fit all, it is intended to answer to the needs of the owner.

Detomasi (2006) points to **regime theory** to explain the development of governance systems. Regimes[3] (Krasner, 1983, as cited in Detomasi, 2006) are defined as "sets of implicit principles, norms, rules and decision making procedures around which actors' expectations converge in a given area of international relations" (p. 231). Other definitions give more nuances to the phenomenon. Keohane and Nye (1977, as cited in Detomasi, 2006) defined regimes as "sets of governing relationships that involve networks of rules, norms and procedures that regularize behaviour and control its effects" (p. 231). Young (1999, as cited in Detomasi, 2006) defined a regime as "a governance system intended to deal with a more limited set of issues or a single issue area" (p. 231).

This definition seems compatible with the starting point of the Norwegian Quality Assurance Regime and the Concept program: "Governance regimes for major investment projects comprise the processes and systems that need to be in place on behalf of the financing party to ensure successful investments. This would typically include a regulatory framework to ensure adequate quality at entry, compliance with agreed objectives, management and resolution of issues that may arise during the project, etc., and standards for quality review of key governance documents" (Concept, 2006).

A regime is a system put in place to govern a limited set of issues or a specific focus area. Without saying it explicitly, it seems the basic regime definition is closely related to the traditional procedures and tools definition of systems. We do not think it has to be. Norms are mentioned by both Krasner (1983) and Keohane and Nye (1977). Krasner also mentions that the implicit principles are important. That is interesting

---

3. A very different meaning of the word 'regime' is used by Fainstein and Fainstein (1983) in their studies of urban politics referred to in Altschuler and Luberoff (2003). "The Fainsteins define a regime as 'the circle of powerful elected officials and top administrators' who are formally responsible for determining local policy and who are 'susceptible to electoral forces'" (p. 62).

and gives new and important aspects to the governance regime. This will be discussed further in a later chapter.

A framework can be two things: (1) abstract: a set of rules, ideas, or beliefs used in order to make sense of facts or events or to decide how to behave; and (2) concrete: a structure that forms or supports something (in our case "something" would be a public investment projects).

The concrete interpretation may be useful as a metaphor, but is not discussed here. It seems that the limitation of a regime to "a limited set of issues or a single issue area" is the only thing that really differs in the definitions of a regime and a framework. It points to goal orientation: who is this framework/regime relevant for? It seems a framework is of a very general nature, and a regime directed towards a certain target group or issue.

	Implicit		Implicit or Explicit			Explicit			
	Ideas	Beliefs	Norms	Principles	Rules	Structure	Procedures	Methods	Tools
Framework	X	X			X				
Regime			X	X	X		X		
System						X	X	X	X

FIGURE 2-2.　　RELATIONSHIP BETWEEN THE CONCEPTS OF SYSTEMS, FRAMEWORKS, AND REGIMES.

Figure 2-2 illustrates the relationship between the concepts as defined by other authors previously mentioned. By putting the words used to define them on a scale from the most abstract—ideas, to the most concrete—tools, a picture of the difference emerges. This picture does not offer a hard or precise definition; rather, it indicates the different nuances between the terms as we are using them in this report. Strict definitions of the limits between the concepts are not easy to obtain. Rules of a framework can be explicit and concrete enough to make it look like a system. A system may be very general and without detail, making it look like a framework. The term framework is also often used in combinations with limitations, for example, framework for analysis, a framework for the discussion, etc. When doing so, the definition tends to come closer to that of a regime. Systems, as we have defined them in this limited sense here, also have to have their specific limitations, as used in "a system for ...."

According to these definitions, a framework is a wider, more general concept than a regime, which again is more general than a system. Does this also apply when combining the concepts as several authors do? Look at combinations referred to in the beginning of this section: institutional framework, regulatory regime, and governance system. Words like institutional, regulatory, and governance include limitations. These limitations add to the complexity to the discussion of definitions and terms. But it is, of course, done on purpose in each case. These combinations of words are used to point to an issue, a target group, or level to which the framework, regime, or system apply. A governance regime is used about a regime on a higher level (across sectors/institutions), and the institutional framework works within a specific institution. Therefore, a governance regime may be a wider concept than an institutional framework.

For example: A governance regime is a broader concept than institutional framework according to Samset,[4] the program manager of the Concept Research Programme. In the description of a governance regime by the Concept program mentioned previously, the regulatory framework is obviously a subset, a limited part of the regime. Both statements are correct.

Koch and Buser (2006, p. 551) used the term "metagovernance" to describe a regulatory framework and pointed out that it originates from political science where it overlaps with governance of networks.

To make it easier for ourselves, we choose to limit our use of these concepts and word combinations. We will primarily use the following terms:

> **(Governance) Framework:** Installed by government, a framework to secure successful public investment projects.

> **(Management) System:** Installed by management of the entity (corporation or programme/project), a system to control the operations within its area of responsibility.

We will avoid the use of the word framework on management level and avoid using the word system on governance level. Other words than these will occur due to the fact that parts of the report cite sources like documents and interviews.

2.7   SUMMARY: GOVERNANCE WITHOUT PROJECTS

We have excluded the international governance for the purpose of this report and concentrated on national public and corporate governance. There has to be a general governance framework defining how resources and risks are distributed

---

4. Professor Knut Samset, Norwegian University of Science and Technology; from personal discussions with one of the authors (2007).

among stakeholders (i.e., the society at large). Laws and regulatory mechanisms make up the structure, and information, auditing, and other control measures are actively used to secure the intended results. The literature mentioned previously is about governance regulating society and corporations. Public governance points towards the public sector (the society). Corporate governance is pointing to the private sector (corporations and companies), but the elements are also relevant towards regulating the enterprise of public affairs. Private and public sectors are parallel in the world of governance. According to some scientists, the difference is getting smaller and smaller. We have also mentioned the difference in levels between the society at large and the institutions. But so far, we have not focused on projects at all, just mentioned them briefly. That must change.

2.8   ENTER THE PROJECTS

The typical definition of a project is: *"a temporary endeavor undertaken to create a unique product, service or result"* (PMI, 2004, p. 368).

The obvious point in the project definition is that projects are a means to achieve goals. When discussing the **major public investment projects**, focus is on large (not only physically or economically big, but influential, complex, critical) investments (resource-demanding choices in order to benefit later) to achieve goals based on the society's needs or demands (defined by the society at large, its institutions, or decision makers).

We established as a conclusion to Section 2.4, the distinction between governance (of the public sector) *through* projects (the corporate level within public sector), and governance *of* (public investment) projects (the project level). Both have to be considered, and we are going to look into both. First we have to sort out some more words used to describe the area we are studying.

2.9   PROJECT GOVERNANCE

Miller and Hobbs (2005) formulated a new trend in project management: "Project governance has only recently become an issue of importance in the project management community and literature. Over the last ten years there has been more interest in the governance of projects in general and the governance of large complex public projects in particular" (p. 47). Darshana Patel goes even further, referring to the growing number of project management offices (PMO); she refers to a "project governance movement" (Patel, 2007, p. 1).

Let us focus on the term *project governance*. What does it comprise? Miller and Hobbs (2005) use the phrases project governance and governance of projects without defining them exactly. Are they synonyms? Patel (2007) does not define the term either. Other terms frequently used contributes to this confusion.

Management by projects was originally introduced by Roland Gareis (1990) as a concept of managing the whole organization ("a strategic option for the project-oriented company") based on project management principles and tools. Despite Gareis' unstoppable enthusiasm and continuing effort to spread the concept, today it seems mostly to be used as a selling point in marketing project management courses to organizations traditionally not project driven in Europe. It is mostly used as a buzzword with no precise definition. In the United States, it seems to be used to sell project management to industry by pointing to this as a new way of operating, which lets companies tailor products and services for individual customers.

Strategic management of projects usually points to the management processes and techniques used to make sure projects are designed to fit the business and organizational needs and demands. It is often connected to concepts like program management, value management, and feasibility studies. These are management techniques—good practices—not governance.

Graham M. Winch uses the phrase "governing the project process." He uses transaction cost economics to propose a comprehensive theoretical framework for governing the construction management process. Winch also points out that "the range of governance options open to any firm is limited by the institutional context within which it trades" (p. 799), so there is a link between the governance principles on a high level and on lower levels, and a link between the internal processes (company, project) and its surroundings (the trade, the sector, the industry, etc.) (Winch, 2001). Similarly, "The reality that project governance is the context, not the content, must be reinforced. Meaning, project governance is the space in which the day-to-day project activities occur" (Patel, 2007, p. 2).

We acknowledge that all these authors (and many more in the project community) have contributed to the better understanding of important sides to the issues in question here. But there is still a need to sort out the meaning of the words. We returned to Wikipedia to try to find some general introductions on project governance, shown in Figure 2-3. It is understood that there is a great deal of confusion.

This figure shows a large collection of management aspects gathered under one umbrella. It appears to be an attempt to settle for an "everything is governance approach." This action is rather typical for a new emerging field. We aim to avoid falling into this trap.

Project Governance

The term **project governance** is used in industry, especially in the information technology (IT) sector (see Information technology governance), to describe the processes that need to exist for a successful project.

Project governance will:

- Outline the relationships between all internal and external groups involved in the project,
- Describe the proper flow of information regarding the project to all stakeholders,
- Ensure the appropriate review of issues encountered within each project, and
- Ensure that required approvals and direction for the project is obtained at each appropriate stage of the project.

Important specific elements of good project governance include:

- A compelling business case, stating the objects of the project and specifying the in-scope and out-of-scope aspects,
- A mechanism to assess the compliance of the completed project to its original objectives,
- Identifying all stakeholders with an interest in the project,
- A defined method of communication to each stakeholder,
- A set of business-level requirements as agreed by all stakeholders,
- An agreed specification for the project deliverables,
- The appointment of a project manager,
- Clear assignment of project roles and responsibilities,
- A current, published project plan that spans all project stages from project initiation through development to the transition to operations,
- A system of accurate upward status- and progress-reporting including time records,
- A central document repository for the project,
- A centrally held glossary of project terms,
- A process for the management and resolution of issues that arise during the project,
- A process for the recording and communication of risks identified during the project,
- A standard for quality review of the key governance documents and of the project deliverables.

FIGURE 2-3.   PROJECT GOVERNANCE ACCORDING TO WIKIPEDIA

We will start at the beginning, according to PMI's definitions (PMI, 2004):

- **Project:** a temporary endeavor undertaken to create a unique product, service, or result. (p. 368)
- **Program:** a group of related projects managed in a coordinated way to obtain benefits and control not available from managing them individually. Programs may include elements of related work outside of the scope of the discrete projects in the program. (p. 368)

> • **Portfolio:** a collection of projects or programs and other work that are
> grouped together to facilitate effective management of that work to meet
> strategic business objectives. The projects or programs of the portfolio
> may not necessarily be interdependent or directly related. (p. 367)

All of these are tools to reach the organization's strategic goals or support the owner's strategies. They represent management methods and tools; normally, they would formally be connected to the use of systems. From the bottom up (from project to portfolio), they increasingly comprise a wider perspective than the single task at hand. They even explicitly link the projects to strategy. Sometimes this link is forgotten: "A number of textbooks and papers….have suggested program processes that, albeit their different designation, are in most instances just transpositions of the project paradigm into program management….It is now generally agreed that programs need to produce business-level benefits and are a link between strategy and projects" (Thiry, 2004, p. 114). Still, in the definitions of this report, these are all aspects of management, not governance. Governance has to do with the perspective of the owner/financing party, not that of the individual project, program, or portfolio manager.

Governing the Project Process

Winch (2001) argued that construction management has developed a process approach in recent years. This means we need to ask how these processes are governed. Drawing on transaction cost economics, he proposed a comprehensive theoretical framework for construction management. He used a set of phrases like transaction governance, construction governance, and governance of supply chains, and uses phrases like horizontal and vertical transaction governance to discuss phenomenons within construction projects.

This illustrates that there may be a defined, separate set of governance principles (constituting a framework) for different function areas or aspects of doing business. These are obviously subsets of corporate governance. To the extent that the function area or aspect is project related, it will also be a subset of project governance. Winch discussed this topic on a more detailed level than the discussion in this paper. Governing project processes is what we would call this (not the whole process, but different partial processes). Winch (2001) points out that the appropriate transaction governance depends on three dimensions: asset specificity (because of opportunism), uncertainty (because of bounded rationality), and frequency (because of the need for learning). These dimensions may be useful for further discussion.

Furthermore, Winch (2001) also said that "the range of governance options open to any firm is limited by the institutional context within which it trades" (p. 799).

This statement means there is a link between the governance principles on a high level and on lower levels, and that there is a link between the internal processes (company, project) and its surroundings (the trade, the sector, the industry, etc.). This comment is not surprising at all, but it points out that we need to understand these links. In a later contribution, Winch introduced the concepts "macro analytical perspective" and "micro analytical perspective" and explicitly places his own work within the micro perspective (Winch, 2006, p. 328).

Project Strategy

Strategy management is well-known and dealt with in the literature (e.g., Mintzberg & Quinn, 1996). "Strategy is the direction and scope of an organization over the long-term; ideally, which achieves advantage in a changing environment through its configuration of resources and competences with the aim of fulfilling stakeholder expectations" (Johnson & Scholes, 1993, p. 3). But as we turn to projects, Artto et al. (2004, 2007) are concerned with the link between projects and strategy. They report a major literature study revealing the way project literature has been (and still is) looking at the link between strategy and projects. There are three different tracks (Artto et al., 2007, p. 5): In the first and most dominant track, projects are viewed as subordinate to the parent organization where project strategy is derived from more significant business strategies of the parent....In the second track...projects have been considered as autonomous organizations connected loosely or tightly to a parent organization. In such literature, projects themselves develop their own strategies and plans independent of the surrounding organizational context....In the third track, projects have been considered as organizations that are not subjected to a clearly defined governance or authority setting in relation to their surrounding organizations or stakeholder organizations. In such cases, projects interact with their uncertain and complex environment and adapt to the ongoing changes as strategic entities of their own. (p. 5)

The first track is indeed dominant. "Project strategy has to be developed to support larger organizational plans," says perhaps the father of modern project management, Cleland (2004, p. 212). Partington (2000) has a similar (low-level) view of program/project strategy. He divides strategy into three levels: corporate, business, and operational, and puts programs/projects into the latter category. Another similar view is taken by Kerzner (2000)—author of a very well-known text in project management—who looks at the corporate strategic plan at the top-level, divided into top-level function plans, which are then divided into supporting business unit plans and budgets, which are then cascaded into plans for individual projects, products, brands, manufacturing plans, and so on. A clearly operational perspective is used by Seider (2006) who presents optimization of project portfolio as a tool to enhance productivity and effectiveness in engineering.

The tightening of the relationships between corporate and project strategies is given in the well-known book by Turner (1999), who showed business strategy aligned with portfolio objectives, giving the portfolio strategy aligned with program objectives, giving program strategy aligned with the various project objectives and thus project strategies. Other literature in this field includes Shenhar et al. (2005) who introduced the division between strategically managed projects (focused on achieving business results) and operationally managed projects (focusing on getting the job done). Of course, it is generally not individual projects but programs or projects through which strategy is pursued, and it is these that need to be aligned with the strategic objectives of the organization (Turner & Simister, 2000). The Office of Government Commerce (OGC, 1999) said that a key benefit of program management is the alignment of projects to organizational strategy. Rietiker (2006) looked at projects in their corporate and social context that forms an environment in which projects are based on the needs of the enterprise.

The two main questions in the perspective of this report concern whether the project is connected tightly or loosely to the responsible public entity, and to what degree the objectives and strategy are defined (given) by the owners. These are obviously relevant issues and points to governance and the use of governance frameworks. One particular mechanism that we mention in this report is the public-private partnership (see Ive, 2004 for a discussion), in which the project is more self-standing, and thus connected particularly loosely to the responsible public entity.

Artto et al. (2007) tried to clarify the concept by introducing a new definition and interpretation of project strategy. The new definition is: "Project strategy is a direction in a project that contributes to the success of the project in its environment" (p. 11).

They "derive different alternative project strategies from literature, characterized by two important dimensions in a project's environment: project's independence and number of strong project stakeholder organizations" (p. 2). This definition underpins the point that projects are dependent of their environment, and thus of the framework they are executed within.

The project literature seems to be slowly turning over from the traditional operational focus to more of a strategic focus (Klakegg, 2006). But still the general impression of the project literature is that the perspective is that of the project and program managers.

Complexity
The contributions mentioned previously point to the issue of complexity. Complexity is, of course, an important characteristic of both the public context and the major projects we are studying. Clearly, governance of a complex project or a program in a

complex environment or organizational structure needs particular mechanisms to be successful.

Amin and Hausner (1997) looked at acting in the context of a complex society, with the aim of looking at the governance of complexity and the "practicalities of governing complexity in various national and cultural settings" (p. 4). They say: "The argument we advance is that the successful governance of complex economic systems ... requires a strategic interactive approach. Such an approach can be summarized as one combining central strategic guidance with decentralized associative governance" (p. 4).

Furthermore, Amin and Hausner stated that "any attempt to build effective governance mechanisms should include:

- Simplifying models and practices which reduce the complexity of the world....
- Developing the capacity for dynamic social learning about various causal processes....
- Building methods for coordinating actions across different social forces.....
- Establishing both a common world view for individual action and a system of meta-governance to stabilize key players' orientation, expectations and rules of conduct." (p. 100)

They also stated that objects of governance do not simply pre-exist the governance, but "the very processes of governance co-constitute the objects which come to be governed in and through these same processes" (pp. 104–105). "This leads this author to the idea of the 'negotiated economy' — a 'third way' between market economics and central planning" (p. 117).

Artto et al. (2007) concluded that the project, as a response to its complex environment, should be allowed to develop its own strategies, providing direction as a continuous process throughout the project life cycle as a dynamic scheme. The project's strategy may be different from that of the parent organization.

Winston and Mallick (2007) studied the effect of incorrect representation of uncertainties in governmental planning, showing examples of how uncertainties are used as assumptions in project planning—hiding the truth and giving a flawed basis for decisions as a result. Müller and Turner (2005) studied the impact of hierarchical management and contract type on communication between project owner and manager giving recommendations for risk-minimizing owner–manager communication.

2.10   LINKING GOVERNANCE AND PROJECTS

Ownership

Several authors have pointed out the role of the owner as important to success in projects. We will not go deep into this subject here, but only make a few remarks. Ownership is naturally one of the important links between governance and projects. Governance is in the perspective of this report naturally installed on behalf of the owner. Olsson, Johansen, Langlo, and Torp (2007) pointed at the owner as a special stakeholder. Certainly, this stakeholder will have a central position in our work. Foss and Foss (1999) stated that the owner is the party that has residual control rights and residual profit responsibility over the output of the project. Control rights give the owner right to use, possess, and dispose of a resource. Profit responsibility means the owner is responsible for both the cost and the income/benefit related to the resource. Residual means the owner can delegate the authority to others (Grünfeldt & Jacobsen, 2006). Samset (2003) noted that the owner (he uses the term financing party) is first and foremost interested in the long-term effects of the project. The responsibility to finance the investment is also a natural part of ownership. The ownership functions are organized in many different ways (see the indications in Section 2.3 in the discussion on new public management). According to Eikeland (2001), the project owner is characterized as the one taking the risk related to the cost and future value of the project. Both these risks can, to a certain extent, be transferred to other actors in the project. Ownership could be a major subject to discuss in a report like this, but instead of taking the broad view and deep discussions on the owner role, we choose to highlight a few aspects of special relevance to the discussions to come later in this report.

Organizations and Projects

The obvious link between the owner and the project is expressed through the formalities defined as organizational structures. The organizational structures describe roles and responsibilities, reporting lines and control spans, and internal and external interfaces. This is important to bear in mind as we go into the study of governance frameworks and project cases. The organizational structures may take many shapes and forms and can be discussed at several levels, just like governance. The following are a few general aspects.

The key roles in the perspective of this report can be listed as owner, decision makers, managers, assessors, users, and other stakeholders. In a public setting, the owner will often include functions like the financing party, commissioning party, operating party, asset management party, etc. The decision makers include two main categories: political and administrative. For the executing party, managers are responsible for the execution of the tasks, portfolio directors, and program and project managers. Assessors are the independent experts doing reviews and audits on behalf of the owner or other stakeholders. Important aspects are: Who is responsible for what? Who is legitimately influencing the decision at what stages of development? Organizational elements like project steering committees and project boards are means directly aimed at linking governance and projects.

Projects may be internal or external to the parent organization; internal meaning the project is a direct subordinate of the parent organization and thus strongly linked. External projects may have a more independent position, be more loosely linked to the parent organization, even its own juridical entity. See the discussions on project strategy and complexity. Then we have the hybrids, like the partnerships, PFIs, etc., where the interface between internal and external has a different nature.

The project organization may be internalized, meaning its organization is mainly composed of internal resources—employees of the parent organization. This result is, of course, a close link to the parent organization—normally the project owner. Project organizations may be composed of external resources (the function outsourced or the service commissioned); in this situation, the owner is a client and the interface defined by a commercial contract. This is a weaker link. Then there are the hybrids again, which can involve integrated teams where both internal and external people work together.

There are many aspects of these formal structures linking organizations and their projects. We need to understand these to understand the ways governance can be implemented from the owners in a strategic perspective.

Governance and Management
This report discusses the building of effective governance mechanisms from the owner/financing party's perspective, supporting the implementation of successful portfolios, programs, and projects. In this report lies a link to management. A simple illustration is shown in Figure 2-4. It shows the levels of organizational contexts (environments). In this report, the two outer layers are defined as the macroanalytical perspective. This perspective is the owner and financing party. The three inner boxes are the manager's perspectives. In this report this is called the microanalytical perspective.

Each box in Figure 2-4 is a framework for the next box within. Every box is a new level of governance (two outer boxes) and management (three inner boxes). Every box is interdependent of each other (influences each other). Each box defines the environment of the next box (level). Every box (inwards) has a more limited perspective, constitutes a framework for the next level, and includes an increasing level of detail in the appurtenant guidelines and methods.

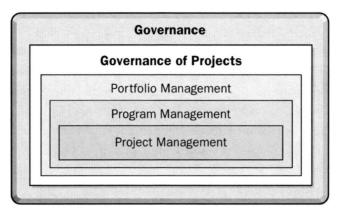

FIGURE 2-4.   BOXES WITHIN BOXES—DIFFERENT LEVELS OF CONCEPTS IN THIS DISCUSSION

Governance and Accountability

One way of explaining the vertical dimension in Figure 2-4 is proposed by the Norwegian Centre for Project Management (Olsson et al., 2007) and shown in Figure 2-5. Governance represents the owner's effort to ensure the projects are carried out in accordance with the overall objectives of the organization. Accountability can be used synonymously with such concepts as answerability, responsibility, and liability. As an aspect of governance, accountability has been central in discussions related to problems in both a public and business context. It is not less important when looking at projects.

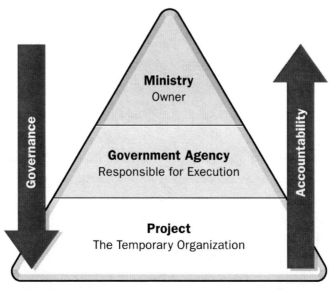

FIGURE 2-5.   GOVERNANCE VS. ACCOUNTABILITY

Accountability is frequently seen as an important means of achieving governance. In Britain, accountability has been formally identified by government since the mid-1990s. The Committee on Standards in Public Life was established in 1994 by then Prime Minister John Major and is still active. "The Committee on Standards in Public Life … is an independent advisory body to the Government, we monitor, report and make recommendations on all issues relating to standards in public life" From the committee's web-pages (Committee on Standards in Public Life, 2009);

Accountability is one of the seven principles of public life (Committee on Standards in Public Life, 1995, p. 6). The principles are still present in the committee's 11th report as well (2007). The seven principles are:

- **Selflessness**—act solely in public interest,
- **Integrity**—do not place yourself in obligations influencing your performance,
- **Objectivity**—make choices solely on merits,
- **Accountability**—be responsible for your actions and open for scrutiny,
- **Openness**—give reasons for decisions and only restrict information when needed,
- **Honesty**—declare your private interests and take steps to resolve any conflict arising, and
- **Leadership**—promote and support these principles by leadership and example.

The committee has performed surveys to map the public's attitudes towards these principles and expectations towards the behavior of Members of Parliament (MP's) and government ministers as well as senior public officials (Committee on Standards in Public Life, 2005). They find the importance of these principles is stable over time, but that the actual perceived performance has had a negative development. People hardly make any distinction between the groups when it comes to expectations and perception of performance.

Accountability is much of the answer to the challenge of governance. The other six principles support the accountability in interest of the public. The seven principles are an example of general guidance for good governance, but fit well also in the context of governance of projects.

It is not undisputed, though. An example is Jeremie Hardie. He stated the following:

"For full public accountability to work, two apparently banal but tough conditions need to be met. First, the decision must be made transparent by setting out a clear account of how it was arrived at. Second, the public must be capable of making an assessment, in the light of that account" (Hardie, 2005, p. 1).

He argued that it often is hard, not to say impossible, to make the problem well behaved (structured, clear) and even more common, the public is not able to assess the decision (lack of knowledge). Hardie suggested the rationality of decisions is not working and instead we need something else. He summed it up in the word *trust*. This action is also relevant in the world of projects.

Others, for example Næss, Flyvbjerg and Buhl (2006), noted (investigating major transport projects) that: "Due to their complexity and lack of transparency, transport model calculations will often be impossible to penetrate for other people than a narrow group of experts" (p. 21). There is strong evidence that the reality behind good principles like transparency and openness is shadier than we like to think. In this report we accept the fact that there are no such things as perfect governance and accountability. The development and implementation of governance frameworks is the tool to improve it.

The underlying thesis for the study is that the framework under which the investment project is planned and executed is important in determining the effectiveness of cost estimation and reducing the problem of cost overrun. This brief survey of project literature has shown that there have been many initiatives to enter the field we are studying, and the frequency of such contributions is increasing. Many important issues have been touched upon. It has also revealed that there is a confusion about the use of words and definitions in this field, probably also reinforced by lack of clarity of which perspective the authors of many contributions are having. To make sure we do not end up increasing this confusion, we chose the following for the rest of the report:

- We will NOT use the term project governance. Project governance is here restricted to describe governance within the project. We use the terms governance of projects/governance through projects.
- We place ourselves in a macroanalytical perspective as defined previously.
- Our perspective is defined by originating from the owner/financing party's view.
- We acknowledge the complexity of the project environment and accept that the project strategy is not necessarily given by the parent organization (the owner). There is a dynamic interrelationship between the project and its environment—regulated by the governance framework.

2.11 GOVERNANCE OF PROJECT MANAGEMENT

APM defined governance of project management as the following:

> *"Governance of project management (GoPM) concerns those areas of corporate governance that are specifically related to project activities. Effective governance of project management ensures that an organisation's project portfolio is aligned to the organisation's objectives, is delivered efficiently and is sustainable." (APM, 2002, p. 4)*

GoPM is explicitly a part of corporate governance. Comparing the APM definition to the definition of governance systems by Monks and Minow (2004) (section 2.4), there is a clear parallel between the governance of project management and the internal governance processes. Not all internal governance processes seem to be included, however. The focus is that "effective governance of project management ensures that an organisation's project portfolio is aligned to the organisation's objectives, is delivered efficiently and is sustainable" (p. 4).

Interpreted for our purpose, the three main goals may be derived from the APM definition:

- Choosing the right projects,
- Delivering the chosen projects efficiently, and
- Making sure the projects (their effect) are sustainable.

The last bullet point is very important. Logically, it could be an important reason underlying the two previous ones: choosing the right project means choosing a sustainable alternative, and efficient delivery also means delivery in a sustainable way (taking economy, environment, and other aspects into consideration). Nevertheless, these goals are important focal points in governance of projects. They are also important goals of the Norwegian Quality Assurance scheme. From this standpoint, the following deconstruction is possible:

Both governance through projects and governance of projects are embedded in the APM definition: choosing the right projects (to make sure the right objectives are achieved) and making sure the projects (actually the goals and the effects of the project) are sustainable. This is governance through projects—the context in which the critical decisions are made. This is the true project governance on a public or corporate level.

Delivering the projects efficiently is also important. In the setting of this report, it is about how to avoid wasting (public) resources. The framework established around the project execution (from the time that it is decided upon until it is put into operation) determines how well the project organization is able to perform its task (of course, this also depends largely on competence and capacity), and thus how efficient delivery can be obtained. This is governance *of* projects—the context in which project management is working. This is project governance on a project level.

Why did APM focus on **project management** in their definition—not at the project itself? "It follows from our basic purpose and understanding of the problem with the governance of projects—that there is insufficient understanding by boards of the significance of project management and a discipline and a collection of tools, resources, and skills in their organizations. The way to better projects is through better governance of project management."[5] This statement reminds us that the people involved are of vital importance to the end result, and the reference to the project organization underlines that this is not a technical problem which can be managed only with structures and systems.

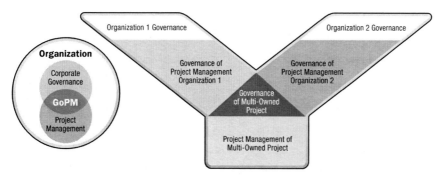

FIGURE 2-6.   LEFT, GOVERNANCE OF PROJECT MANAGEMENT IN CONTEXT (APM, 2002). RIGHT, GOVERNANCE OF MULTIOWNED PROJECTS (APM, 2007).

The APM Governance of Project Management Special Interest Group has developed two sets of guidelines which are very relevant to the subject in this report. These guidelines are developed by a group of senior experts with a wide range of experiences from public and private sectors. They are individuals with many years of experience as practitioners and academics. The guidelines are practical tools for improving the governance of project management. The first one that covers single projects came in 2002 and is widely distributed. The second one covers multiowned projects and came late in 2007. In these two references, a set of governance principles are defined. These are shown in Table 2-1.

5. David Shannon. Chairman of the GoPM Special Interest Group in a personal e-mail to one of the authors, October 2007.

TABLE 2-1.   GOVERNANCE PRINCIPLES OF THE APM GOPM SIG

Directing change - 11 principles (APM 2002)		Co-directing change - 12 principles (APM 2007)	
1	The board has overall responsibility for governance of project management.	1	There should be formally agreed governance arrangements.
2	The roles, responsibilities, and performance criteria for the governance of project management are clearly defined.	2	There should be a single point of decision making for the project.
3	Disciplined governance arrangements, supported by appropriate methods and controls, are applied throughout the project life cycle.	3	There should be a clear and unambiguous allocation of authority for representing the project in contacts with owners, stakeholders, and third parties.
4	A coherent and supportive relationship is demonstrated between the overall business strategy and the project portfolio.	4	The project business case should include agreed, and current, definitions of project objectives, the role of each owner, their incentives, inputs, authority, and responsibilities.
5	All projects have an approved plan containing authorization points at which the business case is reviewed and approved. Decisions made at authorization points are recorded and communicated.	5	Each owner should assure itself that the legal competence and obligations and internal governance arrangements of co-owners, are compatible with its acceptable standards of governance for the project.
6	Members of delegated authorization bodies have sufficient representation, competence, authority, and resources to enable them to make appropriate decisions.	6	There should be project authorization points and limiting constraints to give owners the necessary degree of control over the project.
7	The project business case is supported by relevant and realistic information that provides a reliable basis for making authorization decisions.	7	There should be agreed recognition and allocation or sharing of rewards and risks, taking account of ability to influence the outcome and creating incentives to foster co-operative behavior.
8	The board or its delegated agents decide when independent scrutiny of projects and project management systems is required and implement such scrutiny accordingly.	8	Project leadership should exploit synergies arising from multiownership and should actively manage potential sources of conflict or inefficiency.
9	There are clearly defined criteria for reporting project status and for the escalation of risks and issues to the levels required by the organization.	9	There should be a formal agreement that defines the process to be invoked and the consequences for assets and owners when a material change of ownership is considered.

Directing change - 11 principles (APM 2002)		Co-directing change - 12 principles (APM 2007)	
10	The organization fosters a culture of improvement and of frank internal disclosure of project information.	10	Reporting during both the project and the realization of benefits should provide honest, timely, realistic, and relevant data on progress, achievements, forecasts, and risks to the extent required for good governance by owners.
11	Project stakeholders are engaged at a level that is commensurate with their importance to the organization and in a manner that fosters trust.	11	There should be a mechanism in place to invoke independent review or scrutiny when it is in the legitimate interests of one or more of the project owners.
		12	There should be a dispute resolution process agreed between owners that does not endanger the achievement of project objectives.

The first one, called directing change, focuses on the board and its responsibilities. Given that the board is representing the owner, this focus is similar to the one in this report. The setting is a single project with one owner. The second guideline, codirecting change, is developed for the situation where there is more than one owner. This practice is not unusual in public projects.

The principles described in Table 2-1 are basically consistent with the current best practice in project management. Therefore, it should be expected that these principles may be implemented without creating a conflict with the principles by which the project organization is working. On the contrary, these principles are defined to help project management reach success. We would suggest these guidelines could be a part of the toolset to improve the overall success of all kinds of projects in all sectors. Since these guidelines are not included in any of the frameworks compared in this study, we do not use them directly in the further work.

2.12 GOVERNANCE FRAMEWORKS FOR PROJECTS

Winch (2006) says a project belongs to a broader *governance framework* that includes the context of incentive systems and distribution of risks and resources in the market. Such a context includes both economic actors and political actors. Our view is also that this context should include both hierarchy and market as regulating mechanisms.

The government of the two countries included in this study have both chosen to establish a formal governance framework for major public investment projects with the purpose of improving their way of handling these projects and have more value for the public funds spent on investments. As will be shown later, they both believe in a framework established as a common resource and support for all major projects within a portfolio. With reference to the theoretical approaches presented earlier in this chapter, this approach is clearly instrumental-structural initiatives backing up an economic-rational perspective. At the same time, they have elements best explained in a cultural-institutional perspective in that they are implemented to modernize and improve the governing organization.

A definition of governance frameworks may go something like the following: "Governance regimes for major investment projects comprise the processes and systems that need to be in place on behalf of the financing party to ensure successful investments" (Concept, 2006, p. 2). This definition, however, is very closely connected to the specific setting of a regulatory regime for major investment projects. Therefore, we try to make it more neutral by reformulating it. Based on previous theory (see Figure 2-2), we exchange the word *regime* with the word *framework*, and the word *system* with *rules*. The result is the following definition: "Governance framework: an organised structure established as authoritative within the institution, comprising processes and rules established to ensure projects meet their purpose").

An organized structure means it is put there with a purpose, defines structures, roles, and responsibilities, etc. Authoritative within the institution means it is anchored on a high level and has a strong position, but is limited to the institution within the borders of which it is supposed to work. Comprising processes and rules—this is its explicit content to ensure projects meet their purpose, which is the purpose of the framework.

The project meeting its purpose is a way of defining its success. It implies both delivering the relevant solution in an effective way and achieving a sustainable effect. The initiatives in the United Kingdom and Norway represent a common framework for all (major) projects. In practice the smaller projects are not included, for operational (mostly resource) reasons. Some authors question the idea of having a common framework. For example:

A specific governance regime must adapt to the particular project and its context. The approach taken is, therefore, not the design of a governance regime but rather the identification of design criteria that should be brought to bear when developing a governance regime for a megaproject. Several of the criteria contrast to the traditional conception that governance is a static, binary, hierarchical process. Governance regimes for megaprojects are time-dependent and self-organizing. They involve a network of actors in a process through which the project concept, the sponsoring coalition, and the institutional framework co-evolve (Miller & Hobbs, 2005, p. 49).

Miller and Hobbs used the description of project governance to enter into a systems thinking approach, not unlike the one we are trying to establish here. Their work is based on large engineering projects of a scale equivalent to megaprojects (definitions discussed earlier in this chapter). The views of Miller and Hobbs are particularly relevant to the discussions in this report.

We do not want to limit the definition to megaprojects in this report. Governance of projects (as a concept) has to be relevant to projects of all sizes and characteristics. The focus of the Concept Research Programme is major projects (chosen to establish a distinction—they are big and important but not limited to the definition of megaprojects) with a proposed budget of 500 million (NOK)/$80 million (US) or more. This choice coincides with the lower cost-limit defining that projects have to go through in the Norwegian QA scheme. The United Kingdom governance framework includes a criteria based on criticality (where cost is one component). These initiatives implicitly assume that all projects should adapt the same principles, although the practical solutions may vary in different types of projects and projects of different sizes/complexities.

Few of the projects in question would meet the definition of a megaproject defined earlier. At the other end of the scale, there are strong resource limitations in small projects, suggesting they might have to be treated differently. A typical element of a governance framework is some kind of *stage-gate* or *gateway* process in which the projects are subject to scrutiny—typically at decision points in the development process. Cooper, Edgett, and Kleinschmidt (2002a, b) suggested that all projects should be subject to stage-gate process due to the fact that all projects take up resources. Eskerod et al. (2004) showed that the small projects in practice are excluded from the governance, upper level decision making, and portfolio management.

In this report the same starting point is chosen as in developing the national frameworks. In doing this we accept the aspect of stability and common regulations embedded in a governance framework. At the same time, we support the idea that the real mega-projects are of a different class that in many cases demand individual adaptation—many of them cross borders between different governance frameworks (countries, states, etc.), and if for no other reason, adaptations may have to take place to handle this. On the other hand, a governance framework may be flexible enough to handle mega-projects as well. Like the national frameworks studied, we accept the notion that small projects can be treated by simpler means, and thus argue again for flexibility. The research presented in this paper focuses on major projects within the normal governance framework defined for the two countries.

We have, so far, only talked about single projects. Clearly, projects that are interlinked into a *program* of projects need to be looked at as a whole entity. Equally clearly, our structures of governance through projects need to look at the overall *portfolio* of projects and see how the corporate strategy is realized through that portfolio

(Morris & Jamieson, 2004). Alternatively, we may ask how aligned the portfolio is with the overall strategy of the organization—this reflects the first (and third) of the APM definition. We will come back to these questions in the analysis.

2.13   SUMMARY: GOVERNANCE AND PROJECTS

There are many levels of governance with different perspectives and problems attached to each. This chapter has illustrated some of these and given a theoretical platform for discussing the consequences of them. The awareness of the different levels is important, but not enough. The levels represented by society, institution, and project are well-known and widely used. Placing them together gives the illustration in Figure 2.7. Note the limitations to project governance. This report represents a macroanalytical perspective on projects and the governance frameworks installed to define, choose, and control them.

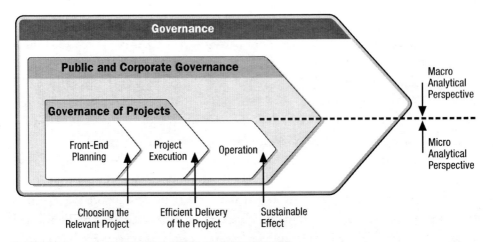

FIGURE 2-7.   DIFFERENT LEVELS OF GOVERNANCE

The different settings in the public and corporate sectors imply there are important differences in substance. As shown in Figure 2-7, the two different perspectives, public governance and corporate governance, are placed on the same level. Even though they are getting closer to each other over time, they are not synonymous. Still, we have chosen to put them on the same level and argue that this is correct in this context. We will acknowledge the difference and choose different forms in abstract formulation and choice of words. However, the public sector is focused on here and will dominate our description.

The public agencies and corporations are different, but at the same time governed and managed more and more by the same principles. The corporate (private sector) thinking over the last decades has also dominated the public sector. The increasing use of projects as an organizational tool is a result (and driver) of this development. Therefore, we accept a strong link between corporate governance and project governance independent of whether we discuss projects in public or private sectors.

We have defined our starting point in a position where we accept the need for and appropriateness of a governance framework to secure the owners' success. We acknowledge there are extremely large, complex projects with special needs and resource limitations connected with small projects. Therefore, there is a need for flexibility in the frameworks, and perhaps in some cases special adaptations. We have seen that there are a large number of principles to guide us on what is *good governance*, and these will be part of the basis for further analysis.

2.14   CONCLUSION TO THEORY: OUR DEFINITIONS

We need to choose some words and establish a set of definitions to use in further work. The standard definitions of project, program, and portfolio are according to PMI.

Governance can be defined as: "The use of institutions, structures of authority and even collaboration to allocate resources and coordinate or control activity in society or the economy."

We will not focus more on this level—thus any of the definitions given in the paragraph on public governance will do. The other definitions mentioned may be interpreted a bit wider than this one. The one chosen is the one that fits best with the purpose of this report.

Public governance is defined as (OECD, 2005): "Governance refers to the formal and informal arrangements that determine how public decisions are made and how public actions are carried out, from the perspective of maintaining a country's constitutional values in the face of changing problems, actors and environments." (p. 16)

Corporate governance is defined like this (OECD, 2004): "Corporate governance involves a set of relationships between a company's management, its board, its shareholders and other stakeholders. Corporate governance also provides the structure through which the objectives of the company are set, and the means of attaining those objectives and monitoring performance are determined." (p. 11)

In a project context, this phenomenon could alternatively be called governance through projects, pointing to the link between the organization's strategic objectives and chosen initiatives. We have pointed out the choice of relevant projects that gives a sustainable effect as a main motivation. The alternative name for the phenomenon is only useful in a setting where the corporation or public agency has explicitly defined that conducting projects is their dominating management strategy.

Governance of projects is defined as the following (based on APM): "Project governance concerns those areas of governance (public or corporate) that are specifically related to project activities. Good project governance ensures relevant, sustainable alternatives are chosen and delivered efficiently."

The concepts of governance through projects and governance of projects together make up a useful whole. Note that we do not use the term project governance. Use of that phrase should be limited to describing governance within the project. That is not the topic of this report.

Governance framework is defined like this (our definition): "Governance framework is an organized structure established as authoritative within the institution, comprising processes and rules established to ensure projects meet their purpose."

A specific governance framework must be able to adapt to the particular project and its context. Governance is a dynamic, multidimensional, interactive process involving a network of actors. The governance framework is time-dependent and self-organizing.

In this form, the definitions are clearly pointing towards structure and may be seen as formed in the instrumental-structural perspective. It is not our intention to limit the definitions, or the following analysis, to this perspective. The problem at hand surely demands other views as a supplement. We argue that these definitions are open for use of the cultural-institutional perspective as well, although we are determined that the project (the task and the temporary organization), the organization, and the framework are to a large extent possible to design and control. Losing this position would make both governance and planning meaningless (see Næss, 2004).

3 Methodology and Working Process

3.1 RESEARCH PHILOSOPHY

The aim of this work is to look at how the governance regimes for major investment projects in different countries determines or affects project performance, as well as comparing this with the intended effect of these frameworks.

This type of *how* and *why* question cannot be properly answered by a positivist approach, it can only be approached by a phenomenological approach (Easterby-Smith, Thorpe, & Lowe, 1991), looking in depth at a small number of cases. This step is important to the proper understanding of such systems. Several researchers, among others Flyvbjerg (2006), have argued very strongly for this kind of approach. We need case studies offering context-dependent knowledge to comprehend fully the platform for expanding theory into this field of study. Once this step is complete and initial understanding gained, it could be confirmed or expanded in the future by a wider, positivist study.

There are essentially two types of such phenomenological study: action research (Eden & Huxham, 2006), in which we could affect the course of the projects under consideration, or case studies (Yin, 1994), in which effects are observed by an essentially neutral observer. In this study we essentially have to take the latter role, although it should be noted that the very existence of the QA regime, of which the Concept program is an integral part, has a significant effect on the estimation process in the Norwegian projects studied.

Such a study will enable us to investigate *how* and *why* underestimation occurs, rather than simplistically comparing estimates with out-turns, such as the Morris and Hough (1987) work admitted, but is also in the Flyvbjerg et al. (2003) work, which cannot distinguish underestimation and the early governance phase from execution-phase effects, such as mismanagement, scope changes, and the "double-dip" effect of underestimation (Eden, Ackermann, & Williams, 2005).

While it is clear that empirical study of cases needs to be carried out to establish the effects of the governance framework, we are not entering the cases blindly. First, we have already established in Chapters 2 and 3 the underlying theories of what project governance is. Second, since we want to compare frameworks, we can establish the variations between frameworks to point us to how to carry out the case studies. Therefore, these studies will be pointed and directed, rather than the very open studies carried out under, for example, grounded theory (Glaser, 1992; Strauss & Corbin, 1998).

The study was a small study aimed to find initial results. It was, therefore, proposed to analyze a very small number of projects as case studies, in just two countries. Norway and the United Kingdom were chosen as having a fairly new public sector project governance framework and a well-established one, respectively—and they were the frameworks to which the authors had significant access. Two projects were studied in each country. As described in Chapter 5, it was found as part of the United Kingdom study that defense projects (the largest public projects) were governed under a different framework in the United Kingdom from other public projects (using the OGC methods). So it was decided to study a defense project in each country and a civil project in each country.

The main source for identifying case studies for the Norway projects was the research database established and maintained by the Concept Research Programme. This database counts at present 71 projects, so far dominated by transportation infrastructure projects (40%), public building projects (30%), and defense procurement projects (25%), which constitute the other major parts of the material. The case projects were selected from this portfolio of projects, and the position of the Concept program gave access to interview participants as required.

On the United Kingdom side, as discussed in Chapter 5, the main owner of the governance framework for public projects apart from MoD is the Office of Government Commerce and discussion with the OGC executive director of "Better Projects" enabled a civil project to be selected which had passed through most of the governance process. The professional head of project management within the MoD's procurement agency similarly identified a defense project to form part of the study.

We had a number of criteria for choosing case studies, such as to seek projects that satisfied:

- Easy to find documentation and information, and well documented— and this to cover the history as well as the current status of the project,
- Useful for comparison with other projects (not too special),
- Open (not secret),
- Preferably normal complexity and characteristics, in a sector known to the authors,

- Easy to find people concerned to interview, and
- There were arguments for looking for projects at various stages in the project life cycle—the later in the cycle, the more history there is, but the later you get, the less likely it is that they will have had contemporary governance methods, particularly as these were new and evolving frameworks. (Note that knowing the outcome does not tell us directly how good the cost estimation was, so there was not a particular push to look at finished projects.)

Perhaps the two most important criteria were the following:

- Similarity between the projects in each country was sought (which helped to determine the domain—the UK OGC had targeted IT projects whereas these were scarce in the Concept database; on the other hand, the Concept database had many transport infrastructure projects but few of these were available on the UK side; civil building projects were available in both sets of available projects.
- The main criteria though were determined as in most case study research: access was difficult and to a certain extent, the team had to accept what projects were available.

3.2   STRUCTURE OF THE STUDY

This section, therefore, sets out the logic of the study and also the structure of this report, which directly follows the study logic.

The literature gives us a theoretical underpinning for governance in general and the main concepts involved. This area was covered in Chapter 2.

We can draw from the literature to specify the characteristics of a governance framework for public projects and set these characteristics into a clear structure. This structure is, therefore, firmly based on the literature and provides the structure on which to base the remainder of the study. In this sense, we can study cases with a clear agenda of where to look. This structure is laid out in detail in Chapter 4.

The study involves investigating the frameworks for public projects in two specific countries: the United Kingdom and Norway. There are experts in these frameworks who can reflect on them and characterize them.

The study, therefore, took the structure built up in Chapter 4 and rephrased it in the form of a questionnaire (shown in Appendix A), which was then sent to the interviewees prior to the interview. The structure was then used as the basis for semi-structured interviews with these experts to determine the nature of each of the frameworks with respect to the characteristics of the frameworks that the structure implies is important. The results of these interviews are given in Sections 5.1–5.4.

As part of these interviews, it became clear that one major section of the UK public sector used a different framework from the remainder—the Ministry of Defence. This difference meant that, rather than investigate the two frameworks—the United Kingdom and Norway—we looked at the United Kingdom (except MoD), the United Kingdom MoD, and Norway frameworks.

Documentation on the frameworks was also extensively studied and is referred to in the descriptions in Sections 5.1–5.4.

The results of these interviews and document study, being already structured, could then easily be compared to give a structured analysis of their differences. The comparison was laid out in tabular form for the purposes of the analysis, and is described textually in Chapter 5.

This comparison and analysis gives us the foundation of our main results and enables us to describe how the different governance frameworks have arisen, and in what ways they differ. But as described previously, the study is to look at how these differences actually play out in practice in case studies, and the analysis so far gives the foundations for the case studies. The structure was taken and set out in areas to look out for (see Chapter 4), and a brief summary of this was given to the case study projects prior to the first meetings (see Appendix B). While the investigators were not blindly limited to these areas, this structure did give the foundation for the areas to study.

In parallel, the literature on the theoretical perspectives on governance allowed us to look at the governance frameworks through the lenses of these various perspectives. Consideration of the case studies in the light of various theoretical ideas highlighted aspects of establishing governance frameworks which could be supported by theory; this shows a set of different perspectives and theories which can be helpful in the design process and hopefully aid transferability of the results.

Figure 3-1 shows this logical process pictorially. The main activities are shown in the boxes with borders, while the outputs that are necessary for the logic are shown in italics. The relationships with the chapters in this report are also shown.

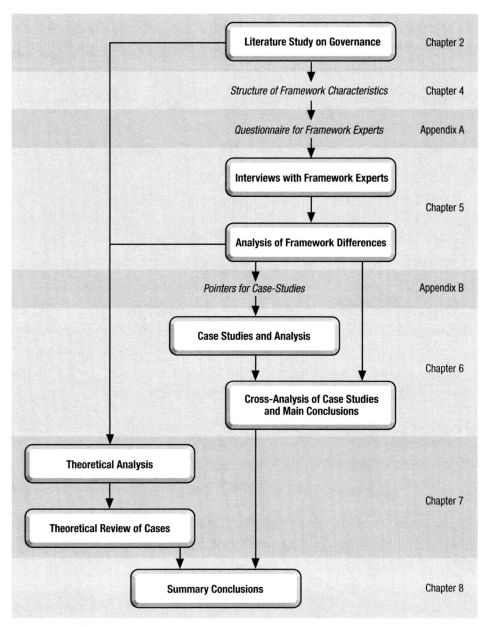

FIGURE 3-1.   STRUCTURE OF METHODOLOGY USED IN THIS STUDY

4 Characteristics of a Governance Framework

4.1 INTRODUCTION TO CHARACTERISTICS

Remember the definition we concluded earlier: A governance framework for investment projects comprise the processes and rules established to ensure the project meets its purpose. To make sure the society's interest in getting value for money when using its resources, any country will have a governance framework of some kind. This framework defines principles and procedures established to make the governance of public investment projects possible and effective. There is no known standard or commonly accepted description of such governance frameworks.

This chapter ends in a description useful to characterize the process of developing such a framework and the framework itself. It may be developed into a systematic checklist to produce systematic information about such frameworks. An example of such a checklist is shown in Appendix A. This list is used in this study. Having such a theoretical framework gives the opportunity to produce comparable descriptions of governance frameworks. This is important, both to be able to describe systematically and to make a meaningful comparison.

4.2 GOVERNANCE FRAMEWORKS CHARACTERISTICS

The characteristics of a governance framework are useful in several analytical contexts. This version is developed for the specific purposes of this study; to make it possible to explain how the frameworks influence cost estimation and time planning. The use is not, however, limited to this purpose. As stated in Chapter 1, our main hypothesis is that the framework under which the investment project is planned and executed is important in determining the effectiveness of cost estimation and reducing the problem of cost overrun.

For the purposes of this analysis, the characteristics can be divided into four different categories: (1) the development process, (2) embedded governance principles, (3) the structure of the framework, and (4) detailed governance elements.

The first part is needed to understand why the framework has come to be, and how it is formed. The second and third part is the core of the subject matter; it describes the framework itself and the governance principles built into it. The fourth part is flexible, open for addressing special issues of interest. This version is designed for this particular study concerning the effect on cost and time planning. This explains why this version only addresses these issues. In other studies, this part could be different, depending on the purpose of the study. Other obvious subjects of interest could be contracts, risks, organizational models, etc.

The structured list of characteristics developed in this chapter is derived from the analysis of the literature described in Chapter 2, as well as literature and other sources that follow on from that work. The list was further refined slightly as the research progressed, through incorporating some experience from interviews and performing the actual analysis of findings described in later chapters.

The aim of this structure here is to form the basis of a systematic comparison of the Norwegian and United Kingdom frameworks, which itself will guide empirical analysis of real cases to investigate the operation of these frameworks. This methodology was described in Chapter 3.

4.3   THE GOVERNANCE FRAMEWORK AND THE SYSTEM

The phenomenon of governance and governance frameworks are discussed in Chapter 2 of this report. At this point, it is important to make clear the difference between the part of the system architecture provided by owner (the governance framework) and the part of the system architecture provided by the executing body (the system) (see Figure 4-1). The latter is the solution demonstrating accountability from the executing body towards the owner—the governing body (this idea is extracted from a working paper from the Norwegian Centre of Project Management; Olsson et al., 2007).

Examples of how these system elements are described can be found in several references. To illustrate this, we have picked a couple of classics:

In Figure 4-2, Bemelmans-Videc, et al. (1998) gives an overview on policy instruments defining, on a high level of abstraction, the elements of a regulatory regime or governance framework. This description focuses on the principles and incentives embedded in the framework, but it needs a supplement to cover the structure.

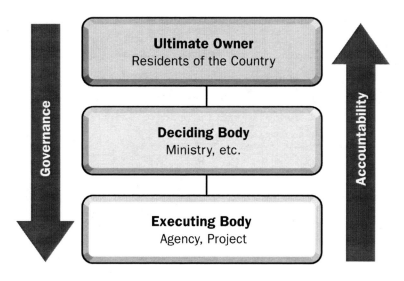

FIGURE 4-1.   GOVERNANCE AND ACCOUNTABILITY

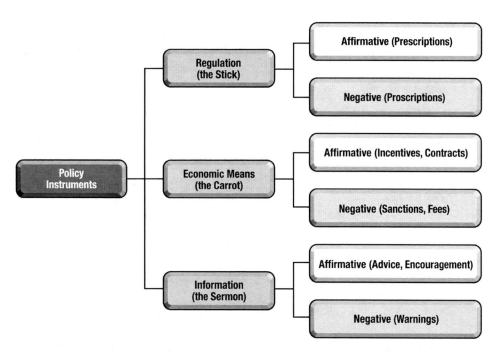

FIGURE 4-2.   POLICY INSTRUMENTS TO IMPROVE GOVERNANCE IN PUBLIC SECTOR
(BEMELMANS-VIDEC ET AL., 1998)

Another relevant example is found in Miller and Floricel (2000), where 30 devices to install governability used in the projects covered by the IMEC study are discussed; these are shown in Figure 4-3. Miller & Floricel describe them as follows: "Each device can contribute to governability by enhancing bonding for internal cohesion; long-term coalitions; presence of reserves or stocks; flexibility options; generativity; and modularity and diversification. Through the presence or absence of devices, sponsors can hope to enhance the governability of project structures." (p. 140)

Relationships between owners and lenders
- Alliance of equity owners
- Diversity of competencies
- Leadership of major investors
- Business linkages (prior)
- Partners' agreement

Relationships with affected parties
- Negotiation-compensation
- Sustained engagement

Relationships with clients-markets
- Power purchase agreements
- Tolls – public support
- Revenue guarantees
- Client is owner

Relationships with banks and institutional investors
- Strong equity position
- Financial architecture – covenants
- Selection of responsible leaders
- Government guarantees
- Adaptability protocols

Relationships with contractors
- Number of work packages
- Consortium
- EPC firms involved in ownership
- Degree of specification at cut-off
- Owners' involvement
- Incentives in engineering
- Incentives in construction
- Owner-contractor collaboration

Relationships with the state
- Founding contract
- Agreement with state
- Involvement of multilateral agencies
- State participation

Relationships between owner and operator
- Owner(s) operate
- Contract operator

FIGURE 4-3. **DEVICES TO INSTALL GOVERNABILITY IN LARGE ENGINEERING PROJECTS (MILLER & FLORICEL, 2000)**

According to Miller and Floricel's description, these are examples describing the left side of Figure 4-1—devices installed by owner/sponsors. They should then define **what to do/achieve** to make sure the owners/sponsors are satisfied. However, the discussion in the book shows that there is more focus on the structure than on what to achieve. The structural elements are found in words like relationships, work packages, and agreements. These elements supplement the contribution by Bemelmans-Videc et al.(1998) mentioned previously.

The right side of Figure 4-1 can be illustrated with any management system defined in order to make sure the performance in execution of given tasks (management, administrative, planning, or production) is according to demands from the owner. We have chosen to illustrate the point by pointing to the management method PRINCE2 (see Figure 4-4).

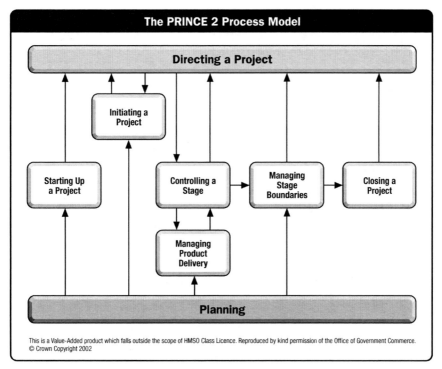

FIGURE 4-4.   THE PRINCE2™ PROCESS MODEL—EXAMPLE OF MANAGEMENT SYSTEM STRUCTURE. Available at; http://www.prince2.org.uk/web/site/About PRINCE2Management_Overview1.asp

This system defines how to do the things needed to make owners satisfied. The systems are made for executing parties and give guidelines for good practices. As shown in Figure 4-1, this contributes to building the organization's accountability towards the owner of the project. Governance of projects is in PRINCE2 referred to as directing a project. A well-known basis for design of such management systems is the *PMBOK® Guide* – Fourth Edition (PMI, 2004).

These examples, together with the literature in Chapter 2, are what make up our basis for developing a general descriptive structure to characterize a governance framework.

4.4 FRAMEWORKS CHARACTERISTICS

We are now in a position to identify those elements which can be used to characterize a governance framework. As described previously, these will be in four categories, looking at the process of development, the structure of the framework, embedded governance principles, and detailed governance elements, especially those specific to this study. This structure will form the basis for our study of the governance frameworks in the two countries compared. Three different governance frameworks are presented and discussed using these characteristics in Chapter 5.

4.4.1 The process of development

1. Explicitly stated purpose of the framework

This part identifies the official policy, the statement the framework is funded on.

- Any explicit statement of purpose (political), made by the decision makers.

1. Background—why and how the framework came to be

This part is important for setting the stage, to understand the context, and explain the framework's initiation and development up to the current edition.

- Political setting (who was in power, democratic system, political traditions),
- Administrative setting (who was responsible for what, different sectors, etc.),
- Social economics (economic situation at the time of initiation, trends),
- Sociocultural setting (specially at the time the framework was initiated, trends),
- Traditional market mode of operation (transactions or relations, sectors),
- Triggering incident (what started the development of current framework),
- Initiators (who initiated, who made the decisions),
- The espoused aim of the initiators in originally initiating the development,
- How was political and administrative anchoring achieved (at what level, how, by whom),
- Development process (what means have been used to develop the framework and promote its use),
- When was the framework officially introduced (previous and current editions),

- Changes in the framework during its working period, and
- Characteristic/important changes in the political or administrative setting during the working period of the framework, consequences.

2. Current status and how the framework is maintained and developed
This part identifies how the framework is implemented, improved and developed.

- Political and administrative anchoring (who is responsible, and who are the important stakeholders),
- Policy/strategy of implementation,
- How the framework is promoted/informed about/available to users,
- Policy/strategy of further development and assessment of the framework, and
- Results of the implemented framework (performance measurement, evaluations).

4.4.2 Embedded governance principles

1. Governance principles
This part includes descriptions and characteristics of embedded governance principles. Characteristics describe in which way/to what extent these are used:
- Establishing a common world view for individuals' action,
- Establishing a system to stabilize key players' orientation, expectations and rules of conduct,
- Differentiation between projects based on
  - criticality
  - their level of complexity
  - asset specificity
  - uncertainty
  - others
- Mechanisms (e.g. practices or models) to reduce complexity,
- Principles for distributing risk among participants in projects,
- Ensure that contractors cannot exhibit collusive behavior, abuse of dominant position etc.,
- Mechanism to trigger governance processes in response to turbulence in the project environment, and
- Developing capacity for dynamic social learning.

4.4.3 The structure of the framework

1. Current structure of the framework

This part includes descriptions and characteristics of the current framework structure.

- Objective of the framework,
- Explicitly stated ends/goals for the framework (or/and responsible party),
- Users (sectors, levels, etc.),
- Framework elements (control measures, arenas for coordination etc.),
- Framework structure (how elements are put together and interact),
- Project model (timeline, phases, milestones),
- Vertical integration (level of integration, value chain/supply chain),
- Horizontal integration (level of integration, across sectors),
- Organization (structure, levels, anchoring within the public administration),
- Roles and parties within the organization supporting/operating the framework, and
- Extent and control of outside engagement (private sector engagement in governance procedures).

4.4.4 Detailed governance elements

This part includes descriptions and characteristics of more detailed elements and governance mechanisms. This part has to be adapted and extended to the purpose of the analysis in which it is planned to be used. In this study we are looking specifically (but not solely) at how the frameworks influence cost estimation and time planning.

1. Framework elements concerning cost estimation and time planning

This part includes descriptions and characteristics of framework elements concerning cost estimation and time planning in early phases of the project.

- Explicit statements or framework elements specifically addressing the development of cost and time estimates in the established framework,
- Governance principles concerning cost estimation and cost control, and
- Systematic analysis of the effect of these principles.

2. Governance of transactions (example—not used in this study)
Look for any explicit statements or framework elements specifically addressing transactions between actors, contracts, etc.

- Explicit statements or framework elements specifically addressing tendering and contracts in the established framework,
- Governance principles concerning tendering and contracts, and
- Systematic analysis of the effect of these principles.

This part can be expanded to support the needs of any defined study of regulatory frameworks. Added categories could be focusing on risk, organization, human resources, etc. We acknowledge all these issues are also relevant for cost and time, but our study is limited to the elements explicitly direct referring to cost and time.

This framework now gives us the structure by which we can start the empirical study, as discussed in Chapter 3. The characteristics checklist is shown in Table 4-1.

TABLE 4-1.   **CHARACTERISTICS OF A GOVERNANCE FRAMEWORK**

Category	Theme	Explanation	Characteristics (examples from the complete list)
1. The process of development	Background—why and how the framework came to be	Setting the stage to understand the context and explain the framework's initiation and development up tthrough current edition.	• Political setting (who was in power, democratic system, political traditions) • Administrative setting (who was responsible for what, different sectors, etc.) • Social economics (economic situation at the time of initiation, trends) • Traditional market mode of operation (transactions or relations, sectors) • Initiators (who initiated, who made the decisions) • When was the framework officially introduced (previous and current editions)
	Explicitly stated purpose of the framework	Identify the official policy, the statement the framework is funded on.	• Any explicit statement of purpose (political), made by the decision makers.
	Current status and how the framework is maintained and developed	Identify how the framework is implemented, improved and developed.	• Political and administrative anchoring (who is responsible, and who are the important stakeholders) • Policy/strategy of implementation • Policy/strategy of further development and assessment of the framework • Results of the implemented framework (performance measurement, evaluations)
2. Embedded governance principles	Governance principles	This part includes descriptions and characteristics of embedded governance principles.	• Establishing a common world view for individuals' action • Establishing a system to stabilize key players' orientation, expectations, and rules of conduct • Differentiation between projects based on complexity, asset specificity, uncertainty, criticality, other factors. • Mechanisms (e.g., practices or models) to reduce complexity and distribute risk • Mechanism to trigger governance processes in response to turbulence in the project environment

Category	Theme	Explanation	Characteristics (examples from the complete list)
3. The structure of the framework	Current structure of the framework	Describe and define the current framework structure.	• Explicitly stated ends/goals for the framework (or/and responsible party) • Users (sectors, levels, etc.) • Framework elements (control measures, arenas for coordination, etc.) • Framework structure (how elements interact, the timeline) • Vertical and horizontal integration (level of integration, value chain/ supply chain, across sectors) • Extent and control of independent/ outside engagement.
4. Detailed governance elements	Framework elements concerning cost estimation and time planning	Descriptions and characteristics of framework elements concerning cost estimation and time planning in early phases of the project.	• Explicit statements or framework elements specifically addressing the development of cost and time estimates. • Specific governance principles concerning cost estimation and cost control • Systematic analysis of the effect of these principles.
	Governance of transactions	Explicit statements or framework elements specifically addressing transactions	• Explicit statements or framework elements specifically addressing tendering and contracts. • Specific governance principles concerning tendering and contracts • Systematic analysis of the effect of these principles.
	Etc.	-	-

5 The United Kingdom and Norwegian Frameworks

This chapter describes the frameworks studied. The frameworks are:

OGC Gateway Process by Office of Government Commerce (UK)

MoD Acquisition Operating Framework by the Ministry of Defence (UK)

Quality Assurance Scheme by the Ministry of Finance (Norway)

The report compares the frameworks as they were implemented in practice mid-2007.

As described in Chapter 3, the analysis of the frameworks follows the generic analysis developed in Chapter 4. The following descriptions follow the structure developed in Chapter 4. This structure divides the story into four separate aspects with importance for the issue in this report, followed by some discussion. The sections in this chapter are as follows:

5.1 The development process (the story)

5.2 Governance principles (the values)

5.3 Structure (the content)

5.4 Detailed level (elements addressing cost and time)

5.5 Latest development (transitions in 2007 and beyond)

5.6 Summary discussion on frameworks comparison (practical perspective)

Within Sections 5.1–5.4 of this chapter, there is a generic structure:

- A short introduction, including a table of illustrative excerpts from interviews,
- UK OGC,
- UK MoD,
- Norway, and
- Discussion (including a summary table).

The basis for this chapter is several sources: interviews and document studies are the most important ones. This basis includes a picture that is rich on details, anecdotes, and personal judgment made by key people knowledgeable about the development and implementation of these frameworks. The authors' job has been to extract a consistent and complete overview of the frameworks without going into all available details.

5.1　THE DEVELOPMENT PROCESS

This section covers the story of the shaping and implementation of the framework from the events leading up to the initiation of the development up to the implemented governance framework in mid-2007. Chapter 5.5 covers current and further developments. Table 5-1 gives an overview of the key attributes and acts as a map to the subsequent text where more details and discussions are added.

TABLE 5-1.　　KEY ATTRIBUTES OF THE DEVELOPMENT PROCESS—EXCERPT OF QUESTIONS AND ANSWERS.

Question asked	Norway	UK MoD	UK OGC
Triggering incident (What started the development of current framework?)	Media and public interest and attention to a series of unsuccessful major investment projects during the 1980s and 1990s.	Projects were not delivering to time/ cost performance. The main motivations were towards cost control and reducing risks—summarized in value for money— and procuring capability rather than equipment.	In the late 1990s, Peter Gershon was asked by the then prime minister, to review civil procurement in central government in the light of the government's objectives on efficiency, modernization and competitiveness
Initiators (who initiated?)	The Ministry of Finance	The Ministry of Defence	The Prime Minister
What was the espoused aim of the initiators in originally initiating the development?	The intended effect is to make the state able to choose the right projects and execute them well.	Managing MoD's projects as a single program to get the best capability for UK defense as a whole.	Originally to improve delivery, the espoused aim of the framework later became to achieve financial targets of money saved.
What is the policy/strategy of implementation?	Mandatory for all major investment projects	Mandatory	By influence (towards the end of this project it actually turned mandatory)

Question asked	Norway	UK MoD	UK OGC
Political and administrative anchoring	Parliament and the cabinet	MoD main board, supported by investment appraisal board.	A treasury department, but framework also involves the prime minister's office
Any explicit statement of purpose (political), made by the decision makers?	Yes. It is stated by the prime minister´s office that better projects and better execution of investment projects is a political goal.	Through-life capability management, covering all the defense lines of development.	To work with public sector to achieve efficiency, value for money in commercial activities, and improved success in project/programs delivery.
Development process (what means have (typically) been used to develop the framework and promote its use?)	The framework came as a consequence of an investigation. Development through implementation of framework and consensus on principles.	Original framework developed by consultants. Later developments came from a parliamentary report (McKane).	Development by the OGC organization based on influential reports by Gershon in 1999 and 2004.
When was the framework officially introduced?	First generation: QA2 in year 2000. Second generation: QA1 in addition to QA2 in year 2005.	In 1998 after McKinsey work–Major changes in April 2007	OGC was established in 2000, the Gateway Process shortly after. Major changes introduced during 2007.
Does the framework have a clear objective?	It should help the cabinet sort out relevant elements with correct price tags and realistic assumptions on utility when deciding on projects.	It is to achieve maximized capability, through-life capability management on the extended life-cycle and value for money	The espoused aim of the framework is specifically to achieve financial targets of money saved. Later came the ambition to change the culture of departments
How is the framework promoted/ informed about/ available to users?	In the form of demands. Users need to ask for more information if they need it.	Mandatory and well-known. Outside MoD, it is available from websites.	This is part of standard procedures for government departments—in common with UK civil service culture. Available from websites.
Changes in the framework during its working period?	Not within the framework contracts in any of the two periods, but between the two periods—the introduction of QA1.	Changed in 2007, following the McKane report and the merger into the new DE&S organization.	It has gradually developed, bringing in categorization, centers of excellence and the project initiation process.

Question asked	Norway	UK MoD	UK OGC
Results of the implemented framework (performance measurement, evaluations)	For the bulk of quality assured projects, it is too early to make a verdict. Indications on improvement are plenty.	Results are incorporated into the DE&S corporate targets. Also overview from the NAO major projects report.	Target was achievement of £8 billion savings through efficient public procurement. They have met their targets.

5.1.1 UK OFFICE OF GOVERNMENT COMMERCE (OGC) FRAMEWORK: THE OGC GATEWAY™ REVIEW

Introduction

In the late 1990s, Peter Gershon, then at GEC Marconi, was asked by the then prime minister to look at procurement in government. Gershon wrote his influential report in April 1999 (known as the Gershon report but actually called the *Review of Civil Procurement in Central Government*). This report coincided with the merger between the two main parties of the UK defense industry (then known as British Aerospace and General Electric Company (GEC)), and Peter Gershon was asked (formally by Andrew Turnbull, the then Head of the Civil Service with the support of the prime minister) to set up the Office of Government Commerce (OGC), which he did in April 2000. The OGC is now formally part of the HM Treasury (the UK's finance ministry).

The new OGC pulled together other parts of government commerce. It took on the staff of the Central Computer and Telecommunications Agency (CCTA), Property Advisers to the Civil Estate (PACE), the Buying Agency (TBA), and some procurement staff from the HM Treasury and the Cabinet Office. CCTA had been the organization that established PRINCE in 1989 (which is in the public domain; PRINCE is a registered trademark of OGC). The PRINCE2 project management methodology (OGC, 2002a,b) had subsequently published in 1996, having been contributed to by a consortium of some 150 European organizations. These types of methods are influenced by their origins in the IT sector.

The methods developed in the Gershon report covered general procurement of commodities and project procurement. The Gateway™ Process eventually established in the OGC reflected practice in GEC (Harpham & Kippenberger, 2005) and the buying solutions also established in OGC utilized Peter Gerson's experience from the private sector (particularly GEC).

The main initiators here were thus initially the prime minister, who (via the appropriate civil service route) asked Peter Gershon. The subsequent OGC with Gershon and subsequent CEO's (John Oughton until the end of March 2007) who reported to the UK Treasury are the initiators of developments.

Political and Administrative Setting in the United Kingdom

The United Kingdom is a constitutional monarchy and parliamentary democracy. It has a strong public administration tradition and a large influential civil service. Government business is divided into departments, such as defense, home office, etc.

Responsibility for a project is entirely within the department. The minister is the person responsible for his or her remit, and the two people responsible are the elected politician and the permanent secretary (the civil servant in charge of the department). Wider government responsibility only comes in through the minister who reports to the cabinet. The permanent secretary will talk to the treasury about funding, initially about the yearly allocation for the department, but also for special cases requiring more funding. Contractual decisions are the responsibility of officials, and accountability for decisions rests with the department's permanent secretary.

There is, however, a number of mechanisms by which there is parliamentary review of government work, including various parliamentary committees, although the power of parliament is generally thought to have been weakened in the late 1970s and early 1980s.

In 1997, the UK government changed parties to New Labour, after 18 years of (right-wing) conservative government. New Labour is avowedly socialist but market-oriented and private-industry friendly (see for example the rapid development of the Private Finance Initiative, with 835 projects signed by the end of 2006, to a total value of GBP 61.7 billion (http://www.ifsl.org.uk/uploads/PB_PFI_2007.pdf)).

While not seeking to make sweeping generalizations about the UK national character, it may be that there is more of a blame culture within the United Kingdom—or at least within the UK civil service (Williams, 2007), which is geared towards hiding the facts to avoid blame. Gateway™ Reviews are looking to tease out the hidden facts. It may be that participants (from the projects) sometimes fear the reviews—they think it is about blame so they are looking to hide the facts. However, it should be pointed out that Gateway Reviews are there to assure the health of programs and projects and offer help; reviews are carried out in accordance with a very strict code of conduct and avoiding blame is one aspect of this code; other key aspects stress confidentiality of the information provided by interviewees, etc., and objectivity in the way information is reported and used. Reviewers encourage project team members to be open and honest, so that the Gateway Review team can add meaningful value and offer help. Information offered during the interviews is always nonattributable.

Economy and Market Mode

The economic circumstances of the United Kingdom have influenced the establishment and subsequent development of the framework. As described at length in Section 1.5, while the United Kingdom has a large economy, it has considerable limitations in public funds and considerable unemployment in the time period we are considering. There is less public money available than in Norway, so there is more emphasis on value for money. OGC Gateway Reviews are, therefore, looking at questions, such as whether public money is being wasted, and looking for "gold-plating" and so on. And there is a general perception that the availability of public money is getting tighter, so value for money if anything is becoming more of an issue. This has not really changed the actual framework but is shown in the flavor of the reviews. But it is why there is more regular and prevalent so-called "Gateway 0's (the fundamental Gateways described in the following paragraphs). In addition, a new idea of project initiation is geared towards looking at the question, "Is it worth spending money on this?"

Espoused Aim and Political Anchoring

In the beginning the aim of the initiative was to improve the performance of government procurement. Our understanding now is that the espoused aim of the OGC is specifically to achieve financial targets of money saved (as a combination of the work on commodities and the work on projects), and the espoused aim of the OGC project framework is specifically to improve financial outturns.

Later developments (e.g., centers of excellence) were aimed to change the culture of the departments, all the way up and down the department, and to establish governance—it was wanted to get a culture shift within departments to business management (and the OGC was to be a catalyst for this).

But the aim of the Gateways now is to help programs/projects reach a more successful outcome. This aim is reflected in better financial outturns but not necessarily specifically to achieve financial targets of money saved, which is more true of the commodity-procurement side of the OGC's work. The work was originally geared towards IT projects and IT-enabled change projects, but this is not the case now, and the framework is used throughout.

How is the project-oriented work of the OGC politically anchored? Reports on a particular project go only to the senior person responsible (the person known in the framework and PRINCE2 as the senior responsible owner [SRO]) and the OGC. But the OGC does not consider individual project reports once they have reported on them; rather, they look for systemic trends. Therefore, in that sense governance of a project is limited. However, there are a number of mechanisms to provide anchoring further up, particularly political anchoring.

Within the wider civil service:

- There is a general trend within departments that the permanent secretary (i.e., the top official in a government department) and the head of the center of excellence also see the Gateway reports.
- There is a steering committee for the OGC consisting of a collection of permanent secretaries who comment on initiatives.
- There is also the National Audit Office (NAO), who looks at projects "in an audit sense" (they are looking at a higher level than individual projects and will regularly report on series of projects, as noted in the MoD).

In terms of political reporting:

- There is a list of "mission critical" projects, specified in agreement with the prime minister's office. The head of OGC reports regularly on these projects and directly to the prime minister's office.
- When a program or project attracts two consecutive red ratings, this is escalated to the permanent secretary for the department concerned, the National Audit Office, and to the head of the civil service.
- The OGC is a relatively autonomous independent office of the treasury that in 2007 was reporting to the financial secretary to the treasury. The chief executive of the OGC is at the permanent secretary level, so while this person reports to the permanent secretary of the treasury, he or she is, in a sense, at a similar level in the hierarchy.
- Other stakeholders include the prime minister's delivery unit (PMDU), which also reports to the prime minister's office, but is interested in "delivery" and specifically the overall departmental public sector agreement targets as a whole (i.e., the specified top-level targets that each government target must meet). These stakeholders (such as PMDU and NAO) are gradually getting more "joined up" and liaising (e.g., the Centers of Excellence are there to help guide towards the departmental public sector agreement targets).

The OGC works by influence and recommendation. At the time of starting this research study, their recommendations are never mandated. SROs request Gateway Reviews. However, it should be noted that, since this is normal practice, if an SRO did not request a Gateway Review, and the project went wrong, then there would be difficult questions asked. This is in the traditional UK civil service culture. However, during this study there were changes towards making their work mandatory. John Healey, MP Financial Secretary to the Treasury stated in January 2007: "To meet these challenges and opportunities OGC will be given stronger powers to set out the high standards of performance required, monitor departments' performance against them, insist improvements are made where necessary and demand departmental collaboration where that improves value for money" (HM Treasury, 2007b), These developments and their implications are discussed in Section 5.5.

Development Process

These developments began with a request initiated by the then prime minister, which eventually resulted in the setting up of the OGC and its Gateway Review system. The McCartney Report in 2000 (Cabinet Office, 2000) produced the peer review concept.

Later, there was a general concern that 'We need better programme management,' giving rise to the development of the Centers of Excellence part of the framework.

In September 2001, a cross-departmental project, Improving Program and Project Delivery (IPPD), was set up by the Office of Public Services Reform (OPSR) to look at the civil service's general weakness in this area. Their IPPD report in 2003 identified the Centers of Excellence (CoE) concept.

The assessment of the work of the OGC continued and major changes have been announced during this study and will take effect in 2008. These are discussed in Section 5.5. The discussion in Sections 5.2–5.5 describes the current (2007) situation.

Results

The OGC is given agreed savings targets, with a process for estimating the figures approved by the National Audit Office, who claim to deploy expertise in support of the Government's target of £21.5 billion[7] efficiency gains a year by 2007/08, which includes the achievement of £8 billion savings through efficient public procurement.

The National Audit Office procedures for estimating monies saved were agreed upon with the OGC. Basically, they are simply estimates of the reduction in costs from what the project would have cost had the review not proposed different actions, i.e., it is just a theoretical spend. The key to this work is the Gateway framework. Their 2005–2006 report states that "Gateway has now delivered over £1.5 bn of value for money savings. In 2005/6, 34% more Gateway Reviews were completed a total of (360) compared with the previous year" (Office of Government Commerce 2006, p. 19). In the early days, there were great savings as there were quite a lot of points at which big problems were identified and diverted, but having got projects on track, there are fewer savings available now. The OGC also has an ongoing review of the results of the Gateways, showing the trends in red/amber/green results.

---

7. Current exchange rate is 2. Efficiency gains £21,5 is equivalent to $ 43,0 and £8 billion savings is equivalent to $16 billion.

But the OGC's work is also about changing culture and awareness, and this work is more difficult to measure. However, the highest political levels within the United Kingdom seem to feel that the office has done well. In its major reform paper on transforming government procurement (HM Treasury, 2007b), the overall summary says that "Following the publication of Sir Peter Gershon's report 'Review of Civil Procurement in Central Government' in 1999, the Office of Government Commerce (OGC) was established as a central 'one-stop shop' procurement organisation. It has since played a key role in delivering over £8 billion of efficiency savings from public procurement. However, the pursuit of value for money for the taxpayer must remain uncompromising" (p. 1). So the report gives an idea of OGC's development in the future, as quoted previously:

"To meet these challenges and opportunities OGC will be given stronger powers to set out the high standards of performance required, monitor departments' performance against them, insist improvements are made where necessary, and demand departmental collaboration where that improves value for money. More intelligent government procurement also has the capacity to shape the market in offering more innovative and effective products and services. To achieve these changes the OGC will have to reform. It will become a smaller, more focused, higher calibre organisation, with the skills and powers needed to drive through the necessary changes within central government" (p.1).

These developments are discussed further in Chapter 5.5.

Concluding Remarks on the Development Process
PRINCE2, Gateways, and the Centers of Excellence now have a track record and have been well-received. However, there are significant developments in the way that OGC operates, and these developments may have implications for the tool-set it uses. What the authors understand about the forthcoming changes is described in Section 5.5.

5.1.2 UK MINISTRY OF DEFENCE (MOD) FRAMEWORK: THE ACQUISITION OPERATING FRAMEWORK

Introduction
The one major section of the UK public sector that uses a different framework is the Ministry of Defence (MoD). MoD has always had an "extended life cycle," going back before the "project" and after. The Downey Report (1969) put the emphasis on the early stage of projects, giving percentages of time and money to be spent preproject. Two projects which were "triggering incidents" to better governance of MoD projects were TSR2 and the Nimrod early warning radar projects, both cancelled after

significant sums of money were spent on them. The projects were not delivering to time/cost performance, and technology was becoming increasingly complex. The main motivations to change were towards cost control and reducing risks, which could be summarized as value for money.

What is called the CADMID process, part of the SMART acquisition, came in around 1998 following work by the consulting firm McKinsey. Contracting defense budgets gave motivations to value for money (and to getting more accurate in their predictions). The McKinsey work showed the need for a "stronger customer" (the customer being MoD Center, often termed "main building" after its home, who needs the capability). Thus, there was a move more towards procuring capability rather than equipment. This move led to the establishment of the key development: integrated project teams (IPTs).

A big change came from a report entitled *Enabling Acquisition Change* report by Tom McKane (Ministry of Defence. (2006), often called the McKane report). This report prompted the formation of the Defence Acquisition Change Program in 2006. It was a result from the Defence Industrial Strategy (DIS).

The terms of reference for the report begin,

"The Defence Industrial Strategy has signposted the need to review our pan-departmental approach to acquisition. Building upon smart acquisition the department needs to understand where our current structures, organisation, processes, cultures and behaviours support, encourage, hinder, or obstruct our ability to deliver through-life capability management, and to address these obstacles where they are encountered" (Ministry of Defence 2006, p. 45).

Through-life capability management (TLCM), the key to the DIS, was the motivation to the report. TLCM implies procurement so that all the requirements for through-life capability are considered rather than the procuring one-off bits of equipment. And this needs to cut across all of the different aspects of capability that need to be brought together to create the desired capability—the so-called defence lines of development (DLoDs).

A first major outcome from the McKane report was the merger of the Defence Procurement Agency and the Defence Logistics Organization in April 2007 to create a single entity, Defence Equipment & Support (DE&S). These were already huge organizations: at the time of the McKane report, the DLO had 25,000 staff, operating costs of 2 billion (GBP)/$4 billion (US), and project/equipment costs of 3.7 billion (GBP)/$7.4 billion (US) in the previous financial year; the DPA had 4,700 staff, operating costs of 0.5 billion (GBP)/$1 billion (US), and project/equipment costs of 5.3 billion (GBP)/$10.6 billion (US) in the previous financial year.

Political and Administrative Setting in the United Kingdom

The political and administrative setting in the United Kingdom was described in Section 5.1.1. The Ministry of Defence is one of the government departments described there.

Economy and Market Mode

The economic setting in the United Kingdom was described in Section 5.1.1, and the Ministry of Defence is subject to the same limitations as other government departments. As described in Section 5.1.1, the government is market-oriented and friendly to private industry. In the Ministry of Defence's case, though, it has a particular interest in private industry as a whole, and so the relationship with industry is fundamentally different from the civil world:

- There is a substantial industrial strategy to ensure the industrial base is looked at as a whole (Secretary of State for Defence, 2005). This paper looked at the strategic overview for defense procurement and considers "how best the MoD should seek to engage with the industrial base in order to meet our requirement." It is "driven by the need to provide the Armed Forces with the equipment which they require, on time, and best value for money for the taxpayer," while seeking also to "promote a sustainable industrial base" (p. 6).
- The MoD is much more open than previously, involving the industry more in their decision making. They now have a relationship where MoD can essentially say "We have a specific amount of money—what can industry do for this?"
- There are also some parts of sovereign capability that the United Kingdom does not want to lose for its strategic national interest, so the MoD has to bear that in mind in its relationship with industry,
- There used to be a system whereby the MoD was the design authority for much new equipment; now there is a move towards industry being the design authority

Espoused Aim and Political Anchoring

The aims of the framework set up for the procurement of defense equipment is, particularly, managing MoD's projects as a single program to get the best capability for the UK defense as a whole. The implications of this are significant, including:

- Capabilities essentially come in combinations, so these need to be managed at the program level rather than the individual project level,

- MoD needs to manage the through-life capability,
- There is a need to manage an extended life cycle, and
- MoD is also interested in value for money.

The Ministry of Defence is effectively directed by the Defence Management Board, the MoD's senior nonministerial committee, chaired by the PUS. The Defence Management Board delegates' responsibility for acquisition governance to two committees: the Acquisition Policy Board (APB), which provides strategic direction on acquisition issues, and the Investment Approvals Board (IAB), chaired by the chief scientific advisor, which scrutinizes major acquisition investments and which is the important board for the purposes of the framework described in the following. The representative of the customer and use is "capability management," led by the deputy chief of defence staff (equipment capabilities) (DCDS[EC]).

Political involvement in this process comes in three ways:

- A minister sits on the defence council, the senior committee in the department, which provides the legal basis for the conduct and administration of defense, chaired by the secretary of state for defence and including the other defence ministers.
- A minister chairs the APB.
- Some IAB decisions need ministerial approval, such as those that are politically sensitive, novel, and contentious, according to specified criteria.

The supplier of the equipment is the head of DE&S, called Chief of Defence Material (CDM).

The defense industrial strategy includes a summary of their overall strategy in procurement: "Our future approach to acquisition must be built around achieving primacy of through-life considerations; coherence of defense spend across research and development, procurement and support; and successful management of acquisition at the departmental level." (Secretary of State for Defence, 2005, p. 10)

There is also a definition of what the Ministry of Defence means by through-life capability management:

There is a general shift in defense acquisition away from the traditional pattern of designing and manufacturing successive generations of platforms—leaps of capability with major new procurements or very significant upgrade packages—towards a new paradigm centered on support, sustainability and the incremental enhancement of existing capabilities from technology insertions. The emphasis will increasingly be on through-life capability management, developing open architectures that facilitate this and maintaining—and possibly enhancing—the systems engineering competencies that underpin it. (Secretary of State for Defence, 2005, p. 17)

Development Process

The main person who "owns" the process is the second permanent undersecretary (2nd PUS)—this person is the same as a second permanent secretary, who runs the defence acquisition change program (DACP). (This program has around 10 workstreams, one being the DPA/DLO merger.)

The system had a major restructuring in April 2007 and some aspects are still in the process of final formation.

There is a professional head of project management and a head of project governance within the DE&S, but it is not clear what influence, if any, they have on the definition of the actual framework.

Results

CDM (the head of DE&S) reports to corporate targets that look at the agency's overall performance. Much of this work is project-related and thus by implication assesses the procurement framework. Within the DE&S, there are eight "cluster" directors who report different aspects of the work (in military terminology, they are at the "2*" level).

3 Categories of Measures Identified in the Department Review	Number of Instances	Total Cost Reduction (£m)	Percentage of Total Cost Reduction
Re-allocated to enable more appropriate management	18	448	57
• Suppliers' corporate costs	3	17	2
• Re-allocated to other parts of the Department	15	431	55
Re-assessments of quantities required	3	139	18
More appropriate accounting treatment	5	32	4
Re-definition of some elements of the projects	18	162	21
• Re-assessment of requirements	2	6	1
• Commercial and contract management	8	138[1]	18
• More cost effective methods of delivery	8	18	2
	44[2]	781	100

Source: National Audit Office

NOTES
1 This includes a cost reduction of £91 million due to a rebate and exemption from HM Revenue & Customs.
2 The Project Summary Sheet for Astute records one Department Review measure for decreasing costs regarding nuclear safety cases. For the purpose of analysis, this has been broken into six separate measures.

FIGURE 5-1.   RESULTS OF IMPLEMENTING THE MOD FRAMEWORK (Source: Major Projects Report 2006, NAO).

There are also regular national audit reports on major projects (National Audit Office, 2006). The report includes the table in Figure 5-1 which shows the 44 main measures they are actually taking.

As the table in Figure 5-1 shows, there have been good indications of positive results so far, according to estimates made by the Ministry of Defence and the National Audit Office.

Concluding Remarks

The establishment of DE&S, at the time of writing this report, is too recent to have accumulated evidence of its performance specifically. But the moves over the last decade emphasizing capability rather than equipment, towards IPTs, towards the extended life cycle, and then more consideration of TLCM and program management, does seem to have brought a more holistic view, suggesting a more effective management of the overall supply of capability to the UK armed forces.

5.1.3 NORWAY MINISTRY OF FINANCE FRAMEWORK: THE QUALITY ASSURANCE SCHEME

Introduction

In Norway, major investment projects involve big money and tend to draw much attention. The triggering incident in Norway was a series of unsuccessful major projects during the 1980s–90s. Repeated project overspends turned into a political problem. Deputy Secretary General of the Ministry of Finance, Peder Berg, led a government committee investigating a number of project cases and the report documented the problems (Berg et al., 1999). The Ministry of Finance initiated the development of an obligatory quality assurance scheme in the year 2000. The goal was to ensure improved quality-at-entry in large public projects.

It was a bottom-up process within the ministry with Peder Berg as a driving force. Upon initiation of the QA regime, it was important to achieve anchoring on a high level within the ministry. The decision to introduce this governance framework was eventually made by the cabinet, which in turn informed parliament. For both the first and second generation of the QA regime the intention was to establish a system where politics and administration is well divided, with the interplay between these two sides well understood. Our interviewee said: "From an administrative point of view the important thing is to make sure there is always a basis for decision addressing all relevant sides of the issues involved, and an independent assessment confirming its professional quality. The intended effect of such a system is making the state able to choose the right projects and execute them well."

The QA regime was a new initiative from the Ministry of Finance, and the Ministry of Finance is still responsible for it. An important limitation to the QA regime is that it encompasses only large investment projects (>500 million [NOK]/ USD $85 million [US]). The numbers would look slightly different if smaller projects were included, according to our interviewee.

Political and Administrative Setting in Norway

Norwegian politics are founded on a long parliamentary tradition going back to 1884. Norway is a constitutional monarchy and parliamentary democracy. As a characteristic, one could say "mainstream Western Europe." The first generation of the QA regime (year 2000) was the initiative of the first government (minority coalition) lead by Prime Minister Kjell Magne Bondevik (Bondevik I) consisting of political parties in the "center" of Norwegian politics. The second generation of the QA regime (year 2005) was the initiative of the second government (minority coalition) lead by Prime Minister Kjell Magne Bondevik (Bondevik II) consisting of political parties in the center and conservative wing of Norwegian politics. In the periods between and after these governments, the QA regime has also proved to be very well anchored in the governments of Prime Minister Jens Stoltenberg (currently leading a majority coalition government with parties from the center and socialist wing of Norwegian politics).

In Norway, constitutional responsibility for the budget, including investment projects, rests solely with the relevant minister (ministerial responsibility). With few exceptions, the management of larger projects is delegated to directorates/crown entities reporting to the relevant sectoral ministry. Ministers are jointly and severally responsible for formal cabinet decisions. These decisions are made in the name of the king (the king in council). There is a possibility for individual ministers to file formal dissensions, which happens, but indeed not very often. If a minister has committed any sort of wrongdoing (infringing the constitutional responsibility) or done something politically unwise without the knowledge and consent of the cabinet (infringing the political responsibility), it is an issue for the prime minister to decide on that particular minister's future in the cabinet. One specific public sector element of responsibility is that the Norwegian state is responsible for the actions of their employees. The state can be sued, but not the person. On the other hand, the state can seek recovery from the employee, but this rarely happens unless there is a case of proved fraud. Bad performance often has no consequence.

Economy and Market Mode

Norway has a strong national economy. The GDP growth rate is satisfactory, unemployment is low, and the financial situation is sound. Due to considerable revenues from oil and gas, the public sector is run at a surplus. A scheme for financial savings in abroad instruments is employed. Savings thus accumulated currently, amount to more than $300 billion (US). The overall financial ease implies considerable budgetary challenges in the public spending sectors.

The commercial setting is pretty much like other countries in Europe. There is a peculiar characteristic of the Norwegian culture, though: in general it is easier to get forgiveness than permission. Actors tend to be allowed to try again and again even when not having shown signs of learning from previous tries. Contract strategies are often a result of traditions and habits. Seldom is the contract strategy considered explicitly in the early phase of projects. There is a strong tradition for splitting projects up into many small contracts, especially in the building and construction sector. In procurement sectors (defense and others) the tradition is different, with a tendency to buy complete delivery in a package.

Espoused Aim and Political anchoring

For both the first and the second generation of the QA regime, the intention was to establish a system where the political and administration roles are thoroughly divided, and where the interplay between these two sides are well-understood. From an administrative point of view, the important thing is to make sure there is always a basis for decision making addressing all relevant sides of the issues involved, and an independent assessment confirming its professional quality. The intended effect of such a system is to make the state able to choose the right projects and execute them well. Our interviewee said:

> *Anchoring on a high level is very important. We would never have accomplished anything without it. Especially when addressing problems across sectors. It also has to survive changing political settings and new governments. Introducing rules are not enough. The QA regime is also anchored in Parliament, even though they never made a formal decision about it. By introducing it as an orientation about cross sector budget issues, the Parliament Financial Committee was compelled to have an express opinion on the subject. Anchoring has to go all the way to the top.*

This anchoring is well-documented through the budget proposals for the relevant years. First generation: QA2 introduced in year 2000. The necessary political decisions were made one year before this date. See the text of the state budgets for 2000. (Finansdepartementet [1999]; Budget Proposal for 2000 Ch. 7.4. [original text in Norwegian])

Based on the study [of existing systems and 11 project cases, cf. pre-study conducted by the Ministry of Finance], the government has concluded that there is undoubtedly a need to improve the control of state investments. The state's mechanisms for project management have to be improved. This will involve organizational changes, building up of competence and changing of rules. It will inevitably take time to have all the necessary changes in place. It seems practical to start with the introduction of more rigorous demands concerning the management/ administration of the major projects. For all investments with a total cost exceeding 500 million NOK [60 million EURO], the government will demand an external quality assurance before the project can be brought before Parliament.) (Author's translation)

Through this document it is stated by the government (prime minister's office) that better projects and better execution of investment projects is a political goal. The parliament (financial committee) was unanimously positive in 2000 when QA2 was introduced. In 2005 when QA1 was introduced, only one party (FrP—right wing) suggested it might not be such a good idea. Second generation: QA1 in addition to QA2 in year 2005. New framework contracts signed in June 2005. (Finansdepartementet [2004]; Budget Proposal for 2005 Ch. 10.2. [original text in Norwegian])

Based on experience to date, the [quality assurance] scheme nevertheless is considered to have been working well; in as far as it goes. It has, however, been shown to be not sufficient to ensure that the project concept is relevant to the needs of society, and that it is the best alternative to meet these needs … The choice of concept is the most important decision for the project and for the state as project owner. It is of limited value to ensure realistic frames and good control documentation for a project that should not have been approved. In connection with the tendering of new framework contracts for quality assurance of major projects, it is therefore considered worthwhile expanding the scheme. The Government will introduce a new quality assurance scheme for the choice of concept, supplementing the existing QA scheme, which will be continued with a few adjustments. …The basis for QA1 is to ensure that the choice of concept is subject to true political governance.) (Author's translation)

This development gives power back to the government (see Chapter 2, post-NPM reform). Government is given the real power to decide whether a preproject of a major state investment project should be started or not. The ones responsible should also make the decision. Earlier, one could see a disorderly process where lower level managers and local organizations could promote a project to a point where the government has little choice. It is, at the same time, an increase in responsibility at other levels—sectoral ministries and top management of directorates and crown entities. Sectoral ministries have to answer for the cost frame (financial limit), directorates, and crown entities for their cost baseline.

Development Process

As shown previously, it all started with an investigation into a selection of good and bad investment projects, a prestudy performed in the period 1997–1999. The framework came as a consequence of the investigation; it was not a part of it. Development of QA2 took 1 year and the framework contracts were signed in June 2000. When QA2 was introduced in 2000, the intention was to have an external assessment of projects before the budgetary deliberations in the cabinet and the subsequent appropriation decisions by parliament. The effect was as planned.

Experience through 2000–2004 highlighted that there was a need to do something on an earlier stage. Some of the projects that parliament was invited to decide on had not matured sufficiently, or (in a few cases) suspicion arose that the proposed projects would not be the right response to identified societal needs. This idea had also been discussed earlier and the QA2 experience served to confirm the need for additional remedies. In 2005 QA1 was introduced and the current framework contracts are valid through 2008 with an option of two more years. The development of QA1 took a little less than 2 years.

An important part of the Norwegian governance framework is also the coordination arenas. There are several, and they all play a significant role in the development of the governance framework and its use:

- From the beginning, a project control forum was established. The purpose was coordination and horizontal integration. An important function was achieving consensus on principles and best practices related to the quality assurance (definitions, use of words, procedures, roles, reporting) and its contents (uncertainty analysis, organization, contract strategy, etc.). In this forum, the ministries meet with the QA consultants and the researchers. This forum was later called the project owners forum.

- In 2005, it was supplemented by the project management forum based on the experience that there was a need for an arena to discuss best practices in management of major public projects. In this forum, the government agencies meet with the QA consultants and the researchers. The forum is open for the ministries.

- In 2002, the concept research program was established to support development of competence and improved QA performance. Its primary task is to perform trailing research on the projects undergoing quality assurance. Copies of the QA reports are sent to the research program and data is entered into a database containing all major public projects in Norway since 2000. Information about this research is available at the Internet: www.concept.ntnu.no.

Promotion is more an implicit issue than a function or task connected to the Norwegian framework. Our interviewee said: "The QA reviews are mandatory and exemptions are an issue for the minister of finance and the line minister jointly, or for the cabinet. It is a more profound challenge to ensure that the spirit filters through to line ministry executives and to those responsible for project execution. There is clearly a positive development, but the pace has not been entirely satisfactory, and there is still much work to be done."

This shows that promotion is a continuous process. By the practical use of the governance framework, and by systematic motivational contact between Ministry of Finance and the ministries and directorates involved, the framework is promoted. The most important means is probably to mediate the intention and interest of the state in using the framework. By making the users understand why the Ministry of Finance is doing this and convincing them it is also in their own interest. The comments made by the interviewee also indicate some of the challenges attached when trying to change the culture and procedures of the civil servants.

There is no organization set up to promote the use of the governance framework. The promotion is simply in the form of demands. The ministries and directorates have to use it or their projects will come to an end. If they need more information, they come to the Ministry of Finance and seek information.

Changes through the working period: There have been no changes within the framework contracts in any of the two periods. But between the two periods a major change occurred—the introduction of QA1.

The interviewee said:

> QA2 was the important first step. In 1999, we concluded this was necessary. This made everyone involved in major investment projects aware that "business as usual" was not good enough anymore. When we discussed how to further develop and extend the QA regime, a QA3 at the time of evaluating tenders was an alternative. We chose instead to extend to the earlier phase—the QA1. This was not a consequence of change of setting, but a result of a process of maturization combined with fresh inputs from QA 2 reviews. By and large little has changed in the formal political and administrative settings. If we go a little further than that, it is now a trickier task to justify overruns. I think we can conclude that there is an ensuing increase in responsibility at all levels—sectoral ministries, directorates/crown entities, and project managers.

Current status: The current framework contracts are valid through 2008, with options to prolong for another two years. The implemented model defines a two-step decision gate model. It is all mandatory. The projects will have to pass through the gates, or else they will be stopped.

Projects have always been forced to go to parliament for financing. The new principle is connected to the early decision gate. Earlier it was quite usual to involve a lot of local stakeholders and make preproject documentation/design alternatives long before the government was involved—and when they where, their room for action was small. This way the regime gives political control back to the government. The consultant's advice has no formal standing/authority, but their report will give the ministry the arguments they need to enforce changes/responses.

The Norwegian framework is managed on a full-time basis by only two executives at the Ministry of Finance. However, the work is done in close cooperation with the staff at the Ministry's budget department, which is responsible for the budgetary follow-up. This works very well according to our interviewee, not the least as a result of top-management support and encouragement.

Results

Our interviewee responded:

> *This is very difficult to answer for the time being. For the bulk of quality assured projects, it is too early to make a verdict. The most important result is connected to the bad projects we do not have to use resources on at all. Success is first and foremost to avoid using time and resources on bad projects. We will never know how many project plans were abandoned before they reached us, while they alternatively would have been pursued in the absence of the QA hurdles. This absence is and will remain a fundamental problem when trying to evaluate the regime.*

The following are indications of positive changes identified:

- *In the first period of the QA regime, 52 QA2's were executed. For a few of these, serious doubt arose as to whether they were the "right" projects. The answer to this challenge was the QA1. This result indicates that the framework is able to promote further changes/improvements.*
- *The results of QA2 as such were according to expectations. Focus was on cost estimation, and several projects benefited. An example is the Ministry of Defence GOLF-program. Through QA2 this program was put back on track by QA2 initiating replanning and reorganization to make it manageable. A policy was implemented in the program; you have to show success in implementing the first step, then you can be allowed to go to the next step. Thus, manageability and a sound set of incentives were secured. There was a very high risk of total project failure, if the project had been allowed to proceed according to the original plans. According to our interviewee, the implicit*

savings in this program alone was more than the QA regime will cost for decades ahead.

- *All government agencies know they are monitored through the QA regime. This knowledge gives increased cost-awareness and self-discipline. An example is the Rv150 Sinsen-Ulven motorway-project. The Norwegian Public Roads Administration (NPRA) stopped the project after QA2 and demanded redesign to reduce cost. This redesign was completed, and afterwards, the project was allowed a second try which succeeded. These two examples indicate that the framework is able to promote improvements to single program and projects.*

- *A few projects have actually been stopped after QA2. However, there is not always a clear connection between the stop and QA2. In addition, the responsible ministry sees the benefit of a common benchmark. It helps them identify the wrong candidates and stop them. Although this indication is not evidence that the framework gives the decision makers a basis on which they can actually stop bad projects, it shows that the process promotes the critical debate that opens up for this.*

- *There has also been a clear improvement in the documents going through QA2. They represent a better basis for decisions and management than they did before the QA2 was introduced. It is too early to conclude the same for QA1. Our interviewee commented on the QA2 document: "The guidelines for the Strategic Management Document forces projects to address the important challenges. But we still need a better discussion on why old habits nevertheless have a strong tendency to survive, even when no one can claim that they are anything near best practice."*

- *Good project practices like uncertainty analysis of the cost estimates have become well-established in all Norwegian governance agencies and investment projects. This development was started before QA2 was introduced in 2000, but it has given an equalizing effect and learning across sectors.*

- *The effect on cost estimates have been subject to investigation.* (Magnussen & Olsson, 2006).

The authors conclude:

Two important results are highlighted and discussed: The differences in the proposed cost estimates appear to have decreased systematically since the introduction of the quality assurance and the project owners rely to a large extent directly upon the cost estimates from the quality assurance when the decision to execute the project is taken. (p. 281)

The concept research program is performing trailing research on all the projects going through QA1 and QA2 in Norway. Still, too few projects are finished to make an assessment of the effect on the projects. A separate study (Torp et al., 2006) has been done on different sides of the cost estimation and uncertainty analysis part of the quality assurance. The report discusses eight different aspects of the problems in question, but comes up with more questions than answers. This research is planned to be followed up continuously as more projects are finished.

There is no formal measurement of the effect of the executed projects. Effect assessments are discussed right now—focused on the investment projects. It is too early to conclude whether this will initiate changes or additions to the Norwegian governance framework.

Concluding Remarks on the Development Process
The Norwegian framework is still new. It should, therefore, be expected to represent the latest developments in governance of projects. It is still in the making, as far as QA1 goes. There is still no established common practice in this field. QA2, on the other hand, has been around for six and one-half years now and is well-established. The experience still has to be considered as limited since few projects have finished yet. Indications point in a positive direction.

5.1.4 COMPARISON AND DISCUSSION ABOUT THE DEVELOPMENT PROCESS

The three initiatives seem to have been prompted by similar developments: Uncertainty due to repeated failures of major projects and concurrent changes in market during the 1990s, lack of success in public investment projects, and motivated initiatives to improve the basis for having successful public investment projects. In the MoD case, it seems that a stronger relationship between projects and the delivery of capability was an additional motivating factor. Strong individual contributions put focus on the importance of how public investment projects were decided upon and executed. With support at a high political level, the responsible ministries were ready to act. Better use of public funds may be said to be the underlying aim in both countries, and the development of new, improved governance frameworks were the choice of strategy. However, as shown in Table 5-2, there were still considerable differences.

TABLE 5-2.   COMPARISON/SUMMARY OF DEVELOPMENT PROCESSES.

	NO	UK MoD	UK OGC
Initiative	The Ministry of Finance	The Ministry of Defence	The Prime Minister
Established	2000/2005	1998/2007	2000
Scope	All sectors (except Oil&Gas[8])	Defence	All sectors
Anchoring	Pol: Parliament and the Cabinet Adm: Ministry of Finance	Adm: MoD Main Board	Adm: HM Treasury
Motivation	Cost control and increased value	Cost control and reduce risk	Modernizing government
Espoused aim	Choose the right projects and execute them well	Maximized capability for UK Defence as a whole	Improve delivery
Current objective	Maximized value	Value for money	Achieve financial targets
Creation	Expert/Consensus	Consultant	Expert
Changes	Stepwise	Stepwise	Gradually
Implementation	Mandatory	Mandatory	By influence
Promotion	Mandatory. Information on request	Mandatory. Available from websites.	Standard procedure. Available from websites.
Results	Positive indications found	Positive results documented	Targets achieved

In the following, we will comment on and discuss the significance of these differences.

The OGC and Norwegian initiatives are both anchored at top political level (although the anchoring is formalized in different ways and at different levels as indicated in Table 5-2 they go all the way to the political top level) and organized under the Ministry of Finance. The process, however, was genuinely different. In Norway, the initiating process was bottom-up, as was the implementation of the improvement and following learning processes. In the United Kingdom both

---

8. The hospitals where excluded by an owner reform in 2001. They are now owned by self-financing regions and thus no longer subject to this framework. The health regions have installed a separate framework.

processes were top-down, as was the implementation of the management system (the toolbox attached to the governance framework). These differences are believed to mirror the administrative culture in the two countries. Norwegian culture has a tendency to go for consensus solutions based on low-level initiatives within an administration having a relatively weak position to impose solutions in the face of opposition. The UK administration has a stronger position and introduction of top-level initiatives is consequently easier. Consensus is not a basic demand in the United Kingdom, and therefore, it was easier to ask for a consultant/expert solution to be imposed from the top.

Both initiatives being anchored at top political level and organized under the Ministry of Finance seems reasonable, based on the background and motivation coming from cost overspend and the means pointing to economic control. For the purpose of horizontal coordination, it seems natural not to choose any of the sector ministries/departments as responsible for the framework working for all sectors (there will be more on horizontal coordination later in this chapter). Using an existing control unit, like the National Audit Office, could have been an alternative. This might have created confusion because there are fundamental differences between the reviews used in the governance framework and the audits performed by NAO. It could easily create confusion about NAO's role. The UK MoD is naturally organized within its own ministry, according to its area of responsibility. The specific reason why MoD has a separate framework from the other sectors was not made explicit to us, but it was felt that MoD's situation was special due to the need to manage programmatically to provide capability, and the much longer development projects; there might also be historic, cultural reasons based on the special situation described. The Norwegian case implies that this might not always be necessary.

The situation is quite compatible in the two countries. Norway has its own "excluded" sector—not defense but oil and gas (not covered here, as explained in Chapter 1). Due to an owner-reform in the Norwegian health sector in 2001, hospital projects are no longer subject to the reviews of the Norwegian framework. The sector is now self-financed and implements its own similar governance framework. With these exceptions, the Norwegian framework is implemented across the whole range of investment projects made by the state just like the OGC framework in the United Kingdom.

Responsibility is another main concern in the process of developing a governance framework. As already explained, the responsibility for development and implementation of the governance framework is important. In Norway, the same entity is responsible for the framework in all sectors. This framework is expected to give the same governance across sectors. In the United Kingdom, responsibility mainly rests with OGC but there is also responsibility with the department, prime minister's delivery unit (PMDU)—to whom the status of critical projects are reported—and

NAO (for audit purposes). This may potentially give differences in governance across sectors. Note that the department for work and pensions (DWP) is licensed by OGC to carry out their own Gateways, as indeed is MoD. MoD responsibility is entirely within MoD. Even though the responsibility is shared by several units, it is expected to be at least an equally good governance across sectors.

Responsibility to plan and execute the projects is another important matter. In Norway, the responsibility is with the minister, but delegated to a subordinate government agency or crown entity. In the United Kingdom, the responsibility is within the department with the minister and the permanent secretary, obviously also delegated. There is a stronger tendency to put high rank people in formal (project related) positions in the United Kingdom (SROs and members of Acquisition Approval Board, etc.), whereas in Norway a Ministry of Finance official would very seldom accept a formal position in any project (except the Ministry of Finance' own projects, of course). The same would probably yield other high rank officials because they might be apprehended to talk for their Ministry and risk ending up as hostage in the further process. This effect is less significant in the United Kingdom where the personal responsibility is stronger anyway. Only lower rank people would be represented in boards, etc., in Norway. Then again, project boards are rarely used in Norwegian state projects. There are internal boards in sectors like defence and coordination groups across ministries (steering committees).

The implementation strategy is very different in the frameworks in this study. The OGC currently works by influence and recommendation; the projects do not have to go through reviews, and its recommendations are not mandated. The review report is meant as kindly advice from experts in the field. We call these "friendly gateways." This advice is in the traditional UK civil service culture. Even if the review signals severe problems, the project may go on. In Norway, as in the UK MoD framework, the reviews are more critical (critical gateways) and the problems identified may stop the project. Having a review is mandatory before passing the gateway. The recommendations, however, are not mandated but have a strong position among the decision makers. As already mentioned, the UK OGC framework is going in the same direction as this study is progressing.

In the United Kingdom, there are a substantial number of people involved in implementing the framework, many of them giving advice to users of the tools and methods attached to the framework itself. In Norway, this is not the situation. The whole framework development and implementation involved two people in the Ministry of Finance (with some support from the budget department in the ministry according to specific needs). The remainder of the development work is a process involving all parties on a voluntary basis. The framework was implemented without organizational changes. It does not involve anyone other than the two people mentioned (see the next chapter for description of how the actual project related activities initiated by the framework is organized). The keys to understanding the difference here is the size and complexity of the context (UK vs. Norway as described in Chapter 1), the scope of the framework itself (horizontally and vertically as explained in the next section), the rigidity of implementation, and the degree of methods and tools attached to the framework.

In the United Kingdom (OGC and MoD frameworks), goals are more explicit, administratively focused, and measured in terms of money. This practice corresponds with the tradition in the United Kingdom. In Norway, there are more clearly politically anchored goals, but the expected effect of implementation is not specified. This practice corresponds with the tradition in Norway, where performance measurement is less accepted.

The Norwegian framework is a bottom-up process of learning from cases, transferring experience to other sectors by coordination and building "the new profession," based on the sharing of experience and discussion of common standards in the coordination arenas. The UK OGC and MoD frameworks have the characteristics of a top-down introduction of a common "quality system." The centers of excellence represent the "new profession" aspect in the United Kingdom.

Both Norway and the United Kingdom (OGC) have established a support organization looking for systemic trends: the United Kingdom as a permanent public administration entity and Norway as an external research program. MoD reports on systemic trends at a top level within its own organization. OGC looks only at systemic trends across projects—Norway and MoD also on single cases. Norway has centralized coordination arenas in the project owners' forum and project management forum (ministries, agencies, QA consultants, and researchers meeting to discuss principles and practices). OGC has established distributed Centers of Excellence, in addition to its own professional staff. MoD is already a single, organized entity with a professional staff and internal boards.

The Norwegian development process appears to be more of a step-by-step process. Partly implemented in 2000, scope expanded in 2005 and has been stable in the intermediate periods. OGC and MoD, on the other hand, was straight to full scope, based on structured reorganization of existing agencies. MoD has a similar process like the Norwegian (stepwise), although not expanding like the Norwegian one, but still reimplemented in 2007. OGC has had a continuous improvement process from the start, implementing new features and initiatives (gradually). Note that these differences are minor details (the Norwegian framework has had continuous development in practices during the process, and the OGC framework is going through a major reimplementation now in 2007–2008).

The chosen meta-strategies seem to be different: Norway breaking with tradition and introducing a mandatory new arrangement; UK OGC building on tradition and improving current processes, through influence; UK MoD forcing a reform of its system and practice within the limits of its area of responsibility—a position somewhere in between the two others.

As this description and comparison show, there are many ways to develop and implement a governance framework. The starting point, the aims of the initiative, and the context obviously has to be considered and the detailed solutions chosen carefully in order to make the complete new system work as intended. In this case, all frameworks seem successful and well adapted to each of the three settings. The changes and improvements along the way confirms that (1) everything does not fall into place at once, and (2) there will be changes over time forcing the frameworks to be regularly updated and changed as well.

5.2   EMBEDDED GOVERNANCE PRINCIPLES

By which governance principles are these frameworks working? This statement identifies interior key elements of the framework; it opens up the "black box." It identifies the value dimension of the framework. Identifying the embedded governance principles is not an easy task. This probably goes for any framework. They are hardly ever expressed explicitly. When they are mentioned, the issue tends to end up mixing with description of structure and elements on one side and management best practice issues, on the other hand. Thus, this chapter is one of the more difficult to investigate and report. However, the authors of this report believe that we should try to be clear on the use of principles, both to raise awareness and to be able to systematically compare and choose how the governance frameworks should be designed.

This study is not the first time the issue of governance principles has been raised. Two sources are explained to some detail in Chapter 2: (1) the seven principles of public life, and (2) the GoPM (11 principles) and GoPPM (12 principles).

Both of these sources originate from the United Kingdom, but neither are parts of the UK frameworks. Still they are relevant because they explicitly define principles of good governance. These principles could be expected to influence individuals working within the UK frameworks both in public and private sector.

To the degree that these principles are embedded in the practical work and not only meant for speeches in the cabinet, they will influence the performance and thinking of the individuals. They could, in the future, be influential also in other countries through the development of common practices in government and project management. The governance principles are vital in defining "the way we do business."

TABLE 5-3.   KEY ATTRIBUTES OF THE GOVERNANCE PRINCIPLES—EXCERPT OF QUESTIONS AND ANSWERS.

Question asked	Norway	UK MoD	UK OGC
Governance principles (explicitly stated and implicit)	• Performed best practice in planning and execution • To make oneself (one's work) available for scrutiny. • Transparency • Willingness to change, to learn • Conclusions based on professional standards • Different priorities and values are appreciated • QA should never become political • Work by 'management of expectation'	• MoD is a single customer managing a single portfolio to get the best capability for UK defence as a whole • A lot of derisking pre-projects • Governance of the extended life cycle • System needs trust	• Independent scrutiny • Tease out the hidden facts while avoiding blame • Differentiated according to level of criticality • Senior experts giving good advice to the project • Bring 'best practice' to the departments • Use a systematic initiation process • Have a single responsible individual represent the owner (SRO)
Does the framework differentiate between projects based on their level of complexity? Cost? Asset specificity? Uncertainty? Other?	Only size, measured as expected cost.	Yes. Four types of projects; each of these have different categorizations into A–D. Each type has (different) categorizations into A–D. For equipment and support this is based on cost.	Yes. Criticality. Political significance is an important factor in criticality. The assessment of criticality would be different for different levels of risk and cost.

5.2.1 UK OFFICE OF GOVERNMENT COMMERCE (OGC) FRAMEWORK: THE OGC GATEWAY™ REVIEW

Accountability was formally identified as a principle by the previous government in 1995, during a period of public concerns about "sleaze" (Committee on Standards in Public Life, 1995, p. 6). The following seven principles were identified:

- Selflessness—act solely in public interest,
- Integrity—do not place yourself in obligations influencing your performance,
- Objectivity—make choices solely on merits,

- Accountability—being responsible for their actions and open for scrutiny,
- Openness—give reasons for decisions and only restrict information when needed,
- Honesty—declare your private interests and take steps to resolve any conflict arising, and
- Leadership—promote and support these principles by leadership and example.

While these principles are still valid (it is included in the latest report from the Committee on Standards in Public Life, 2007), our interviewee did not recognize these principles as affecting OGC practice at all.

The OGC framework was built around the idea of having independent scrutiny of the projects, in order to "tease out" any hidden facts. It has utilized PRINCE2's key idea of having a single responsible individual for the project (the SRO). Rather than being directive, it uses senior experts to give good advice to the project, leaving the decision making to the SRO. Clearly, the OGC cannot carry out all assessments for all government projects, hence, the ideas of differentiating projects according to level of criticality, and the Centers of Excellence to bring best practice to the departments. We also looked for more detail about how the governance was actually applied.

Projects are differentiated by risk (since that affected their criticality categorization) as described in Section 5.3.1, but it seemed that the process did not really differ between projects by complexity or uncertainty. Simply, if the project was very complex, it would be broken down into parts, and they would have individual project-level Gateway. There were no obvious mechanisms to reduce project complexity otherwise.

While the framework tries to allocate action between the parties and get a common view and agree with the expectations and rules of conduct through its recommendations and findings, mechanisms generally provide assistance rather than direction. In circumstances of turbulence in the project environment, it is up to the project to ask for a review rather than have reviews imposed upon them. The regular Gateway 0's are on a time schedule, and each recommends when the next one should take place; turbulence, on the other hand, would lead to the project (SRO) asking for a review (although OGC people could suggest that the SRO asks). Centers of Excellence could go to the permanent secretary and suggest a review if there were problems in the environment. Centers of Excellence are also there, for example, to protect against collusive behavior by contractors. Departments can ask for assistance from the OGC and reviews do look for such behavior by contractors or abuse of dominant position (using their experience and highlighting any issues they feel).

5.2.2 UK MINISTRY OF DEFENCE (MOD) FRAMEWORK: THE ACQUISITION OPERATING FRAMEWORK

The MoD position is rather different from OGC, in that MoD is a single customer managing a single program to get the best capability for UK defence as a whole, and governance of the procurement process is based upon this premise.

This means that it is the governance of the overall capability program that is important. It has implications, for example, in the distribution of risk among participants in projects since ultimately, MoD keeps the risk. They need the military capability (although partnerships and the new openness with industry help here, there is ultimately no mechanism to ensure that a contractor does not exhibit collusive behavior or abuse of a dominant position). The framework does help to stabilize key players' expectations and rules of conduct, since MoD is a unified whole and now has an increasingly open relationship with industry. If there is turbulence in the project environment, the customer (equipment capability) monitors the environment to make sure he or she has the capability wanted (although there are also mechanisms to help: incremental acquisition, plug-and-play technology, the ability to re-role equipment, etc.).

As part of the governance of the extended life cycle, there is a great deal of derisking preprojects as a way to getting to the equivalent of OGC Gateway 0. Having said that, there are not specific mechanisms to reduce complexity, but rather MoD and DE&S are trying to understand and cope with the complexity and ambiguity—indeed, working on the basis of acquiring capability (rather than simple procurement of individual pieces of equipment) increases complexity—our interviewees were unsure that MoD/DE&S had fully comprehended program management.

This framework does differentiate between the four types of projects: equipment and support, IT-enabled business change, public-private partnerships, and estates have different categorizations into levels A–D, and these categorizations capture the different levels of complexity, asset specificity, and uncertainty typically within each of the four categories.

It was also interesting to note the degree to which the system incorporates trust, specifically concerning cost and time estimates, as discussed in the following section.

Many of the values underlying these points are operationalized in the detailed defense values for acquisition (DVfA), which are endorsed by the acquisition policy board and are shown in Figure 5-5. These include through-life thinking; quantification of risk and the recognition of the need to stop a project before Main Gate sometimes; the close relationship with industry and the different motivations; the identification of performance/time/cost trade-offs; avoidance of time-slippage; and openness and transparency.

MoD as a whole at the very top level is governed by its public service agreements (PSA) with the prime minister's office. See, for example, the PSA resulting from the 2002 Spending Review covering 2003/4–2005/6. The PSA is structured around three objectives structured into seven targets: objective three is "build for the future" consisting of two targets, target six is to "develop and deliver to time and cost targets military capability for the future, including battle-winning technology, equipment and systems, matched to the changing strategic environment" (HM Treasury, 2002, p. 1)

This objective is defined more precisely in the service delivery agreement for this target, which includes a promise to achieve, on average, in-year slippage of equipment in-service dates of less than 10 days for new major projects (specified as those under CADMID) and less than four weeks for pre-existing major projects with, on average, no real terms increase in costs and 97% of key requirements attained. It notes that

Progress on the delivery of major new equipment projects is reviewed annually by the national Audit Office and published in the Major Projects Report. It also notes that the target refers to military capability, rather than equipment: the central MoD customer defines its requirements and the Defence Procurement Agency is then able to achieve that requirement in the most effective way possible (National Audit Office 2006).

Target 7 is:

> Increase value for money by making improvements in the efficiency and effectiveness of the key processes for delivering military capability. Year-on-year output efficiency gains of 2.5% will be made each year from 2002/3 to 2005/6, including through a 20% output efficiency gain in the Defence Logistics Organisation. (HM Treasury, 2002, p. 1)

For example, the service delivery agreement for this target includes agreement to achieve 0% average annual cost growth (or better) for the 20 most expensive approved equipment projects over a year (i.e., the projects contained in the NAO major projects report). The Defence Logistics Organization is now of course absorbed into DE&S.

Another governance mechanism is provided by the National Audit Office, which regularly takes an overview of MoD's largest projects in the major projects report, as noted in 5.1.2.

5.2.3 NORWAY MINISTRY OF FINANCE FRAMEWORK: THE QUALITY ASSURANCE SCHEME

The following is how the interviewee answered directly to the questions.

On professional standards:
"Best practice is a good headline: The intention is to make sure best practice is performed in planning and execution of the projects.

QA1: Making the right choice issue.

QA2: Doing the right thing well issue.

One principle is to make oneself (one's work) available for scrutiny. The transparency is important.

If one's practice is not a best practice, it should be changed. Willingness to change and to learn is an important principle. This practice also implies that it is important to come to conclusions on professional standards."

On understanding of roles:
"The QA reports have to lay out straight the available room of action. And when a report is on the table, we cannot pretend it is not there. But it is of course OK to have a different opinion. Different actors have different priorities and values. That is OK. And there still has to be a room for action on the political side when it comes to decision. One vital principle is that the QA reports and the actors involved in QA should never become political. The reports should not include political pitfalls which can be misused."

On transparency:
"If the QA-reports are going to make a difference, they have to be available and credible. They have to satisfy high professional standards. And they have to conduct according to the framework contract. To make sure the knowledge is available; we want maximum openness and the QA-reports to be publicly available. One intended effect of this is to kill non-viable projects as early as possible."

On the impact of top level expectations:
"One important principle is the management of expectation: When everyone knows there is going to be a QA1 or QA2, they know what's coming and they know they will have to face it. This changes the way they work. Expectation guides the action. And it is working on many levels and in all phases of the development. By starting on a high level (the cabinet) this create a positive spin-off at all levels below. Signals are diffused throughout the hierarchy."

Other governance principles can be extracted from documents. These are presented in the following. Some of these may be viewed as subsets of the major principles pointed out by the interviewee.

Principles concerning the design of the framework:

- Simplicity, robustness. (Described as a quality of the framework. Hereby lifted up to be a principle by which this framework is working. The simplicity and robustness supports clarity of the decision making process and the processes within the framework. It is also vital to the efficiency and determines how often changes can be expected to the framework.)
- Mandatory, no shortcuts. (This principle simplifies the implementation of the framework as soon as there is an authoritative decision that this is how it is going to work. It also increases and expresses the authoritative and normative position of the framework as such.)
- Continuous learning and willingness to change. (This principle is the basis for improvement and a vital assumption for the whole initiative. See the professional standards.)
- External control, independency. (In Norway the whole QA scheme is run by external parties. Partly for practical [capacity] reasons, but the principle of independency is held very high. This supports transparency, credibility,[9] and learning. Maximum independency is achieved by using private sector consultants in the public projects.)
- Political anchoring on high level. (This principle is described as a characteristic of the Norwegian framework. In this perspective it is raised to be a governance principle. It is of vital importance to the system as a whole.)
- QA/Gateway Review is nonpolitical. (Just like the previous principle, this one is an important principle built into the Norwegian framework. By mentioning it as a principle, it is implied that it did not have to be this way, it is an important choice.)

Principles concerning decision making:

- Maximum openness about basis for decisions. (Certainly at the administrative side, expectedly on the decision making side as well, although that would be less obvious and difficult to prove. See understanding roles.)

---

9. The principle of independence supports credibility. This comment does not imply government officials or civil servants are less credible than people in private sector. It works the same way in the private sector.

- Decisions should be made at the appropriate political level. (Typical for a post-NPM reform, there is a focus on placing decisions in the appropriate forum at the appropriate level. This focus demands a clearly defined and transparent decision-making process to avoid projects being approved without having a real choice. Such restrictions may come as a result of growing expectations and political pressure from resourceful minorities.)
- Choose the concept early. (This principle increases the possibility to make a decision on the appropriate level. If the choice of concept is postponed it will open up for growing expectations and pressure, as well as keeping the presumptions for planning open and unclear.)

Principles concerning the quality assurance:

- Setting common, high professional standards. (Combines the two principles: professional standards and continuous improvement. Professional standards should be set high and include specified minimum achievements as a basis for control.)
- Look for big trends, not the minor details. (Both the definitions of the actual documents being subject to quality assurance and the instructions to the QA consultants in their framework contracts are explicitly focused on identifying the important few aspects of the larger picture, not the pity details. This principle helps build an efficient system.
- Base projects on real needs. (The focus on causality in the Norwegian framework is very strong. In the bottom of any suggested project, there should be the real needs of the users, not a construction of arguments to reach other goals.)
- Strong focus on good performance of methods. (The framework contracts and guidelines to the Norwegian QA scheme show a distinct focus on the use of methods. The project management is expected to implement state-of-the-art methods, and the QA consultant is supposed to give advice on how to plan and manage the project.)
- Choose (project) strategy early. (This principle is seen as important to make sure the project has a well-defined and thought-through strategy from the beginning, as well as it improves the possibility of an effective control.)
- Primary project focus. (The quality assurance should have a primary focus—some leading criteria against which the project is assessed. In the Norwegian framework, this focus is very different from the first Gateway to the second. In the first (QA1), the focus is on value. In the second one (QA2), the focus is on cost and risk.)

It would be possible to increase the number of identified principles, by going further into detail. This detail is not necessary or desirable. The principles referred here show how the Norwegian framework is meant to work (formal framework design is described in the previous section). It explains the result of a large number of major choices in the development process. Although many of these principles represent basic assumptions, which should not be changed (if changed, it would become a different framework), some of the principles concerning the quality assurance may be subject to change over time and in light of experience from implementation of the framework.

5.2.4 COMPARISON AND DISCUSSION OF GOVERNANCE PRINCIPLES

Comparing governance principles (the "value" dimension of the frameworks) is difficult, not least because of the difference in the way these are exposed. In the United Kingdom cases, the governance principles are embedded in the frameworks without being addressed explicitly. In Norway, the interviewee was very clear on many principles, and the principles are also more evident in the documents. The comparison may be somewhat skewed because of it.

TABLE 5-4.   DIFFERENCES IN MAJOR GOVERNANCE PRINCIPLES

	NORWAY	UK MoD	UK OGC
Characteristic:	Simplicity, robustness	Completeness	Complex system
Influence:	Management of expectation	Hurdles to cross	Recommendations
Authority:	Mandatory	Mandatory	By influence
Review focus:	Control of input and methods	Output within program (contribution to capability)	Business case
Life cycle:	Choose concept early and choose strategy early	Very early gateway. Extended life cycle.	Initial and repeated strategic assessments within program
Project focus:	Cost/Risk/[Value]	Value for money	Value for money

The following describes the structure of the governance frameworks, their main elements, and how the implementation is organized. To understand how this is actually supposed to work, it is important to understand the governance principles built into the framework. Since the degree of explicit description of the principles is uneven, the authors have had to interpret both direct statements and extract principles indirectly from documents and procedures to find them. In both countries, governments have expressed the intention to ensure best practice in planning and execution of projects. Some of the principles are mentioned by interviewees and can be summarized as follows:

(a) Common governance principles (stated by both sides):

- Transparency, openness for scrutiny, maximum openness about basis for decisions,
- Learning, willingness to change,
- Setting common, high professional standards,
- External control, independency,
- Political anchoring of framework on high level,
- QA/Gateway Review is nonpolitical, and
- Looking for big, important trends, not the minor details.

(b) Expected to be common principles (stated only by one side, but implicitly part of both):

- A good process has the potential to lead to a good result.
- Base the projects on needs of the users and society.
- Decisions should be made at the appropriate political level.
- Use senior competence as owner representative and in assessment.

Many of these are closely related to the common Western thinking about business and government, as well as general aggregated experience from projects. This is the common platform for the frameworks. At this level, they are quite equal.

Significant differences are found in values rooted in the different (administrative) cultures in the two countries and MoD. These are the interior sources for choices leading to the exterior being very different. The indications are given in Table 5-4.

The most characteristic difference has to do with the way of thinking about systems. In Norway, the simplicity in system is a characteristic ideal. In the United Kingdom, the ideal is completeness (taking into account the toolboxes, not only the framework). The MoD framework can be seen as a good attempt to combine these two ideals.

The second is the choice of a mandatory system in Norway and MoD and the persuasive recommendations with OGC. As shown previously, these choices reflect administrative culture in the two countries' government. In the United Kingdom, there seems to be a clear difference in administrative culture separating the defense sector form the rest. This is also the case in Norway, but here other characteristics make it realistic and reasonable to use the same framework also in this sector. The simple, robust ideal is an enabler.

Another characteristic difference between the frameworks is the review focus on business case (results) in the UK OGC, the capability (contents) in UK MoD, and on performance (input and method) in Norway. This corresponds with cultural differences mentioned earlier. The OGC review mirrors the market mode and individual responsibility. The MoD review focus is closely linked to the superior purpose pervading the whole organization (this uniform objective focus is only possible within a limited sector). The Norwegian review focus mirrors the background of the initiative and the strong belief in setting high professional standards combined with the fact that performance measurement has weak support in Norwegian culture. It should be noted that in practical situations the focus of the responsible review team leader will have large influence and may deviate from the general focus mentioned in Table 5-4.

In Norway the control measures are focused on cost and risk (initially at least, but moving more towards benefit and value), whereas the UK side is focused on the business case/value for money. This focus may be a measure of the maturity in the frameworks; the Norwegian being all new and the United Kingdom building on long tradition.

The focus in the reviews on what should be main priority upon assessing the project seems quite different in the three frameworks: In Norway the focus of the QA1 is clearly the value of the outcome of the project—the benefit as such. The focus of the QA2 is clearly cost and risk. The MoD focus is on the capability need and value for money, the benefit relative to the resource input. The OGC focus is on the business case. The expression of these focuses is different according to the purpose in each context, but the values in the bottom are expected to be similar. There is no evidence of significant fundamental differences. The difference between focusing value per se, against value for money may be a simple consequence of the different economic situations in the two countries (see Chapter 1). The result is expected to be comparable.

The life cycle perspective also shows different faces in the three frameworks studied. The MoD framework has an explicit complete life cycle perspective with a very early gateway to set this focus. The OGC has strategic assessments on the program level, repeated when needed. In these assessments the bigger picture defined as the intended change is in focus. It does say explicitly the whole life cycle should be considered (see Section 5.4). In Norway, the framework focuses on defining objectives and strategies early (with a similar intention as the MoD focus). It is implicit that the project should consider the whole life cycle (explicitly expressed as all costs) but the project model (phase model) does not include a complete life cycle, and the guidelines only "touch upon aspects of life cycle cost and life cycle benefit" (see Section 5.4). This may be a less significant indication of governance principles or values since they point in different directions and are not exclusive to each other. We are not indicating that the underlying values have to be different, only that the expression on the surface is different.

Ideally a governance framework would address both the portfolio level, program level, and project level. As an impression of the whole framework, one could be tempted to put the following labels on each one of them: MoD—Portfolio (since it is implemented to instill governance to the whole family of projects within the MoD); OGC—Program (since it mentions programs frequently and puts this label on its strategic level reviews); and Norway—Project (since this is the official label and neither program nor portfolio currently has any significant focus in the framework). As previously argued, the correct label for the MoD framework would be program, since the portfolio is managed as a group of projects to achieve one strategic goal—the maximized defense capability. This has, by definition, the characteristics of a program (see Chapter 2). The OGC framework actually seems to focus mainly at the individual project level, where a project in these terms is some change that the department seeks to carry out, which will often be termed a program and split into a number of output-oriented projects (hence, the explicit requirement for Gateway 0 to concentrate on the desired program outcome rather than the specific project output). The Norwegian framework did have some focus on the portfolio level in the beginning of its first period, but currently there is only a project focus. Both OGC and the Concept Research Programme in Norway look for larger trends (across sectors, portfolios, and programs). This trend has a perspective not limited to any of the mentioned levels of management.

5.3   THE STRUCTURE OF THE FRAMEWORK

The following section focuses on the contents of the framework—its structural elements. This section describes how the framework is designed. It is by this description the framework will be recognized by most readers. It describes the framework's exterior.

TABLE 5-5.   KEY ATTRIBUTES OF THE FRAMEWORK STRUCTURE—EXCERPT OF QUESTIONS AND ANSWERS.

Question asked	Norway	UK MoD	UK OGC
Framework elements (control measures, arenas for coordination etc.)	The whole framework is a control measure. The control rules are documented in the framework contracts and the control subject is the documentation assessed in the QA regime:	Four types of projects, each type has (different) categorizations into A–D. Gates are hurdles to cross—decision on letting the project proceed taken by the Investment Appraisal Board.	Main elements of the framework are Gateway Reviews, categorization of projects and mission critical projects, Centers of Excellence, and (recently) the project initiation process.
Framework structure (how elements are put together and interact)	Two Gateways: QA1: The early choice of concept, the decision to initiate project preplanning. QA2: The GO decision, the decision to finance the project.	Two gates: • the first (Initial Gate) to release funds for assessment, • the second (Main Gate) to release funds for the main project.	Six Gateways: 0: Strategic management 1: Business Justification 2: Procurement Strategy 3: Investment Decision 4: Readiness for service 5: Benefits Realization
Extent and control of outside engagement (private sector engagement in governance procedures)	It is all external. Several private sector companies are approved in advance through framework contracts.	Mainly within MoD, but independent representatives are on the board.	Gateway reviewers/ strategic assignment consultants service, private sector experienced consultants who have been individually selected.
Vertical integration (level of integration, value chain)	QA1 and QA2 give a tool for control from the top (cabinet – ministry – agency). Does not address the private sector.	The entire project including industrial base is included, so in that sense it is vertically integrated. Stops at MoD level.	Gateways look at the ministerial level all the way down to suppliers.
Horizontal integration (across sectors)	The QA regime is introduced across sectors (excluding Oil & Gas sector)	MoD largely independent of other ministries.	OGC looks at all types of project.

Question asked	Norway	UK MoD	UK OGC
Describe the organization (structure, levels, anchoring within the public administration)	Managed by two executives at the Ministry of Finance.	MoD runs its own scheme. The top-level committee acquisition policy board (APB), which reports to the defence management board, gives the policy. Follow up is integrated in the organization.	OGC "better projects" division runs the process. Formally head of OGC (but practically the head of better projects) "owns" the process.
Roles and parties within the organization supporting/ operating the framework	Only the two mentioned previously; coordinating resources, motivating, informing. The QA consultants are important.	None really. The "chief of staff" in DE&S looks after the process.	OGC and external consultants; Centers of Excellence within departments.
Users (sectors, levels, etc.)	Primary users: The responsible ministries, Ministry of Finance, The prime minister's office Secondary users: directorates/crown entities, researchers.	All of MoD projects but only within MoD.	Essentially all government departments and agencies.

5.3.1 UK OFFICE OF GOVERNMENT COMMERCE (OGC) FRAMEWORK, INCLUDING THE OGC GATEWAY™ REVIEW

Purpose and Objectives of the Framework

The overall political imperative is delivery, and OGC has helped drive it. For example, the Centers of Excellence were there to put delivery rather than policy into departments.

The espoused aim of the framework is specifically to achieve financial targets of money saved (as a combination of the work on commodities and the work on projects). These financial targets are set by the treasury. The "savings" are calculated from estimates, with a process approved and certified by the National Audit Office (although our interviewee stressed that this was not in the thoughts of the Gateway Reviewers as they did their work). This was true originally, and it is still true.

Later developments (e.g., Centers of Excellence) were aimed to change the culture of departments, all the way up and down the department, and to establish governance. It was desired to get a culture shift within departments away from traditional civil-service ways of thinking and towards business management, and the OGC were to be a catalyst for this.

Governance before the OGC methods was put into place consisted of "departmental reviews," and it is not clear whether these provided governance: they could be seen simply as reports that money had been spent, with no challenge to the department and with unclear accountability. Each department's procedures were different, and all the governance was kept within the department.

Framework Elements

There is a clear distinction between the program (the overall change) and the projects beneath this program to achieve the change.

The chief elements of the framework are the Gateway Reviews, then later came the idea of categorization and mission critical projects, then Centers of Excellence, and now also the project initiation process.

The six Gateways are well-defined, they are standardized and documentation is available. They fit together as shown in Figure 5.2. Gateways 1–5 are at project level:

> Gateway Review 0: Strategic management (several times where appropriate)
> Gateway Review 1: Business justification
> Gateway Review 2: Procurement strategy
> Gateway Review 3: Investment decision
> Gateway Review 4: Readiness for service
> Gateway Review 5: Benefits realization

They can be summarized as follows. Gateway 0 is an ongoing strategic assessment, during which the need for the program is confirmed, and it is checked that it is likely to achieve the desired outcomes. Gateway 1 is a business justification, which looks at whether the business requirement can be delivered, and if affordability, achievability and value for money can be established. Gateway 2 ensures that the acquisition and delivery strategy are appropriate for the desired business change and implementation plans are in place. Gateway 3 looks at the investment decision; ensuring that the project is still required, affordable, and achievable; implementation plans are robust and the investment decision is appropriate. Gateway 4 looks at readiness for service, ensuring that the organization is ready to make the transition to implementation and that ownership and governance are in place for operation. Finally, Gateway 5 looks at operations review and benefits realization, confirming smooth operation, delivery of outputs, and achievement of benefits.

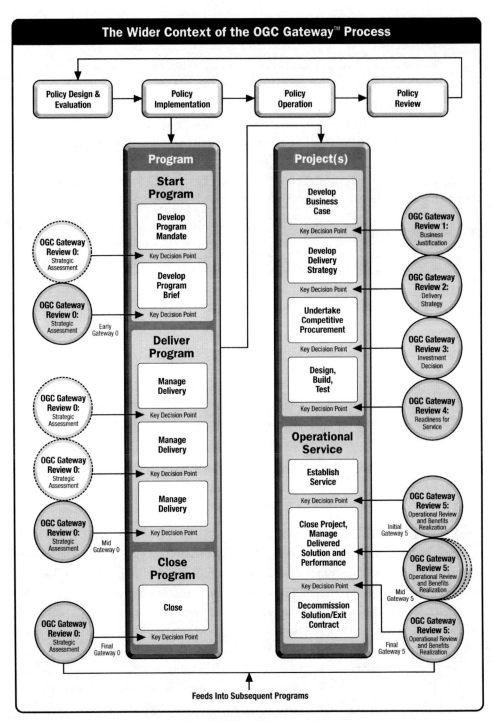

Figure 5-2.   **THE OVERALL OGC FRAMEWORK (OGC, undated)**

Originally there was just one Gateway 0, now (i.e., the framework has developed) the 0's keep on going through in parallel to the project, as the program is going on. This continuation is particularly geared towards change projects, but is equally applicable to equipment and infrastructure.

Gateways look at the ministerial level all the way down to suppliers. Parliament/government level is done by mechanisms outside this study (committees, NAO, etc). Independent reviewers also look at suppliers, as they have relevant experience. The private sector engagement comes from the use of the strategic assignment consultants service (SACS), made up of private sector experienced consultants who have been individually selected. Their accreditation is based on experience, demonstrated through their CV. (Note that people subject to Gateway Reviews feedback their views about the reviewers to OGC, who keep a check that the reviewers are operating satisfactorily, and use this feedback in their allocation of reviewers to projects.) The independent reviewers also look at suppliers, as they have experience of dealing with suppliers. Our interviewee did have a slight worry about independence on the Gateway Reviews. Previously, there had been an emphasis on review teams including independent private sector consultants. OGC had come to consider that it was not necessarily the case that public servants couldn't do reviews as well, so there was possibly an increasing proportion of public sector consultants qualified as Gateway Reviewers, although such reviewers would only review projects well-removed from their normal responsibilities, in order to maintain independence.

It should be noted that reviews are *not* audits and *do not* allocate blame—they are a gateway looking at where you are and whether you are in a position to move forward. They cannot stop projects, but a "red" outcome shows "immediate actions are needed." In extreme cases, they might recommend stopping a project but have no power to do so.

The second element is the categorization by criticality. The assessment of criticality looks mainly at the risk level. This element is based upon a spreadsheet tool called the risk potential assessment. This assessment results in a scoring system to try to measure how much risk is inherent in the project (scores of 30 or less are deemed to be low risk, those of 31–40 are medium risk, and those of 41 or more are high risk). These results are not the only trigger for OGC's involvement; other factors which are taken into account to determine when OGC should get involved include size, complexity, and strategic significance of delivering ministerial imperatives (i.e., level of political significance).

The top level is the "Top 20" mission critical projects; for these projects, the OGC will also sit on the project board. The next level is "high criticality" (essentially those that did not get into the top 20, as there were only 20 allowed there); for these, Gateway Reviews have to use senior people or even all independents. Then there are "medium criticality" projects, for which departments can call on the OGC for help if there is a resource available. Then "low criticality" projects are reviewed within departments. This procedure was necessary because there are so many projects (maybe about 100 high critical as well as the top 20). Criticality assessment is done by a department then between the OGC and permanent secretaries; the mission critical list is also decided between the head of OGC and the prime minister. Reviews of high-risk projects will be led by outsiders, but small- or low-risk projects could be mainly internal. It may be that the level of external input could reduce due to cost considerations.

The third element is the development of Centers of Excellence, bringing "best practice" to the department. Some of these centers report directly to the permanent secretary of the department (the model preferred by the OGC as they feel this works better). They also act as a liaison point within a department for OGC. It is recommended that they are small, around four people. For mission critical and high critical projects, the Center of Excellence will be the department representative; they will be doing mini-Gateway Reviews as the project goes on. For medium criticality projects, the Center of Excellence runs the Gateway Reviews.

There is one further important document which forms part of this structure. The NAO and the OGC identified the common causes of project failure (OGC, 2005), which have become a standard checklist against which all projects are tested. Indeed, the treasury instructed all government accounting officers (in letter ref DAO(GEN)07/04 dated 30th March 2004 and entitled "Delivering success in government acquisition-based programmes & projects") that accounting officers were required to assure their projects against this list of common causes of project failure. The list consists of eight headings, each with between four and eight questions to answer. The headings are as follows:

1. Lack of a clear link between the project and the organization's key strategic priorities, including agreed measures of success.
2. Lack of clear senior management and ministerial ownership and leadership.
3. Lack of effective engagement with stakeholders.
4. Lack of skills and proven approach to project management and risk management.
5. Too little attention to breaking development and implementation into manageable steps.
6. Evaluation of proposals driven by initial price rather than long-term value for money (especially securing delivery of business benefits).
7. Lack of understanding of and contact with the supply industry at senior levels in the organization.
8. Lack of effective project team integration between clients, the supplier team, and the supply chain.

And a typical question, particularly relevant to this study would be one under the fist heading: "Is the project founded upon realistic timescales, taking account of statutory lead times, and showing critical dependencies such that any delays can be handled?".

A later development has been the project initiation process. Recent developments have moved more towards "doing the right projects" rather than "doing the projects right." There is now a "project initiation process" before Gateway 0: OGC go into a department to discuss upcoming projects and to "help get the ducks in a row." This action is aimed to feed into Gateway 0, to make it more effective. (There was a feeling previously that departments were simply waiting for Gateway 0 to do all this work). This will eventually be tied into the Gateway process (no more information is currently available on this initiative).

PRINCE2 also forms part of the OGC toolbox, but it is not really part of the governance framework. Our interviewee commented that "PRINCE2 is not looked for in detail, rather it is the spirit of PRINCE2 that is looked for"; however, he said that some reviewers look more rigorously at the application of PRINCE2; OGC does however recognize the danger of getting overbureaucratic. (Note that while PRINCE2 is not really part of the governance framework, the idea of the SRO is, which originally came from PRINCE2.)

One other document that is extremely influential and is often used as checklist was jointly agreed upon in 2003 by the NAO and OGC: it is a list of eight common causes of failures in major government IT projects, though many of these are more widely applicable (included as an annex to DAO(GEN)07/04 Delivering Success in Government Acquisition-Based Programs & Projects).[10]

Vertical and Horizontal Integration

Gateways look at the ministerial level all the way down to suppliers; this is where the vertical aspect comes in. The only difficulty here is where there is competition (departments possibly being worried about OGC personnel revealing commercial information).

Essentially all government departments and agencies use this methodology (although see the discussion on MoD in this report). OGC tried to look at all types of projects, although their initial focus was IT and IT-enabled change projects. They looked at MoD change projects, but MoD has its own procedures for projects procuring hardware equipment. Another department (the department of work and

---

10. 'Dear Accounting Officer,' or DAO, letters, were used by the UK Treasury to provide specific advice on issues of accountability, regularity and propriety and sent to all Government Departments. They can be viewed on http://www.hm-treasury.gov.uk/dao.

pensions) tends to do its own reviews, having been "accredited" by the OGC (to reduce workload on OGC); but having said that, these two departments are tending to make use of much the same set of independent reviewers in Gateway Reviews.

One complicating factor sometimes occurs when there is more than one department involved. The SRO and the minister will normally be from the same department and designated as "lead" department. The Gateway team talks to the lead departments but also to the others. There are various other models also, for example, some have a "ministerial committee" of equal ministers (or a "steering board" of a number of SROs), but they are being told that this model does not work very well. There could be an SRO in each department, but that too does not work well. It is possible to have a minister in one department and an SRO in another department, then it is not clear who is ultimately responsible (not a Gateway issue but a governmental issue, but it clearly needs sorting), but this is unusual.

Organization and Resources

The head of OGC "owns" or holds the OGC processes formally, but practically the head of the "better projects" part of OGC holds this process. This part of OGC is formed from within OGC; personnel do not get involved in the departments, simply running the framework. (These are to be distinguished from the external consultants described in the following. Until recently there were around 20 "CIMS," people who were like the external consultants but were permanent employees within OGC).

To date, there have been two lists of external private sector experienced consultants: (1) The Gateway list, the set of people who can do Gateways, and (2) The strategic assignment consultants service (SACS) list, a set of independent people OGC has to work on the various OGC assignment.

These lists are heavily overlapping but different, and it is the first item that is important to us. SACS are appointed by the OGC as for any senior job (depending on experience, CV, etc). The Gateway list is a list of people qualified by OGC with a proper laid-down procedure. Many are independent (indeed, many are SACS) but now two government departments (DWP and MoD) have people within them on the Gateway lists so they can do their own Gateway Reviews. Reviews of high-risk projects will be led by outsiders, but small or low-risk projects could be investigated mainly internally, and the MoD or DWP could be investigated entirely internally. Our interviewee wondered whether the level of external input (which has not been laid down) would reduce in the future because of cost considerations; he was thus concerned about independence on the Gateway Reviews, which was a key founding element of the framework. Previously, review teams had been a mix of independents and civil servants, but there were moves to having only civil servants on some reviews.

Gateway reports go technically to the SRO, and that is all that is involved for a particular project. Permanent secretaries will normally be shown the report by the SRO. The OGC will give a brief status report on the mission critical list to the prime minister's office, but only a status report, not the entire Gateway report (perhaps just how many Gateway's have been done and their colors red/amber/green); this is not a formal reporting line—any issues arising from this will be dealt with in the normal part of the prime minister's relationship with a minister. If asked, the OGC would give their views to a parliamentary committee, but not the Gateway Review. They might acknowledge the color of the review, but not the detail. Remember that reviews are not audits and do not allocate blame.

The impact of this on projects has been considered. The OGC has tried to make the requirements on projects minimal. The documentary burden on projects should be very little as they should have the documents that the reviewers would ask for. PRINCE2 is not generally looked for in detail, rather the spirit of PRINCE2. Centers of Excellence tend to be very small.

Concluding Remarks on the Framework Structure

Although at first sight, the Gateway process appears complicated, the OGC has tried to make the burden on projects no more than good governance requires. The framework has gradually developed over time, bringing in categorization (because of the numbers of projects), Centers of Excellence (to improve program management and change culture in a department), and the project initiation process. But there are major changes that took place in 2007, which are very important, and are described in section 5.5

5.3.2 UK MINISTRY OF DEFENCE (MOD) FRAMEWORK: THE ACQUISITION OPERATING FRAMEWORK

Purpose and Objectives of the Framework

As discussed previously, the aim of the framework set up for procurement of defense equipment is particularly, the management of MoD's projects as a single program to get the best capability for UK defense as a whole. The implications of this include the need to manage capabilities at the program level rather than the individual project; the need to manage through-life capability and the extended life cycle, with a continuing eye for value-for-money. Affordability is important but the user need sometimes takes precedence.

Framework Elements

The MoD has four levels of project, Categories A–D, defined by value. Different types of projects, equipment, support, information systems, estate, etc., have different value levels for the categorizations. The private-finance initiative (PFI) projects are dealt with in a separate line. For the purposes of this report, we are mainly looking at equipment and support, and for this type of project category A is defined as a value at least £400 million, and category B within £100 million-£400 million. The categorization helps to give an overall risked portfolio.

The framework consists of two gates only. These are points at which the project is considered by the investment appraisal board (IAB). The first, or Initial Gate, asks to release funds for assessment; the second, or Main Gate asks to release funds for the main project. These are "gates" in the sense that they are mandatory, and a project which does not pass the gate cannot proceed. Submissions to each gate have to be in a standardized format.

It is natural to try to relate these gates to the OGC Gateways. However, this is difficult, partly as OGC is really mainly project-oriented and not concerned with the totality of the overall equipment programme as is MoD. But the Main Gate can be seen as just after Gateway 3 (Gateways 1–3 could go all together), and the Initial Gate would be just after Gateway 0 and 1.

Categories A and B go at the two gates to IAB, via two routes simultaneously:

- The advocate of the project (the SRO), and
- Independent scrutiny, in DG scrutiny and analysis looks at the business cases.

Within DE&S, an internal DE&S investment board (prior to the IAB) for CDM aims to check that the "2*" cluster-director level is happy with the case before the two IAB gates.

The management of projects that are subject to this framework can be described as follows.

- MoD holds the portfolio of projects.
- Equipment capability (the "customer," DCDS[EC]) holds the program of projects, and
- The integrated project team (IPT) holds the project.

Each project thus has an IPT with a two-way responsibility:

- Responsible on the project to the SRO; it reports through the SRO to DCDS(EC) (who reports to main board) for a specific project, and
- Responsible overall within DE&S; it reports through DE&S through CDM to the main board on overall targets; the 2* level in DE&S reports monthly to CDM, and the IPTs report monthly to both the SRO and the 2*.

Work on each project needs to cut across all of the defense lines of development (DLoDs), which provide a way of coordinating the parallel development of different aspects of capability that need to be brought together to create the desired capability, being: training, equipment, personnel, information, concepts and doctrine, organization, infrastructure, logistics, and interoperability. However, it should be noted that only three DLoDs are directly managed by DE&S, the others are managed within MoD, so here the relationship with the customer is key.

It should be noted that the model developed by McKinseys is different from PRINCE2, so the elements of PRINCE2 are used, but it is not required by MoD, other than the idea of the SRO.

Finally, there is a new idea of a foundation review when projects begin. The aim of these reviews is partly to avoid strategic underestimation/optimism. These reviews do exist and are used when IPTs are set up. But there are possibly cracks in the system where a foundation review may not happen (e.g., adding projects into an existing IPT).

Vertical and Horizontal Integration

As discussed previously, the MoD has the defense industrial strategy which looks at the overall defense industrial base at a strategic level. Gates pay due regard to this, and gate reviews look at the entire project including industrial base, in that sense the system is vertically integrated; indeed, the whole system is more open and involving of industry than previously.

The framework is not really horizontally integrated in the sense that MoD is largely independent of other ministries; however, within the defense sector, the framework is mandatory and consistent.

Organization and Resources

The main person who "owns" the process is the permanent undersecretary, who is SRO of the defence acquisition change program (DACP). This process had around 10 workstreams, one initially being the DPA/DLO merger. The 2nd PUS runs the defence change board. The top-level committee acquisition policy board (chaired by a minister as noted previously), which reports to the defence management board, gives the policy.

The IAB carries out all the gate reviews, and it is this body that approves, or otherwise, each submission. In terms of external input, the IAB is chaired by the chief scientific advisor and has nonexecutives sitting on the board, who are non-MoD. The IAB has a secretariat that looks after the administration of the process.

Within DE&S, if anyone can be said to "look after the process," it would be the DE&S chief of staff, who not only oversees the operations but the "ensurance/assurance" within DE&S, making sure this runs smoothly. Other than that, there is not a specific group running the process—effectively the whole of DE&S is a project governance system.

It is up to the sponsor to gather all the material for a gate (Acquisition Management System, 2007); the military analyses, etc., will all be from the customer (see the material on Ministry of Defence 2008). This website also forms a good communication to the industry and the wider defense community on the operation of defense procurement and the framework.

It should also be noted that MoD has been licensed since October 2006 to run the OGC Gateway scheme, and these are being increasingly used in addition. All A and B projects now have OGC Gateways prior to the Initial and Main Gates; these use external advisors to some extent, although it is considered that those outside the defense domain find it difficult to understand MoD projects.

Concluding Remarks on the Framework Structure

The merger of DPA and DLO into DE&S following the McKane Report has necessitated the review of the entire overall governance framework, which became effective in April 2007. It is not clear yet what the implications of the change will be, but the merger matches the MoD's espoused aim of looking at the extended life cycle. It is perhaps true that the wider scope of the frameworks is adding to its complexity. The degree to which the management of defense procurement is military or civilian also varies over time—currently much of the DE&S board is military and might have some effect on the process.

5.3.3 NORWAY MINISTRY OF FINANCE FRAMEWORK: THE QUALITY ASSURANCE SCHEME

Purpose and Objectives of the Framework

The new framework is described in the invitation to tender (Finansdepartementet, 2004). As mentioned earlier, it is stated by the government (prime minister's office) that better projects and better execution of investment projects are a political goal. Our interviewee said:

It is important to understand that this framework is not a template to ensure political decisions with a certain outcome. The decision itself is purely political. The framework itself is an administrative arrangement, but with political implications. We hope the reviews will make it easier for the cabinet to sort out relevant elements with correct price tags and realistic assumptions on utility when deciding on projects. The reviews should also assist the cabinet and individual ministers to withstand allegations based on biased or incorrect information.

The governance framework is arranged to secure the project is subject to a fair and rational choice. If a project is allowed to develop for a long time before the political decision makers (the cabinet) decide whether it is going to be acknowledged, there will be a lot of stakeholders with great ownership to the project. This leaves the government with very little room for real choice/governance. The government needs to take control in an early stage of the development, or else other parties will decide the terms. The point with this arrangement (specifically the QA1) is to put the decision back to where it belongs: at the table of the political decision makers. It is a way to make the political and administrative side have a common interest. The government should define the room for other parties' actions. The administrative side makes sure that the quality of the documents (basis for decision) is good (consistent, clear, realistic, etc.). There is no conflict of interest between the political and administrative sides in this respect, but a common agenda.

The purpose of QA1 is explained in the framework agreement/tendering document (Finansdepartementet, 2004, p. 6) (original text in Norwegian):

3.1 The purpose of the quality assurance

The purpose of the QA1 is that the bidder should assist the client in securing the choice of concept is subject to real political control. In the end the choice of concept is a political process in which the bidder shall not take any part. The bidder's function is limited to support the client's need for control with the professional quality of the underlying documents as basis for decision. (Authors translation)

The purpose of QA2 is explained in the framework agreement/tendering document (Finansdepartementet, 2004, p. 12) (original text in Norwegian):

4.1 The purpose of the quality assurance

The quality assurance (QA 2) shall give the client an independent analysis of the project before it is brought before parliament. The need for control is the dominating aspect to be covered. Partly it shall be a postcontrol of the basis for putting the project with cost frame forward for acceptance, and partly pointing forward to the managerial challenges in the remaining phases of the project. The analysis should support the basis for the final investment decision. The results should also be useful as a control basis for the client. (Authors translation)

Framework Elements

In Norway the whole framework is a control measure. Control rules are documented in the framework contracts (between the Ministry of Finance and preaccepted QA consulting companies) and the control object is the documents assessed in the QA regime. External control and assessment (independent second opinion) of the documents is a key idea.

The QA-regime is made up of more or less well known, standard components, good practices in the areas of cost/benefit, planning, and project management. But the sum seems to be quite unique currently. The framework is simple, consisting of two gateways:

> QA1: The early choice of concept, the decision to initiate project pre-planning, and
> QA2: The GO decision, the decision to finance the project.

QA1 has a wide perspective (open for any alternative), and QA2 has a narrow perspective (only the chosen alternative). QA1 was by far the most difficult arrangement to define and develop, according to our interviewee.

QA1 includes the control of four documents, in a logical sequence. They are all required to pass the quality assurance on a "good enough" basis before the choice of concept is allowed to be submitted before the cabinet. The documents are:

- a needs analysis,
- an overall objectives / strategy document,
- an overall requirements specification, and
- an analysis of alternatives.

A report is presented by the QA consultant at each of these steps (after control of each document). The last report includes the main recommendation and is the formal report from QA1 concerning the project. The project has to pass at all these stages to continue (to be presented to government for formal decision). No shortcuts are allowed. The important logic in QA1 is to base the project on real needs and to choose a strategy and a concept accordingly on a very early stage—it can look at many alternatives. The biggest task of the QA consultant in QA1 is an independent socioeconomical analysis of all major alternatives.

QA2 includes the control of one document with several subdocuments. The documentation is required to pass the quality assurance on a good enough basis before the funding issue is allowed to be submitted before the cabinet, and a subsequent proposal of appropriation is brought before parliament. No shortcuts are allowed.

The document is: the project management plan, with several subdocuments (cost estimates, progress plans, risk analysis, contract strategy, organization, etc.).

A report is presented by the QA consultant two times through this process. The first time after control and the basis for quality assurance is adequate, the second after all analysis is completed. The last report includes the main recommendation and is the formal report from QA2 concerning the project. The focus in QA2 was from the beginning mainly on cost, but the scope of quality assurance also includes contract strategy, pitfalls and success factors, uncertainty analyses, cost and scope flexibility, management, and organization. The biggest task of the QA consultant in QA2 is an independent cost estimation and uncertainty analysis.

The structure of the Norwegian governance framework is very simple indeed. The two Gateways are only loosely coupled. The perspective, focus, and tasks in QA1 and QA2 are very different (see Table 5-6). What makes them related is the initiative and ownership by the Ministry of Finance, the framework contracts covering both and the governance principles embedded in the Norwegian framework (we will discuss those later).

TABLE 5-6.   COMPARISON BETWEEN QA1 AND QA2

	QA1	QA2
Intervention:	Mandatory control	Mandatory control
Timing:	Early (before preplanning is initiated)	Late (before decision to finance the project)
Perspective:	Wide	Narrow
Focus:	Value	Cost, risk
Other key issues:	User needs, owner strategy	Management strategy
Independent analysis:	Alternatives and economy	Cost estimate and uncertainty
Number of reports to owner:	4	2
Main recommendations:	Choice of alternative	Cost limit
Potential to stop project:	Large	Limited

Several coordination arenas are established in connection to the framework. They are close enough to the framework to be considered framework elements in the perspective of this report:

- The Ministry of Finance is acting as an administrator of the framework/ QA regime and has several coordinating tasks on a regular basis. The Ministry of Finance is responsible for developing and maintaining the QA regime and publishes supplementary guidelines.
- The project owner's forum (for ministries, QA consultants, and researchers). This forum was established almost from the beginning (from 2001–2004 it was called the project control forum. It was re-established under a new name in 2005, when the new framework contract was signed).
- The project management forum (for directorates/crown entities, QA consultants and researchers and open for ministries). This forum was established in 2005.
- The concept research program (trailing research) supports the development of the regime and studies the practices of the directorates and QA consultants. It acts as a facilitator and secretary in several discussions and administers several conferences and workshops. The program publishes research results and performs its own studies relevant to the parties involved in QA. All of these activities contribute to coordination, developing consensus, and exchange of experience.

The discussions gather key people from ministries, agencies, QA consultants, and researchers for discussions, often resulting in the common understanding and definition of terms and professional standards.

The concept research program is supporting the development of the governance framework and studies the practices of the governance agencies and QA consultants. Measuring the effect of the governance framework is one of the tasks of the program. It is financed by the Ministry of Finance over the state budget and based at the Norwegian University of Science and Technology. For research purposes, the concept research program clearly expresses its independence of the Ministry of Finance and the QA scheme.

Vertical and Horizontal Integration
Traditionally, the vertical integration stopped at the agency level. The owners decided what should be delivered and at what cost. This decision gave incitement to use the whole budget including contingency (if any was included).

By introducing the QA1, focus is put on the rationale, the objective of the project. It forms a logic sequence starting with the need behind the investment and goes all the way to the effect of the project. It is a tool to secure good foundation for important decisions at a point in time where there still are alternatives. QA1 and

QA2 give a tool for control from the top (cabinet–ministry–agency–project). Every level knows what the other levels know. This works as expectation management, it influences performance, as mentioned previously. As our interviewee said, "This works for us and does not use many other incentives. It is better than imposing a lot of new rules."

The Norwegian QA framework does not address the private sector (suppliers, contractors), but it is a general idea that what is learned from this framework in the public sector will be transferred to the private sector. After all, the private sector is supplier to the public projects and thus meets the consequences of the governance framework through their delivery and service contracts.

The QA regime is introduced across sectors as a means of horizontal integration (excluding the direct public ownership of the Norwegian state in the oil and gas sector and health sector institutions). The QA regime forms basis for benchmarking across sectors. Common guidelines and common definitions are introduced, and the parties meet for discussions across sectors (see the coordination arena).

The fundamental principles are applicable cross-sector wise. There are, however, some sector specific challenges (i.e., defense, transport) as well as related to project types (ICT). Questions about needs, actors and roles, benefits, demands, development of concepts/alternatives, and evaluation thereof are addressed regardless of sector.

Organization and Resources

One specific issue is the extent and control of outside engagement (private sector engagement in governance procedures). The Norwegian QA regime is all external. Our interviewee explained this:

> *"The reason for this choice was that we had to get started fast, and it takes time to build up internal competence. There was no time for an organizational development process in a situation with resistance. Independent control was also a part of the idea. Having several private sector companies approved in advance through framework contracts was a choice made to secure having the best practice (competence) available. We needed to be able to work independent of culture and tools/methods. It also gives the opportunity to benchmark across companies and the companies know that. It has potentially a good effect on discipline. Expectations, again, heavily influence actions."*

The Norwegian framework is managed on a full-time basis by only two executives at the Ministry of Finance. However, the work is done in close cooperation with the staff at the ministry's budget department, which is responsible for the budgetary follow-up. This works very well, not the least as a result of top-management support and encouragement.

The users of the framework are primarily the responsible ministries: the Ministry of Finance and the Prime Minister's office. Secondary users are directorates and crown entities. Researchers are also users, meaning users of the documentation developed within the framework.

Concluding Remarks on the Framework Structure

The Norwegian framework is simple, almost simplistic compared to most initiatives in the program and project management world. It represents a newly found (or at least newly expressed) awareness of governance of projects. There is no accompanying "comprehensive toolbox" like PRINCE2 and others used in the United Kingdom.

Our interviewee explained this:

> "Any good initiative in the political/administrative world should be simple. Simplicity gives robustness. Complex systems are difficult to maintain in a changing world."

It is an important characteristic of a good, robust initiative that it contributes to simple, unambiguous governance structures. The Norwegian QA regime does so. For example, QA1 gives the real decision power on starting basic engineering/development back to the cabinet, where it rightfully belongs in a simple hierarchical model.

5.3.4 COMPARISON AND DISCUSSION OF THE GOVERNANCE FRAMEWORK STRUCTURE

Defining an effective governance framework is the strategic choice of the UK government (both in general and specifically the Ministry of Defence) and the Norwegian government. As we have seen in the introduction to this report, these two countries are quite similar, at least compared to countries in other parts of the world. One might think this would lead to similar governance frameworks, but this is clearly not necessarily so. All the frameworks include defined rules and standards on control, review, documentation, reports, etc. This section of our study shows substantial differences, as shown in Table 5-7.

The first impression is that the difference between the UK OGC framework and the Norwegian one is obviously very big. The Norwegian framework and the UK MoD one seem not so different at first sight. They both have two critical gateways and have similar administrative arrangements. To some extent, this is correct, but as a more detailed analysis will show, there are important differences here too.

TABLE 5-7.   COMPARISON OF FRAMEWORK ELEMENTS

	NORWAY	UK MoD	UK OGC
Number of Gateways:	2	2	6
Control basis	Control rules established by contract	Complete definitive dossier required	Review definitions / guidelines
Review (assessor) roles	Agreed in PE-forum	Defined in detail	Defined in detail
Report format	Standard QA-reports defined	Dossier format defined	Standard review report format
External/Internal resources	External assessment	Mostly internal assessors	External. internal assessors used in some sectors
Coordination arenas	Project owners forum/ project management forum	Coordinated in one ministry	Centers of Excellence
Support organization	None (Research program)	Permanent operational organizations	Permanent administrative organization
Initiation process	-	Foundation review	Project initiation process
Project process owner	Ministry	Senior responsible owner	Senior responsible owner
Decision makers	Politicians	Investment appraisal board	Senior responsible owner

The vertical integration, as well as the horizontal, is quite different. The Norwegian governance framework goes all the way to the top, but stops above the private sector (suppliers). The effect is expected to diffuse down to private sector as results materialize. The UK OGC and UK MoD frameworks, on the other hand, go all the way down into private sector involvement, but stop at the ministry level upwards. Above this level, committees and NAO, etc., supplement necessary governance reports and other functions (apart from the few "mission critical" projects that go from OGC to the prime minister's office). In this respect, the demarcation line goes between the two countries. Horizontally, the UK framework (or its equivalents) is implemented by several responsible parties. The Norwegian framework keeps everything on one hand in the included sectors, as does the UK MoD framework. This simplifies the horizontal coordination.

One important thing to remember is that the implementation of the frameworks in practice is very dependable on the performance of each individual person taking part (especially those responsible for the reviews). Any framework will be subject to this practice, no matter how the vertical and horizontal coordination is arranged. This also underlines the importance of an effective coordination, especially horizontally.

The UK frameworks go all the way down to the executing parties in private sector. This is mirrored in that the UK side is more comprehensive and adequate for more detailed control measures at a lower hierarchical level. Comparing with the literature discussed earlier, it seems like the Norwegian side is purely on macroanalytic perspective, whereas the UK framework also includes the microanalytic. From a program and project management (PPM) point of view, the UK frameworks include a PPM management system, which the Norwegian side does not. The organization implementing the UK governance framework also supplies the answer to the question; "how to achieve…," where the Norwegian framework only answers "what to achieve…."

The use of external consultants is quite similar in both countries, but in Norway, competent companies are assigned, while in the United Kingdom, the main rule is assigning competent individuals. This fact may suggest that there is a need for more experience and credibility on the individual consultant's side in a framework based on influence and recommendations. The Norwegian framework is mandatory and consultants are thus not the ones that have to persuade the agencies and their project organizations. It is probably important that the Norwegian process is one of breaking tradition and building "a new profession." New professions are more likely to attract younger professionals with the aspiration to find new ways of doing things, than a situation implementing best practice. Younger consultants need the support of the company's resource base including seniors, so assigning a company and not individuals may be a good idea. In addition, there are a very limited number of senior experts in Norway with the right knowledge to fill the role as responsible consultant according to the governance framework. This means it will give better utility of a scarce resource to assign them with the backup of all their competent colleagues.

The external/internal dimension is important in understanding these frameworks. The Norwegian one is all-external, the UK MoD one is mainly internal and the UK OGC one is a mix. As described previously all these choices are a consequence of the situation in which the frameworks are working.

The form of support organization is also an interesting question. In this study, we have found three very different forms: The Norwegian framework is implemented without any organizational changes or support organization. Instead, an independent research programme is established to supply new knowledge and document the effect. In OGC, a relatively large support organization is established (by gathering people from several previous units in one) as a permanent entity external to the organizations responsible for the projects. In the MoD case, the support is integrated in the permanent organization also responsible for the projects. This indicates a situation where the control and system is internalized. When a governance framework is designed, the choice of how to implement and support the framework is an important one. As shown here, the several options are open.

Another area where these frameworks show important differences is in the role as "gatekeeper." The project process owner is positioned at ministry level. In Norway, the formal entity is the Ministry itself (according to Norwegian state responsibility described previously). In the United Kingdom, the SRO (senior responsible owner), an individual, is responsible. In Norway, the responsibility for the project is also delegated to a responsible individual within the sector ministry, and this person will play an important key role in the review process as a senior representative on the project's side. The review process, however, is owned (in practical terms, if not in formal terms) by the key individual in the Ministry of Finance. This places the gatekeeper role as an external position to the project. In the United Kingdom, the gatekeeper is the SRO which represents the department (sectoral ministry) responsible for the project—an internal position. Looking at the position of the decision makers makes this even more interesting. In Norway it is the political level (cabinet, parliament), in MoD it is the investment appraisal board (professional,[11] nonpolitical), but in the OGC case it is the SRO. The demarcation between the administrative and the political subsystem is very clear in Norway and the MoD case, but unclear in the OGC case.

One characteristic difference between the two countries is the amount of resources used to perform each assessment. In the UK OGC system, a typical assessment will include a 4–6 day review process, carried out by a senior consultant and a small team, planned, performed, and reported over 11–12 weeks (Howard, 2007). In Norway, the QA team performs complete independent analysis of the project; they may work for 6 months or more, including several meetings. In both countries, the project organization probably spends much more person-hours to prepare and support the assessments than is used to perform them. The total use of resources in performing the gateway reviews in these governance frameworks is substantial. As shown in the previous section on the development process, the investment is worth it according to our sources and the documented effects. At least there are good indications. Solid proof is not available yet.

Figure 5-3 shows all three frameworks phases and gateways loosely indicated on the timeline. The purpose is to point to the importance of choosing the timing well and to define requirements that correspond with the timing. For example, the MoD

---

11. The Investment Appraisal Board has five members; Chief Scientific Adviser, Vice Chief of Defence Staff, 2nd Permanent Under Secretary, Chief of Defence Materiel and Defence Commercial Director.

Main Gate is chosen to come too early for a detailed cost estimate (we have not defined "detailed" so that may be a relative characteristic). The figure also shows how different the phase models are within these fairly similar governance frameworks.

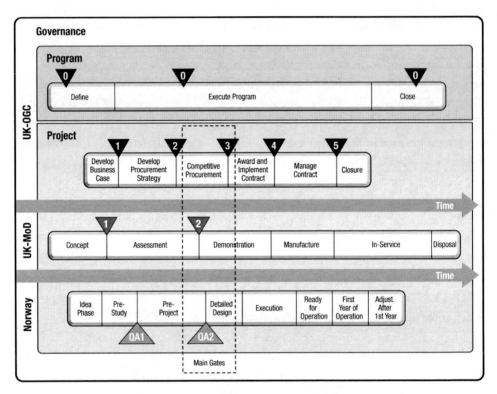

FIGURE 5-3. COMPARISONS OF PROJECT MODELS (PHASES) AND GATEWAYS INDICATED ON THE TIMELINE (IMPRESSION, NOT PRECISE TIMING)

This study of the "exterior" of the governance frameworks shows a wide range of forms and functions. In developing a governance framework, there are many structural choices to be made. These choices have to be made consistent, taking into consideration all major aspects of what is intended to be achieved and the context that it is going to be implemented. The most important and advanced issue in designing the framework structure is choosing elements that work together as a whole. This study has shown that the result may look very different even though the aim and the starting point are quite similar.

5.4   DETAILED GOVERNANCE ELEMENTS ADDRESSING COST AND TIME

This study has had to dive into more details about the frameworks to answer the research question given in the introduction to this report. Because of time and resource limitations, it is not possible to cover all aspects in detail. The framework elements addressing cost and time are the ones that we need to concentrate on here, and the detailed study is limited to these (see Table 5-8).

Value for money is the ultimate goal of the UK governance frameworks by OGC (and MoD). Therefore, the balancing of cost and value (benefit) naturally has a central place in the framework(s). The same can be said about the Norwegian framework, although its focus is placed more towards value as such in QA1 and on cost as such in QA2. One could easily argue that it is all about costs, but in this report's perspective, it is not. We look for elements explicitly and directly focusing cost and time. Based on this fact we should expect a substantial number of elements focusing on cost and time.

We were careful in order to make a fair comparison; therefore, we do not look at the toolbox (PRINCE2) but only the framework itself (the OGC Gateway™ Process and the MoD Acquisition Operating Framework).

5.4.1   UK OFFICE OF GOVERNMENT COMMERCE (OGC) FRAMEWORK: THE OGC GATEWAY™ REVIEW

Reviewers in Gateway Reviews are not making independent cost estimates. The length of the reviews is only around 6 days—much too short for a detailed review. The reviews look at the process carried out. They are generally not concerned with "how to do it" but more on whether they had a good process. In addition, they do comment on cost estimates when they feel they should. They will sometimes recommend getting an alternative or independent cost estimate, although like all other recommendations, it will go to the SRO and be up to the SRO whether the recommendation is acted upon. Furthermore, it should be remembered that Gateways identify issues, they do not resolve them.

We asked whether it was likely that the system would (or could) pick up on poor initial estimates at Gateways 0 and 1. The interviewee said that this does happen and estimates sometimes rise. They have in the past picked up both on "political figures" (i.e., strategic underestimation) and on bad estimating. However, for projects other than mission critical, comments made by the reviewers would only go to the SRO, so in principle they could be ignored if the SRO wished to do so. (For mission critical

TABLE 5-8.   KEY ATTRIBUTES OF THE DETAILED ELEMENTS—EXCERPT OF QUESTIONS AND ANSWERS.

Question asked	Norway	UK MoD	UK OGC
Are there any explicit statements or framework elements specifically addressing the development of cost and time estimates in the established framework? Which?	• Cost is the focus of QA2. • External, independent cost estimate is made. • Estimation is cost without uncertainty. • Uncertainty is analyzed to dimension the contingency. • Time and other planning dimensions are just mentioned as potential focus areas.	• Main gate too early for detailed cost estimates • Based on trust	• Gateway Reviews do comment on cost estimates. • Sometimes they recommend getting an alternative or independent cost estimate. • Focus is on whether they had a good process.
What are the governance principles concerning cost estimation and cost control?	Prestudy, QA1: • We need expected investment costs, operation costs and benefits • Correct, realistic cost estimation • Highlight the systematic part of the total uncertainty • Consider the flexibility in the decision situation Preproject, QA2: • We need both correct expected value and the uncertainty attached to the project • Establish a clear and realistic cost expectation • Get the total picture of the project cost • Establish a control estimate for future management • Control over contingency rests at ministry level	Not sure of any. However, projects use a common cost-estimation resource, the project forecasting group within DE&S.	• Use of experience and "gut-feel" on the overall level of the bid • Note that Gateways identify issues, not resolve them.
Has there been any systematic analysis of the effect of these principles under the current framework?	Too few projects are actually finished yet.	Performance on A's and B's is monitored as part of DE&S organizational targets. Much of it is project related.	Yes. Performance against set targets is followed up more or less continuously by the OGC. OGC also looks for trends in the reports on projects red/amber/ green status.

projects, their comments go to the prime minister's office.) The quality of estimation could perhaps now be tackled in the project initiation process also.

There did not seem to be particular governance principles concerning cost estimation and cost control. The only comments likely to be made by a reviewer are from experience and "gut-feel" on the overall level of the bid. Since this does not depend on laid-down criteria or principles, the operation, of course, depends on the make-up of the team.

It is likely that this framework has not really taken a firm grasp of the issue of underestimation; our interviewee felt that this was clearly still a problem. The system does not appear to provide any challenge on estimating, which the interviewee described as a "big hole" that they do not do adequately. He was not sure that Gateway 0 has enough in there, and he was not sure whether there was any mechanism to do anything about underestimation. It is true that for mission critical projects, a comment might go onto the mission critical report. However, for all other projects, reports just go to the SRO— in other words, within the department—so there is no mechanism for reporting possible underestimation (e.g., strategic underestimation by the department) outside the department.

We can look at the guidelines and written documents of the OGC framework as a primary source of cost and time focus. This part is the formal side of the framework; in practice these guidelines may not necessarily be used as a checklist or questionnaire in reviews. Our interviewee said:

> *"If you have the right people to do the reviews, you will not need these checklists. They have got these things in mind and ask the necessary questions based on their experience instead. However, they may be a good reference when writing up the report as a help not to forget anything important."*

The elements addressing cost and time in the OGC framework are noted in Figure 5-4.

As expected, the OGC framework does pay much attention to cost and time. It is an issue in all phases and on all levels. Gateway 2 is the most important gateway when it comes to cost and time. This comment is reasonable, judged from its purpose: "This Review investigates the assumptions in the Outline Business Case and proposed approach for delivering the project. If there is a procurement, the delivery strategy will include details of the sourcing options, proposed procurement route and supporting information. The Review will also check that plans for implementation are in place" (OGC, 2007, p.7). The pattern is clear: for every step of development, the gateway review checks on whether the cost and benefit still are in keeping with the business case, whether the project development is under control, and whether plans and resources are secured for the next phase. The framework also refers to the toolboxes, services, and guidelines provided to support the successful delivery of

Gateway 0: Strategic assessment

- 2.7 Costs should be for the whole life of the programme and its constituent projects. Check the assumptions on which estimates are based, especially where there is no previous experience of this kind of programme.
- 5.4 Is there a contingency plan? Consider the programme's effects on public services and ensure that decisions are taken about those for which contingency arrangements will be needed. Milestones relating to contingency measures should be defined in plans, and ongoing checks that the milestones are being achieved as expected.
- 6.4 A statement of budget provision should be set out in the programme business case and the availability of ongoing funding confirmed through the corporate investment approval board or equivalent.

Gateway 1: Business justification

- The project initiation process produces a justification for the project based on business needs and an assessment of the project's likely costs and potential for success.
- 3.5 Are the costs and time implications of managing the risks included in the cost and time estimate or treated as a separate risk allocation? Costs and time for managing risks should be identified as a separate risk allocation.
- 4.1 Details should be set out in the Project Plan or Project Execution Plan. See the procurement workbook for an overview of procurement activities; see also the Project Management workbook. Ensure that sufficient time is allowed for the project and that expertise is available to carry out all of the required steps.
- 4.5 Is the time plan realistic? Does it take into account any statutory lead times? See Introduction to the EC Procurement Rules for details of statutory lead times. The time plan should include a realistic assessment of the time needed for pre-procurement activities. Expect to meet the defined project schedule once it has been made known to the industry. See the briefing on faster procurement.
- 4.7 Are there the necessary funds to reach an OGC Gateway Review 2? Budget provision should be stated in the business case; arrangements for financial controls in the Project Plan or Project Execution Plan.

Gateway 2: Procurement strategy

- 1.3 Value for money: Is the proposed commercial arrangement likely to achieve whole-life value for money? The commercial section of the business case identifies the commercial scope for achieving value for money, whether or not it is an external procurement. The project team should seek an arrangement that offers flexibility and the optimum balance of quality, price, and risk over the life of the contract. Where a financial return is not the main objective (e.g., for e-business services to the citizen) the department should set targets for performance as return on investment, based where possible on comparisons with similar successful projects. See the e-government supplement to the Green Book for advice on the treatment of non-financial benefits.
- 1.4 Affordability: Are the costs within current budgets? Is the project's whole-life funding affordable and supported by the key stakeholders? Ensure that whole life costs can be estimated with a reasonable degree of accuracy. Check the basis of underlying assumptions for the estimates, to reduce the risk of over-optimistic budgets being set for the project. There should be financial provision within departmental spending plans, approved by key stakeholders. Including costs that will be borne by the department in implementing the project. See Achieving Excellence Guide AE7;

FIGURE 5-4. **EXCERPTS FROM OGC GUIDANCE ON COST ESTIMATION AND TIME PLANNING IN THE OGC GATEWAY™ PROCESS (source: supporting workbooks incl. checklists for review). (CONTINUED)**

these principles apply particularly to construction projects but provide useful advice for most major projects. See also financial control for projects.

- 1.5 Achievability: Is the organisation still realistic about its ability to achieve a successful outcome? Revisit the project plan and compare with similar projects in the organisation and outside. Make a realistic assessment of the department's track record in achieving successful change; check current capability and capacity available for this project. Ensure that contingency plans are in place and plans for incremental / modular delivery, where applicable. See the risk assessment spreadsheet for questions about achievability.
- 3.1 Is the project under control? Project plans should be continually updated to report progress against time and cost; for construction projects this information is documented in a Project Execution Plan and Cost Report.
- 3.2 What caused any deviations such as over- or under-runs? Any deviations from plans should be recorded in an exception report. Risk allowances should have been agreed at the outset, with budgets for contingency; see the risk management workbook for more information.
- 3.3 What actions are necessary to prevent deviations recurring in other phases? Project Plans/Project Execution Plans should include activities to address any potential deviations from plans, through learning lessons and identifying potential risks from earlier phases of the project.
- 5.1 Is the project plan for the remaining phases realistic? The project plan should set out the key objectives, deliverables, and milestones for the next phase of the project.
- 5.2 Are the project's timescales reasonable? The timescales must be realistic, in line with Introduction to the EC Procurement Rules, and related to the scale/complexity of the project, based on comparison (where possible) with similar projects. Realistic assessment of any potential slippage must be built into the project plan. Note that the industry has a right to expect the project to achieve the published timescales; see the advice on faster procurement.

Gateway 3: Investment decision

- 3.1 Is the project under control? Check that the project is running to schedule and cost within budget. The project plan should include a cost report supported by the updated project plan. See also the document description for financial control and, for construction projects, see Achieving Excellence Guide AE7.
- 5.6 Are all the mechanisms and processes in place for the next phase? The project plan should confirm arrangements for management, monitoring, transition and implementation. See also Achieving Excellence Guide AE3 for construction projects.

Gateway 4: Readiness for service

- 1.6 Can the organisation implement the new services and maintain existing services? Resource plans should form a key part of programme/project plans, supported by current cost reports and confirmation that funding is available.
- 2.2 Is the project under control? Is it running according to plan and budget? Cost reports should show spending against plans for all components of the project. The risk register and issue log should document issues as they arise and actions taken, with updates to project plans as required. Lessons teamed from causes of delay should be documented for the benefit of future projects. For construction projects, see also Achieving Excellence Guide AE7.

FIGURE 5-4.   **(CONTINUED) EXCERPTS FROM OGC GUIDANCE ON COST ESTIMATION AND TIME PLANNING IN THE OGC GATEWAY™ PROCESS (source: supporting workbooks incl. checklists for review).**

- 3.2 If there are unresolved issues, what are the risks of implementing rather than delaying? Updated project plans should include an assessment of all remaining issues and risks and a way forward supported by sensitivity analysis. If delay is inevitable, the SRO must approve the revised plan for implementation.
- 4.6 Have ongoing operation and maintenance been considered in detail? Whole life costs for the operational service must be taken into account, including reasonable allowances for ongoing maintenance. See the briefing on infrastructure management for IT aspects; see Achieving Excellence Guides AE7 and AE9 for construction aspects.

Gateway 5 Benefits evaluation

- 3.1 What is the scope for improved value for money? Can more be done for less? Could the provider deliver better service quality at the same price? Can maintenance costs be driven down? You should seek continuous improvement in value for money from service provision. OGC's Commercial Intelligence Service can provide current information about the supplier marketplace (or call the OGC Service Desk on 0845 0004999). See also the contract management workbook.
- 4.3 Does the department have performance measures to cover all aspects of the contract? Performance measures should relate to: Economy – minimising the cost of resources used for an activity, having regard to appropriate quality. Efficiency – the relationship between outputs, in terms of goods, services or other results and the resources used to produce them. Effectiveness – the extent to which objectives have been achieved, and the relationship between the intended impacts and actual impacts of an activity.

FIGURE 5-4. **(CONTINUED) EXCERPTS FROM OGC GUIDANCE ON COST ESTIMATION AND TIME PLANNING IN THE OGC GATEWAY™ PROCESS (source: supporting workbooks incl. checklists for review).**

the projects. A large number of detailed guidelines, methods, and tools are available from the OGC homepage (http://www.ogc.gov.uk/) to help the implementation of the framework. We will not go into those here.

Furthermore, while the MoD does look at the overall portfolio of projects to see what the total cost is over time, our interviewee was not sure what other departments did. Our interviewee's perception was of the treasury giving a total sum of money to each department (although they do want to know what the money is being spent on). When the treasury cuts a department's budget, departments tend to cut budgets by overall top-slicing rather than looking at the portfolio of projects, which doesn't allow for challenge to the project budgets when revised downwards. However, this was his perception from experience rather than a definitive statement of process.

It was not clear whether there had been any overall systematic analysis of the effect of this framework with regard to keeping to time and cost budgets.

There is also a specific UK issue about whether projects should (or should not) be funded under the Private Finance Agreement, and OGC could look at this question and influence, but had no authority to decide.

5.4.2 UK MINISTRY OF DEFENCE (MOD) FRAMEWORK: THE ACQUISITION OPERATING FRAMEWORK

The vision for acquisition is: *"Providing battle-winning capability for defense and Value for Money for the Taxpayer"* (Acquisition Operation Framework, 2008).

As shown in Figure 5-5, the trade-off between performance, time, and cost is recognized as a basic assumption and should be identified from the start. Slippage in cost or time is damaging for reputation and avoiding them is an important value.

As shown in Figure 5-6, the funding of the assessment phase work is mentioned as a main issue in the Initial Gate. The whole life costs for the equipment procurement and the support solution are similarly focused on in the Main Gate.

A key logistics process is to conduct trade-off analysis. "This process is to ensure that support, performance, and cost are balanced to achieve the best operational effectiveness and optimum operational availability at the least cost." Furthermore, "IPTs must provide evidence that contingency plans are in place to provide risk mitigation against contractors being unable to deploy to, or withdrawing support

---

Defence Values for Acquisition (DVfA)

The Defence Values for Acquisition (DVfA) are endorsed by the Acquisition Policy Board (APB).

They are:

- Recognize that **people are the key to success** – to equip them with the right skills, experience, and professional qualifications.
- Recognize the **best can be the enemy of the very good** – to distinguish between the must haves, desirables, and the nice to haves, if affordable.
- Identify **trade-offs between performance, time and cost** – cases for additional resources must offer realistic alternative solutions.
- **Never assume additional resources will be available** – cost growth on one project can only mean less for others and for the front line.
- Understand that **time matters**, so slippage costs – through running on legacy equipment, extended project timescales and damage to our reputation.
- **Think incrementally**; to seek out agile solutions with open architecture which permit "plug and play" and to allow space for innovation and the application of best practice.
- **Quantify risk** and reduce it by placing it where it can be managed most effectively – stopping a project before Main Gate can be a sign of maturity.
- **Recognize and respect the contribution made by industry** – to seek to share objectives, risks, and rewards while recognizing that different drivers apply.
- Value the **openness and transparency** – share future plans and priorities wherever possible to encourage focused investment and avoid wasted effort.
- Embed a **through-life culture** in all planning and decision making.
- Value **objectivity** based on clear evidence rather than advocacy – ensure that we capture past experience and allow it to shape our future behavior.
- Realize that **success and failure matter**; we will hold people to account for their performance.

FIGURE 5-5. **VALUES EMBEDDED IN THE MOD FRAMEWORK. Source: the AOF website.**

Initial Gate and Main Gate

Initial Gate: The Early Decision Point

Initial Gate remains the first approval point in the life cycle, being a relatively low threshold event to approve assessment phase strategy and funding, projects will return to the appropriate approval authority if agreed targets are breached.

The approvals and scrutiny process is applied to assess whether project maturity remains viable in advance of the Main Gate or whether the Approval Authority should be recommended to direct the CPG to consider another, lower risk approach.

Main Gate: the Key Decision Point

Main Gate approval:

- Remains the key investment decision point for Projects, where the risks to successful delivery (e.g. financial, technical, industrial, defense lines of development (DLoDs)) are considered against the benefit of the proposed solution in meeting an endorsed defense requirement.
- Sets targets against which the acquisition performance of the project is assessed and contains defined trade boundaries for the project – targets are only established at Main Gate, when all the risks are sufficiently understood.
- Considers whole life costs across all DLoDs – crucially, it addresses the support solution as well as the equipment procurement.
- Will require an assurance by the User (generally the Front Line Command) that the proposal can be integrated across DLoDs and with existing systems to deliver an effective military capability from in-service date.

Main Gate requires preparation of a clear, concise business case.

The Business Case:

- Identifies risks, all relevant costs, trade space and limits, and demonstrates affordability and value for money in meeting the endorsed requirement.
- Requires the provision of objective, non-advocate evidence.
- Should increasingly consider a wider range of acquisition strategies (e.g., partnership, incremental acquisition) that allow opportunity for through-life agility or reflect DIS constraints, while demonstrating value for money.

FIGURE 5-6.   GATES IN THE MOD FRAMEWORK. Source: the AOF website.

from, an operation" (Acquisition Operation Framework, 2008, Key Policy and Processes for Logistics).

At the highest level in the MoD framework (the strategic level), there does not seem to be any specific reference to cost and time in the form of precise statements of what to achieve. There are, however, several references (Ministry of Defence, 2008) to support toolboxes and guidelines, like this one. In these references, best practice methods, techniques, and tools are presented and made available for the users.

At the intermediate level of the MoD framework (the operational level), there are governance guidelines for project and program management. We have looked into these guidelines for references to cost and time.

The project delivery charter captures the 10 key principles of project and program management (The AOF website; Acquisition Operation Framework, 2008). Some of these refer explicitly to cost and time, see Figure 5-7.

1. **We lay down the foundations of success early:**
   - Clarify and validate requirements through appropriate challenge, based on a clear understanding of the technical solution and through life capability management.
   - "No project is an island" – identify and assess impact of technical interfaces (interoperability) and DLoDs dependencies / constraints on the project.
   - Risk identification, evaluation and reduction to inform decisions on PTC trades within the project and across programmes. An informed risk provision is made in the Main Gate Business Case and contract with Industry.
   - Build teams with the necessary delivery skills and behaviors, supported by best practice project management controls processes and techniques.
   - Inject realism into detailed planning (time, cost, and resources).
   - Establish an agreed starting baseline with stakeholders.

2. **We maintain a full understanding of the financial, commercial, and technical status of our project:**
   - Project management.
   - Operate cost management process to enable accurate and regular project cost reporting.
   - Adopt commercial arrangements that best fit the required balance between performance, time, cost, risk, and flexibility—use expertise of support groups when assessing industry capability and developing contracting strategies.
   - Apply a level of systems engineering commensurate with the complexity of the solution.
   - Implement and operate configuration management to project documentation and technical products.

3. **We do not underestimate the impact of risks or overestimate our ability to manage them.**
   - Actively manage risk and uncertainty, and take actions in a prioritised manner – there are contingency plans and clear trigger points for implementing these.
   - Risk identification and evaluation covers all dimensions of a project and parent programme.
   - Apply good evaluation and prioritisation techniques, based on a thorough analysis of meaningful data with the right experts.
   - Each risk is owned by those best placed to manage it.
   - Role of risk manager carried out by appropriately skilled and experienced resource.
   - Keep stakeholders and management informed of risk exposure.

4. **We exercise formal change control to preserve the integrity and through life view of the solution:**
   - Establish realistic baselines early and implement change control process which involves our customers and suppliers.
   - Agreed and consistent application of impact assessment criteria that includes consideration of through life, commercial, and contractual implications.
   - Right experts involved in assessment, right authority to approve or reject.
   - Programme oversight to maintain integrity of interfacing solutions.

5. **We ensure we minimise the effects of staff changes on our project.**

FIGURE 5-7.   TEN KEY PRINCIPLES OF PROJECT AND PROGRAM MANAGEMENT. Details kept only where there is some reference to cost and time (Source: the AOF website). (CONTINUED)

6.   **We do not commit to performance, time, and cost boundaries for a project to deliver a solution that we do not understand:**

- Plan to the level of detail necessary to effectively challenge constraints, and assumptions, and to control / influence the project, with a coherent set of plans leading from short term detail to long term expectation.
- "Tell it like it is," backed up by thorough reviews of the project risks, constraints, and assumptions.
- Start Verification & Validation activities early.
- Use approval gates and stage reviews to enable controlled transition based on clear entry and exit criteria.

7.   **We anticipate and act on good quality information.**

8.   **We actively manage our customers and stakeholders, regardless of organisation boundaries.**

9.   **We do not assume our formal agreements to be an irrelevant formality.**

10.   **We establish a common understanding of expectations with our Industry partner.**

FIGURE 5-7.   (CONTINUED) TEN KEY PRINCIPLES OF PROJECT AND PROGRAM MANAGEMENT. Details kept only where there is some reference to cost and time (source: the AOF website).

A key difference between the MoD process and the other frameworks results from the extended life cycle used by MoD, which starts at a very early stage. The Initial Gate is, therefore, very early in what is normally thought of as the project life cycle, and the Main Gate is still quite early in the process, coming before a solution is fully formed. This means that detailed cost estimates could not be carried out at this point since there is not a detailed solution to estimate.

A particular characteristic of the MoD framework (in the perspective of this chapter) is the focus on through-life cost management and life cycle costs rather than the investment cost as such.

One mechanism for normalizing cost and time estimating to bring some commonality to the estimation is the central project forecasting group (PFG) within DE&S. This group has been in existence within the organizations that predated DE&S (the Defence Procurement Agency and previously the MoD Procurement Executive, MoD[PE]) for many years, and has very substantial experience of the historical cost of projects. This service was charged to projects, with one change resulting from the McKane report (Ministry of Defence, 2006). The report, which brought about the existence of the combined DE&S, is that the PFG is now free-to-service and it is now used routinely. PFG will, therefore, set out the framework for estimation, and their approval on estimates will be required for the gates.

The form of these governance elements focusing on cost and time is in a different style than the OGC that is directed towards an internal user and not toward a reviewer. In addition, the level of abstraction seems substantially higher. As mentioned previously, MoD's Main Gate is too early in the process to do detailed cost estimates, suggesting that it is appropriate that the framework does not go into specific details on cost and time.

The system is based to a significant extent on trust, but with appropriate monitoring mechanisms. The IAB has to trust the head of DE&S, CDM, but this person is also governed by overall agency targets (e.g., performance on A's and B's is monitored as part of DE&S organizational targets). CDM has to trust the project teams (the IPTs), but this person will also have been looking at the trajectory over time of cost and time estimates up to the Main Gate. The IPTs trust industry, but the MoD also has "sector management" taking an overall look at particular parts of industry, and DE&S has cost forecasting people. There will also be a financial controller within the IPT; having said that, part of the role of IPTs is to make "judgment calls." An IPT will also have a joint management board, which will look after an open relationship with industry.

To what extents the detailed methods and tools are available in the references (linked up Web pages) are not clear, since some of the lower end links are not available to us (closed to outsiders not working within MoD). Indications found in the available

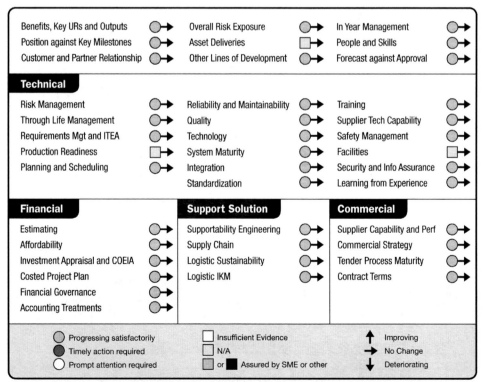

FIGURE 5-8.   PROJECT REVIEW DASHBOARD ASSURANCE CRITERIA VERSION 4.5—APRIL 2007

links point in the direction that detailed guidance is available, more or less like the OGC framework.

The internal reviews is supported by a tool where the main issues looked for in the assessment is marked with a red/amber/green "traffic-light" and characteristic trends. A generic example of a dashboard is shown in Figure 5-8.

The National Audit Office annual Major Projects Report 2006 includes Figure 5-9, which shows the current state of the main 20 MoD projects. This figure shows the results of the implementation of cost and time focus in the major projects has not removed all problems of delay and overrun. This report does not provide enough data to comment on the change over the last years, but the report states that the total delay occurring within this year was "a lower contribution to the total than in any Major Projects Report since 2002" (National Audit Office, 2006, p. 5), and the costs have reduced "equivalent to a 21 per cent reduction in the overall cost increases on projects since Main Gate" (National Audit Office, 2006, p. 5). This report certainly indicates the owner is clearly aware of the challenges and working towards improvement.

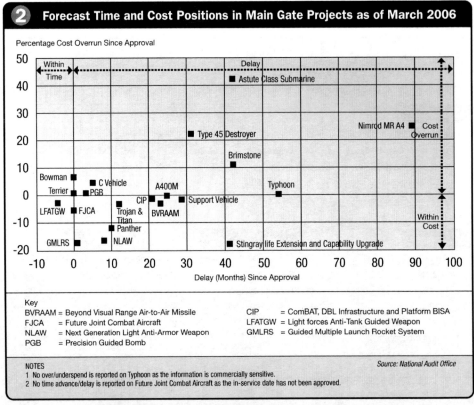

FIGURE 5-9.   STATUS OF THE MAIN 20 MOD PROJECTS. Source: Major Projects Report 2006 (National Audit Office)

5.4.3 NORWAY MINISTRY OF FINANCE FRAMEWORK: THE QUALITY ASSURANCE SCHEME

Project cost overspend was the initial worry that made the Ministry of Finance start questioning the planning and management of major public projects. Consequently, cost had a great deal of focus from the beginning. As described earlier, the first generation of the Norwegian governance framework had one gateway, QA2, that it was focusing on:

1. The document defining the basis for management of the project, and
2. An independent uncertainty/risk analysis of the budget.

Both of these two elements contain subelements focusing on cost. Time is just mentioned.

In the period 2001–2002, two different guidelines and other documents were made based on a joint effort by the QA consultants under framework contract with the ministry. The consultants, on a voluntary basis, participated in group work initiated by the Ministry of Finance. In addition to the guidelines explaining the two-mentioned framework elements, several documents defining the standard reporting format was developed this way. A driving force behind this development was the experience the projects and ministries had. The consultants used different practices and definitions, and the result came out a bit confusing. The aim was to establish a common best practice in reviewing.

The documents made by the consultants were discussed thoroughly in the project control forum (later replaced by the project owners forum) to create consensus about the principles embedded. Here the ministries and researchers from the concept research program as well as the consultants took part. After these discussions, the finished draft was sent formally to the responsible ministries for comments. At this point, the government agencies responsible for the investment projects also made their comments (officially to their ministry, respectively). After this round, the latest comments were included and the final version was approved by the Ministry of Finance as well as the other responsible ministries. At this point in time (second quarter 2003), the documents became officially a part of the framework. In practical terms, the consultants had already started using them and were developing the current practice towards a common practice. The guidelines are used systematically in the major public projects in Norway today and are available on the website of the concept research program (the website is written in Norwegian).

Strategic Level	Purpose, objectives, critical success factors, general terms, and interfaces
Project Strategy	Uncertainty management, strategy of execution, contract strategy, and organizing
Project Control Basis	Scope, work breakdown structure (WBS), cost, time, and quality

FIGURE 5-10.   THE THREE LEVELS OF THE PROJECT CONTROL DOCUMENT (translated by the author)

Basis for Management of the Project

The aim of this guideline is to make sure the projects have the necessary basis for managing the project in the next phase of development. It describes what the consultants are going to look for in their quality assurance assessment. Consequently, it also describes what the projects need to have prepared to make it through this gateway. The introduction of the guideline states explicitly that this document explains *what* the document should include, not *how* it is going to be made. It may be seen as an advice on how to structure the document. This guideline focuses several themes on three different levels (Figure 5-10).

From the text in the guideline for project control document (Finansdepartementet, 2008a, p. 2) (translated by the author): "In a good project control document (styringsdokument), there will be a balanced description of all these aspects, and a clear causal connection between the project purpose, the objectives, the critical success factors, project strategies, and the basis for control."

Basically, all these themes where justified by the need for better (more realistic) cost estimates. Still, we will look only at the two specific issues cost and time here. There is not a voluminous text, so we simply translate the entire paragraph. This paragraph explains what the project control document should include on cost and time (Finansdepartementet, 2008a, p. 5) (translated by the author):

Cost Estimate, Budget and Investment Plan

A description of the project cost estimate, detailed enough to be basis for control of the project, and for the quality assurance of the projects cost limit. Scope of work, unit costs, and total costs should be produced according to WBS. It is important that the contingency is visible as one or more specific posts and not hidden or scattered around as a part of the single accounts in the cost estimate.

Accounts for contingency should be placed on a high level of WBS. The cost estimate should, if possible, include a benchmark of the project cost compared to other, similar projects (this could be unit costs relative to capacity or scope of work), and an overview of how the cost estimate has developed from the earliest phases of the project.

The cost estimate should also be presented as investment, financing, and payment plans, respectively, for a period over the project life cycle.

If the budget is not in accordance with the cost estimate, e.g., by including reserve accounts, this has to be described separately.

In a large project, it will normally not be appropriate to include all details from the complete cost estimate in the project control document (styringsdokumentet). The complete cost estimate should then be attached to the project control document or be referred to as an independent document. (By this is not meant that the document should be detailed more than to the level natural for the current project phase).

Schedule

A presentation of the projects over all schedule, with an overview of the most important activities and milestones, necessary approvals by government, contract awards and important interfaces.

This document put forward demands on how the projects were going to present themselves to the responsible ministries and decision makers. Therefore, the projects also had to choose the appropriate cost estimation methods, etc. to make this presentation possible.

The Uncertainty and Risk Analysis

The introduction to this guideline explicitly states that the purpose of the document is to avoid misunderstandings and confusion. Therefore, the document is in the form of definitions of common terms for uncertainty and risk analysis. Given the nature of the process (see the previous description), this document came to define how the Norwegian government applies uncertainty and risk management in their projects (oil and gas sector excluded) (Finansdepartementet, 2008b, p. 2). The focus of the document is clearly on cost (as illustrated by Figure 5-11 below—this principle is the central illustration of the document).

The document includes a general introduction of uncertainty (and risk) management on project and portfolio management level and defines all 23 necessary concepts as well as two standard graphical presentations (S-curve and priority diagram) to be used in the reports. The principles embedded in this guideline and its definitions are basically in line with international principles of good uncertainty and risk management as defined by PMI, APM etc. The unique combination of these concepts is presented in the Figure 5-11.

The document includes an explicit limitation (Finansdepartementet, 2008b, p. 3). (translated by the author):

"This document does not say how the implementation of these principles within each government agency should be. The principles presented here are meant to be clarifying, but the agencies will have to solve the system needed to apply these principles."

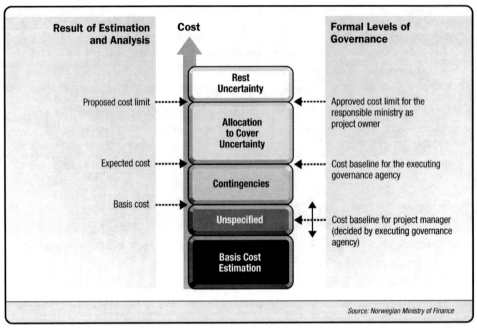

FIGURE 5-11.   ILLUSTRATION OF THE CORE CONCEPTS EMBEDDED IN THE NORWEGIAN GOVERNANCE FRAMEWORK CONCERNING COST UNCERTAINTY ANALYSIS (translated by the author)

Based on this document, the practice rapidly conformed to this standard. However, the use of terms (words) did not easily confirm to the words chosen in the guideline. Each QA consultant (and the agencies) had his or her own preferences and tools. The guideline acts as a mediator and point of reference for translation making clear communication possible. Schedule uncertainty is not mentioned in the document.

Cost Estimation

The above-mentioned documents are still the only official elements of the Norwegian governance framework for major public investment projects focusing cost and time. However, experience over the years since it was introduced show that some critical remarks from the QA consultants tend to come again and again. One of them concerns the cost estimation: The cost estimates and cost uncertainty analysis are not consistent—or the basis for the uncertainty analysis (the basis cost estimation) is not internally consistent and too unclear. Therefore, the Ministry of Finance decided to have a new guideline worked out. This work was initiated in January 2006 within the second generation of the framework. A similar process as in the first generation started with group works including representatives for all the QA consultant companies. The new document, a guideline on cost estimation, is currently being assessed for approval by the Ministry of Finance (along with four other documents—one of them being a new definition of common terms for QA1). (Finansdepartementet, 2008c). See further comments in Section 5.5.

The new (preliminary) guideline is not formally taken into use, but since it has already been worked out by QA consultants and discussed thoroughly in the project owner's forum and project management forum, it is already believed to be influential. This document takes a step closer to a "how to do" guideline, but is still does not decide in detail how cost estimation should be performed. In the introduction to the document, the purpose is explained (translated by the author):

The purpose of this guideline for cost estimation is to make the cost estimation process for large state projects predictable, compliant, and effective in all phases of the project. The guideline primarily deals with estimation of investment costs, but it also touches upon aspects of life cycle cost and life cycle benefit. The guideline defines demands to cost estimation on a superior level. The governance agencies and/or the projects are assumed to establish their own adapted quality systems for cost estimation on a detailed level (Finansdepartementet, 2008c, p. 2).

The guideline includes demands pointed towards the following aspects of cost estimation:

- The (structure of the) cost estimation process,
- Cost estimation competence,
- Include everything and clarify fundamental assumptions,
- Life cycle perspectives,
- Generic cost estimate classification and estimation methods,
- Documentation, transparency, and traceability,
- Use of correction factors,
- Documentation of uncertainty assessments,
- Neutrality in estimates,
- Quality assurance (peer review), and
- Management's role in cost estimation.

The document (current preliminary version) also includes a checklist for the QA consultants to use when assessing the cost estimates. Although on a slightly more detailed level than earlier documents, the characteristics of the document is still more an example of defining demands on "what to achieve" and less instructions on "how to achieve."

The QA consultants performing quality assurance according to the Norwegian framework do their own complete analysis of the uncertainty and independent assessments of cost estimates. This behaviour is different from the UK frameworks. Apart from that, the most characteristic feature is that it is, throughout, a control measure. Advice is also given as to how the strategies of the project should be and what should be in focus of management, just like the OGC framework.

5.4.4 COMPARISON AND DISCUSSION OF THE ELEMENTS ON DETAILED LEVEL

"Detailed governance elements addressing cost and time" was the phrase we used as the title of this section. Of course, this has to be interpreted within the context in which it is written. When we use the word "detailed," it does not imply the detailed level as in a textbook for cost estimators, or a company internal standard or system explaining in detail how to make a good cost estimate. In the nature of governance, the level of abstraction is naturally much higher. When we say detailed here, it means relative to the level used in the previous chapters. As we have seen in the excerpts and quotations from the framework elements, none of them are really detailed or concrete.

The choice of words in all these governance frameworks clearly represents a normative style (do this and do that—do not do this). This style is not surprising given its top-down structure and formal position. Looking at their focus, the level of abstraction (details) in the frameworks and whether they have toolboxes attached, we find differences as shown in Figure 5-12 (the charts are illustrating a qualitative impression, they are not quantified).

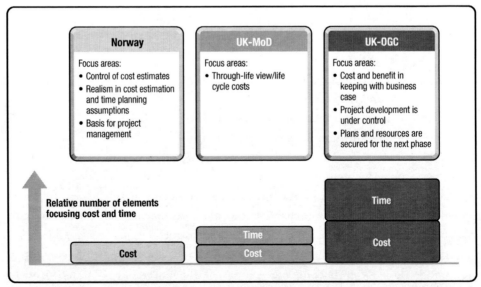

FIGURE 5-12. COMPARISON OF GOVERNANCE FRAMEWORKS AND THEIR FOCUS ON COST AND TIME.

The illustration shows that there are many differences between the frameworks at this level. This is hardly surprising, since we are looking at the most detailed level of the frameworks here. At a detailed level, there is an infinite range of possibilities (of which many can be appropriate ones in given situations). The elements of the framework have to mirror the national setting and the specific challenges the framework is supposed to handle. The possibilities that are chosen should not be a coincidence.

The most characteristic observations are the confirmation of the differences in level of complexity and detail. The OGC framework (including toolboxes) is the complex, complete, and detailed approach covering "all" aspects and lower levels details. The MoD framework being, the high-level approach, combined with linking to concrete guidelines on a lower level. The Norwegian approach is the simplistic approach; most remarkable at this level may be the scarce references to time planning.

In summary, as expected, the three governance frameworks all have elements focusing on cost and time. There are, however, substantial differences. These differences are illustrated in Figure 5-12 and developed further in Table 5-9. The OGC framework is the complex, complete, and detailed approach, the MoD framework being the high-level approach linked to concrete guidelines. The Norwegian approach is the simplistic approach; remarkable at this level in view of the scarce references to time planning.

The other remarkable difference is the choice in the United Kingdom to attach toolboxes giving concrete guidelines on how to do the job properly (like implementing a common quality assurance system) versus the choice in Norway to do an all-independent analysis and cost estimation instead. Both solutions are supposed to increase the quality of the output of the estimation process. One works by telling the professionals how to do their job properly, the other by having other professionals doing the same job check to see whether the answers are the same. Some would probably interpret both solutions as distrust towards the internal professionals, and the historic background for the initiatives in the first place could be used as an argument why this is not without reason. Another interpretation is that all the initiatives, with

TABLE 5-9.   DIFFERENCES IN GOVERNANCE ELEMENTS FOCUSING ON COST AND TIME

	NORWAY	UK MoD	UK OGC
Cost and time focus:	Control	Life cycle	Business case
Depth of details investigated:	Accuracy and detail	Accuracy and detail	General comments
Relative number of elements:	Low	Moderate	High
Toolbox available:	No	Yes	Yes
Independent cost estimate:	Yes	No	No

different weighting of the elements, implement well-proven solutions from business (improvement by quality systems) and government (improvement by control).

5.5   LATEST DEVELOPMENTS (TRANSITIONS 2007)

The descriptions and discussions in this report represent the status of development approximately during the third quarter of 2007. All the three frameworks were developing as this study was performed. We have chosen to include developments already active in the frameworks, but not to include those that are decided, but have not yet come into current practice at the time of writing. Some elements are also left to be described in this additional chapter as we believe the situation earlier this year offers more interesting potential for discussions and learning than the future situation. The fact is that the frameworks in this study are becoming more similar.

UK OGC

The procurement capability has had increasing attention in the United Kingdom over recent years and in January 2007, as we have already quoted, the treasury issued a report called "transforming government procurement" (HM Treasury, 2007b). This report (foreword by the MP Financial Secretary to the Treasury) said that OGC will be given stronger powers to set out the high standards of performance required, monitor departments' performance against them, insist improvements are made where necessary and demand departmental collaboration where that improves value for money…. To achieve these changes the OGC will have to reform. It will become a smaller, more focused, higher calibre organisation, with the skills and powers needed to drive through the necessary changes within central government. (p.1)

There has been much consideration of this new role. The Gateway processes have been mandated. There has been a strategic review of OGC's project activities, and we can summarize the most important forthcoming developments under four areas.

1. Major Projects Portfolio (Integrated Reporting)

Previously, there may had been some ambiguity about how far a government department could go in a major project before the treasury would take notice and "call it in." The mission critical list was an important step to see what the key projects were. This has now been replaced by the major projects portfolio—a list of the key projects across the public sector for delivering the government's service imperatives. A significant innovation in 2008 is the introduction, together with the cabinet office, of a single integrated quarterly report on the health of the government's "major projects portfolio." This innovation will create greater transparency on project performance against common definitions and measures. Exposing problem areas will prompt corrective actions in departments. The OGC will focus help on departments in need of help, which will result in better management of the government's project investments.

2. Major Projects Review Group

Another key change will be a new body, called the major projects review group (MPRG). MPRG is a scrutiny committee for major central government projects and is sponsored by the treasury. Its aim is to deliver better value for the taxpayer by challenging projects on deliverability, affordability, and value for money. The reviews and interventions of the major projects review group will not only be there to help the team (which was the original flavor of the Gateways) but will also be of the nature of a scrutiny so will have much stronger power, and there will be an emphasis on actions to be taken.

The initial plan is for interventions by the MPRG to be at three points:

* When the business case is being developed—where there is maximum scope to influence the project's outcome.
* Before the project goes to tender—to test whether the specification of the requirement is clear and unambiguous, all procurement options have been explored, and there is a realistic prospect of success.
* Following receipt of bids but before award of the contract—to check that the contract decision is likely to deliver what is needed on time, within budget, and giving value for money.

MPRG aims to place departments' most significant projects under an effective, enhanced review process in the early stages. MPRG may advise treasury ministers that a project should stop. However, more generally, it will identify specific issues that need to be resolved before progressing further. In these cases, the department may be provided with recommendations on how to deal with issues and solve problems that the project may be facing.

Projects are selected for MPRG review by the treasury using the following criteria:

* Projects whose whole life costs are above departmental financial delegated authority limits.
* Projects that are high risk.
* Projects that are precedent-setting.

The MPRG initially consists of 11 members, all very senior members of the civil servant or government agencies (including the chief executive of the OGC and OGC's executive director for projects).

3. Enhanced Gateway Reviews

OGC feel that Gateway Reviews have been very successful, but now wish to make tailored changes to their application to increase their impact. There are three particular important areas of change.

- There will be a new overarching rating of "delivery confidence" to supplement the current red/amber/green rating. The latter reflects urgency, and technical issues (such as funding not yet in place) could cause a "red" rating even though final delivery of the project was not in doubt. A delivery confidence rating will in the future indicate the review team's assessment of their confidence that the program or project will deliver its intended outcomes and benefits.
- When there is a "red" rating on the delivery confidence (which now implies a more deep-seated concern), the report will not only go to the SRO but will be escalated to the department's permanent secretary, then to the National Audit Office, and the head of the civil service.
- The reviews will make sure there are action plans, which will be closely monitored by OGC where there are concerns. OGC will thus have a hand in assuring recovery plans. (The authority of OGC in this case comes from their position as expert advisors to the treasury, which is the body that maintains access to the money for the projects).

In addition,

- There is a general intention that reports should be circulated more widely within government departments.
- There should be more flexibility and tailoring of gates and timings to recognize specific needs of complex projects and programmes.

4. Starting Gate

A new intervention is to be introduced, intended to provide assurance at the stage of developing major new policy options, prior to initiation of a project or program, to be termed a "Starting Gate." One aim is to ensure projects or policy initiatives are deliverable before irrevocable announcements are made by ministers. (The need for such a step is actually reflected in the case studies we describe in Chapter 6.) At the time of submitting this report for publication, a careful development plan is just starting, with pilots expected in the fourth quarter of 2008 and a working scheme in the second quarter of 2009.

These developments should not be seen as a complete change, but rather a continuation of the evolving journey, which began with Gateway Reviews, included

Centers of Excellence, then OGC engagements with departments, and so on. OGC is perhaps aiming to change so that their focus of work is at the higher end of the range of government activity (permanent secretaries, boards, etc.) rather than at the lower, more operational, level. However, OGC continues to try to change culture within government departments, in smaller as well as major projects. Further work is ongoing in developing project/program management leadership and professionalism. "Procurement Capability Reviews" are being carried out—these are 3–4 week independent strategic reviews of the procurement activities of a department, including commodities, projects, and PFI, to assess whether departments have the capacity to deliver value for money from their procurement. These procurement capability reviews also incorporate an assessment of whether departments have the program and project management capacity to deliver the intended outcomes successfully.

Finally, the operation of OGC is becoming more focused. This implies reducing the pool of resources (people) within OGC and external consultants. The reduction is primarily in connection with tasks outside the governance framework, but also the strategy for implementation of the framework is changed to be operated by fewer people. The old SACS system (referred to previously) is becoming an external resource framework (ERF) with new contracts as of June 2008. In 2004, there were 90 suppliers giving 350 accepted reviewers, of whom 135 were review team leaders. In the new system, there is likely to be 25 suppliers and 260 consultants for Gateway Reviews. For mission critical or high-risk projects (of which there is perhaps 30–50 per year), the review team leader and some review team members will come from the ERF. For medium risk projects, the review team leader will come from the ERF (some may be done by internal people, some led by external).

UK MoD

Following the McKane report (Ministry of Defence, 2006), MoD introduced major changes to its framework in April 2007. These changes are included in our description of the MoD framework. The themes for this change are given on the MoD website:

Thus, key to these changes are the unification of the customer and the unification of the supplying body (into DE&S).

Norway

As soon as the new framework (specifically QA1) was introduced in 2005, the need for developing new common definitions and guidelines was evident. Using the same model as in the previous introduction period following the original introduction in 2000, a number of development processes were started. This action resulted in a series of new guidelines (titles translated by the author):

- Common terms and definitions for quality assurance QA1,
- Systematic uncertainty (for QA1 and QA2),
- Market uncertainty (for QA1 and QA2),
- Cost estimation (for QA2), and
- Contract strategy (for QA2).

These guidelines are currently being assessed for potential acceptance in the Ministry of Finance. They are not final or made available to the government agencies or QA consultants yet. Even though none of these guidelines gives detailed instructions

---

The ultimate goal for change is to provide battle-winning capability for defense and value for money for the taxpayer. To achieve this goal, four themes have been established to describe how we continue to develop and strengthen our acquisition performance under the DACP and DIS. The four themes are:

Removing barriers to a collective ownership of acquisition and to a truly through-life approach. The key enablers are:

- MoD unified customer (ECC, user, defence equipment and support, science innovation and technology, the center representative),
- Defence equipment and support (DE&S),
- Planning equipment and support over the long term, and
- A more agile research and development program that supports technology pull through.

Better decision making based on a more comprehensive approach to capability management. The key enablers are:

- A unified capability change planning process,
- A stronger focus on through-life management of costs across all DLoDs,
- Closer involvement of the user.

Developing a more effective relationship with industry. The key enablers, delivered through the defense commercial function (DCF) are:

- Commercial management of our portfolio of projects,
- Building and maintaining strategic relations with suppliers,
- Applying consistent commercial approaches matched to the market,
- Developing e-business capability, and
- Evolving the defense industrial strategy (DIS).

Creating the environment for high-performing people and teams to thrive. The key enablers are:

- More sustained and structured investment in skills development,
- Improved reward and recognition, and
- Career development in acquisition.

From http://www.aof.mod.uk/aofcontent/strategic/guide/sg_changethemes.htm

---

FIGURE 5-12.   RECENT CHANGE THEMES IN THE MOD ACQUISITION OPERATION FRAMEWORK.

on how to achieve the demands and professional standards defined by government, this is a step towards developing a toolbox for the framework tasks. The purpose is to develop common understanding and improve performance of the parties involved in the major public investment projects. Only one of them, cost estimation, is used in comparison of the frameworks previously in this report. We chose to do so because the discussions behind it already influence the practice in Norway, and because it addresses specifically the issues which are interesting for this report.

Comparison
This development is highly interesting. Based on experience from implementing the frameworks described earlier in this report, the governments in the United Kingdom and Norway have decided to adjust their frameworks, and the result of these changes and improvements makes the frameworks less different. We interpret this as an expression of several factors:

- Some elements of the frameworks did not give the intended effect and thus had to be changed or strengthened.
- New insight and compiled experience have identified potential for improvement, and this is transformed into new and improved governance framework elements. This shows the frameworks are flexible enough to adjust and that the awareness makes improvement possible.
- The issue of governance of projects has got an increasing attention over the last years and thus the number of available references and sources of impulses are increasing and available in both countries. These can be expected to influence informed key actors within the two countries civil service further in the future.

There has not been any official direct contact in order to exchange experience between the two countries.

5.6   SUMMARY: FRAMEWORKS COMPARISON

This section includes a systematic comparison of the major governance elements, structure, embedded principles, and detailed cost/time element in three current governance frameworks in the United Kingdom and Norway. The main source for this comparison and discussion is interviews with key people involved in development and implementation of these frameworks. In addition, a wide range of documents are studied. Added to this, the personal experience of the authors in how the frameworks are used in reviewing projects. All in all, we consider this a strong basis for evaluation.

This first part of the comparison is practical in the sense that it is not based on theoretical models. It is based solely on practical experience and actual documents from the definition and use of the frameworks. Later chapters will add more practical analysis of cases, and a theoretical analysis based on models and theories presented in Chapter 2. This discussion is not the final conclusion. The following is a summary of the impressions so far:

Development Process
The aims are similar, but the process is genuinely different. In Norway, the initiating process was bottom-up, as was the implementation of the improvement and following learning processes. In the United Kingdom, both processes were top-down. These differences are believed to mirror the administrative culture in the two countries. Norwegian culture has a tendency to go for consensus solutions based on low-level initiatives within an administration having a relatively weak position to impose solutions in the face of opposition. The UK administration has a stronger position and introduction of top-level initiatives is consequently easier. Consensus is not a basic demand in the United Kingdom, and therefore it was easier to ask for a consultant/ expert solution to be imposed from the top. The responsibility of the individual in the United Kingdom and the responsibility of the state in Norway is another context factor influencing initial differences in the frameworks.

The Norwegian and MoD frameworks are mandatory, whereas the OGC framework works by influence through recommendations. This influence is another consequence of the administrative culture and tradition in the two countries, and the military culture in MoD. The frameworks are anchored on a high political level, but in different ways and on different levels. The focus of the Norwegian framework is value, the MoD is value for money, and the OGC is financial targets. In a way the frameworks are similar, but still quite different and very much dependent on the context in which they are going to be implemented. All of the three frameworks in this study shows good indications of success and are thus are considered well adjusted to each context.

Governance Principles
This part of the comparison goes behind the exterior and looks at the embedded principles or "values" with which the frameworks are working. This part of the comparison starts with the notion that these frameworks have to be very different because they express principles or values in very different ways. This changed into realizing that many of the principles are closely related to the common western thinking about business and government, as well as general aggregated experience from projects. This platform is common for the frameworks. At this level, they are actually quite equal.

The real differences are found in values rooted in the different (administrative) cultures in the two countries and the MoD. These are the interior sources for choices leading to the exterior being very different. The most characteristic difference has to do with the way of thinking about systems. In Norway, the simplicity in system is a characteristic ideal. In the United Kingdom, the ideal is completeness (taking into account the toolboxes, not only the framework). The MoD framework can be seen as a good attempt to combine these two ideals. The second most important is the choice of a mandatory system in Norway and MoD and the persuasive recommendations with OGC. These choices reflect administrative culture in the two countries' government.

Framework Structure

This is the part of the comparison that describes the most concrete and apparent differences between the frameworks—their exterior. At first sight, they are obviously different with different type and number of gateways, some are mandatory and some are not. However, even if these choices are different, there is probably more that makes them similar, than what makes them different. They all specify the "rules of the game" supporting the decision-making process and planning and execution of successful projects.

The differences include different means of coordination vertically (from political level on top down to private sector suppliers to projects) and horizontally (across sectors), they have different use of internal/external resources to perform reviews; the support organization is different in form, size, and status. In addition, the roles as gatekeeper and decision makers are very different. All these are another set of indications on the necessary choices of means corresponding to the context in which the frameworks are implemented.

Governance Elements Addressing Cost and Time

As should be expected, the frameworks are different in this aspect. There is an infinite mass of possible choices, and each framework has only chosen a few of them. Including the attached toolboxes, the UK frameworks are much more comprehensive than the Norwegian one. The frameworks themselves are kept on a high level of abstraction, not giving specific details on how to make a good cost estimate or time plan. The MoD focuses on the complete life cycle whereas the two other only mention this aspect. The UK frameworks have relatively many references both to cost and time, whereas the Norwegian one hardly mentions time. On the other hand, the Norwegian framework demands complete independent cost estimates and analyses.

All the initiatives, with different weighting of the elements, implement well-proven solutions from business (improvement by quality systems) and government (improvement by control).

Generalization of These Findings

The point of this comparison, apart from the learning about possible choices, is the potential usefulness in future processes to design new frameworks or improving existing frameworks in other geographical places and situations. Obviously, trying simply to copy the frameworks from one place, setting, and point in time to another will not be a simple way to success. Table 5-10 indicates some main considerations on a superior level.

As shown in Table 5-10, there are different levels of freedom of choice in these processes. There is the least freedom of choice when it comes to governance principles. These are dependent on the whole set of thinking, the business philosophy, and any choice breaking with this process would be risky. The consequences would be difficult to oversee and could lead to major misunderstandings and failure of the whole framework.

TABLE 5-10.   MAIN CONSIDERATIONS IN TRANSFERRING FRAMEWORK EXPERIENCE

ASPECT	CONSIDERATIONS	RELEVANCE
Development process	National culture Administrative culture Tradition	This will have to be unique in each case. No country or corporation will ever have the same starting point or cultural premises.
Governance principles	Regional business and government thinking Administrative culture	This is especially important when transferring outside the western developed countries. This basis may be developed in direction of a standard platform for a region with similar business philosophy.
Framework structure	Purpose/objective Organizational structure/ competence Administrative culture	These are important choices and have to work together with remainder of existing systems and procedures. In this area there is potential for developing a governance 'toolbox' with standard elements to choose from.
Governance elements addressing cost and time	Administrative culture Management culture/style Competence	Same as for the framework structure mentioned previously, but with an even wider range of potential choices.

When designing the development and implementation process, the freedom of choice is great, but it is a bounded freedom. The choices have to fit in with all the elements already in place, the current situation, and all the bearings created by history. This is where there will be a need, not only for objective knowledge of governance frameworks and management systems, but also the skills and talent to make it happen, taking into consideration political issues like power and organizational issues like motivation for change. This part is the most challenging of the whole problem area. A failure in choosing viable solutions for the process will at best waste resources (time and implementation cost) without getting the intended effect. At its worst, it may destroy the good things you had and put you in an even worse situation than before.

When it comes to the framework structure elements, the freedom of choice is large. It is larger the further down you go towards management level. At this level, there are several appropriate choices and each choice does not have the potential to disturb the whole system. A failure can be corrected later. In this area, the number of available choices is big, but not infinite. There could be potential for standardizing a set of good choices within a specific set of presumptions. This way each development of governance frameworks could start with a menu of proven choices to choose from, or at least be inspired by, instead of starting with blank sheets – presumably reinventing the wheel.

On the level below governance frameworks, there is already a tradition for standardization and transfer of system elements and methods between sectors, countries, and regions. The established systems and standards for portfolio, program, and project management are valuable contributions.

6 Case Studies

In this chapter, we present the case studies for this research project. We had access to two civil projects (building projects) and two defense projects (procurement of a new type vessel and a weapons/sensor system). One civil project and one defense project in each country are being studied, in order to investigate more in detail the consequences of the governance frameworks established in the two countries. The cases are presented in some detail, but of course not giving the full circumstances of every aspect. Our initial focus is on cost and time estimation, since these aspects were expected to be well-documented and points towards the starting point of this study—how these frameworks influence cost estimation and cost overrun in projects—but we are also interested in the overall effect of the governance framework.

In each case, there will be references to the governance frameworks as described in earlier chapters of this report: in the United Kingdom the Gateways (OGC) and Gates (MoD), and in Norway, QA1 and QA2. None of the projects have been through all the defined gateways—the frameworks are relatively recent, and a project which today is near its completion started before all elements of the presented frameworks were initiated. In the United Kingdom particularly, the specific choice of project was largely in the hands of the authorities cooperating with the study, that is, OGC and DE&S; we gave some guidelines as to the sort of project we were looking for, but then the choice of project to study was clearly theirs. In Norway, the access to cases was easier to come by, but it is never easy to know which ones to choose before the study starts. There is a feeling in hindsight we did not find the perfect cases for the study, but they all add material that illustrates some aspects of the implementation of the frameworks.

The cases will be presented one by one and there will be an analysis of the total picture in the end of the chapter.

The cases presented here are:

1. The Home Office (UK office building project)
2. NEADS (UK defense system: weapon, sensors, and data communication)

3. IFI2 (Norwegian university building)
4. The Skjold project (Norwegian defense vessel)

6.1   METHOD

There are three main sources of information about the cases:

- General information is gathered from general sources such as official websites and documents published by the government in the two countries.
- Project specific documentation gives facts about each case. Among these, the gateway/quality assurance reports are the most important.
- Semi-structured interviews are performed with key personnel in all cases; this was a main source of information.

The interviews were supported by a questionnaire including a short introduction to the purpose of the research (see Figure 3-1 and Appendix B). The interviews were not bound rigidly to follow the questionnaire, it was more of a structure to follow, and an indication of subjects that needed to be covered through an informal talk. During the interview, the interviewee was sometimes asked to present/refer to documents or proof to back up the observations, if possible. Some of the documents were supplied by the interviewees, others were found in archives by the authors.

This information was compiled into a standardized format by the authors of this report, specially designed to focus on the aspects interesting for our study, but also in order to produce an interesting and informative presentation of each case. To make sure the interesting aspects of each case comes through, we did not want to squeeze the cases into a very tight format, and therefore, there are some structural differences between them in the descriptions. In the end, the cases are systematically compared, with a focus on the effect of the governance framework and the influence especially on cost and time, specifically cost estimation and the potential to avoid cost overrun.

6.2   THE HOME OFFICE

A National Audit Office report in 2003 began as follows:

In March 2002, following a procurement that began in 1996, the Home Office (see Figure 6-1) signed a 29-year contract with Annes Gate Property plc (AGP) for funding demolition of the old Department of the Environment building at 2 Marsham Street (2MS), design and construction of new headquarters accommodation on part of the site and provision of associated services. The Home Office expects to move into its new building in 2005 when it will begin paying AGP a monthly charge for the building and associated services amounting to £311 million [US $622 million] (net present cost) over the life of the project. (p. 1)

FIGURE 6-1.   THE HOME OFFICE BUILDING IN 2 MARSHAM STREET (2MS). Source: http://www.cityoffices.net/properties/2-marsham-street-london.cfm

The home office began the procurement process in 1996 after a review of its accommodation concluded that there were deficiencies in the existing estate and that it needed to be refurbished. In 1998, the Home Office had obtained three competing bids to refurbish the existing estate, proposing the existing building at 2MS as temporary accommodation during the refurbishment. AGP, however, made a developed and cost variant bid for a new building at 2MS. This variant was attractive to the Home Office as, based on based predictions of a decline in staff numbers done at that time, it presented an opportunity to house all Home Office and Prison Service staff in a single building and avoided the business risk associated with moving out to temporary accommodation and back again. The contract provided for 3,450 workstations plus support facilities. The Home Office had also identified other potential accommodation, but it was either too expensive in comparison with 2MS, or the location was unsuitable.

The contract was carried out under the UK Private Finance Inititative (PFI). The building handover was completed in January 2005, amid considerable publicity:

HOME OFFICE MOVES HOME

26 January 2005

The new Home Office headquarters has been officially completed on time and on budget, saving taxpayers around £95 million, Home Secretary Charles Clarke announced today. From next week, staff will begin moving into the new offices at 2 Marsham Street in Westminster. Eventually 3,400 staff who are currently in separate offices in Queen Anne's Gate and Horseferry House will all be working on the one site.

The new headquarters were designed by Sir Terry Farrell, architect of the MI6 HQ and Charing Cross Station, to have a positive impact on those living and working in the area. It is a dramatic improvement on its predecessor - three 20-story concrete tower blocks occupied by the former Department for the Environment, infamously nicknamed 'The three Ugly Sisters' because of the blight they cast on the Westminster skyline.

Home Secretary Charles Clarke said:
"By moving to a newer, more efficient headquarters, the Home Office will save taxpayers around £95 million. This will contribute to the Home Office's programme to save £1.97 billion so that we can target more money at front line services like policing and border control. "2 Marsham Street will be one of the most environmentally efficient public buildings of its type in the UK, with energy consumption designed to be at least ten percent better than Government recommended levels.

"Bringing staff from several Home Office buildings into a single, modern, open-plan office space will considerably improve communication among officials working hard to build a safer, more cohesive society."

Home Office Press release,
http://www.press.homeoffice.gov.uk/press-releases/Home_Office_Moves_Home

---

Two Marsham Street is a single building with three liked blocks named after people who have had an impact on areas of British life within the Home Office's remit: Robert Peel (former prime minister who among other achievements founded the metropolitan police), Elizabeth Fry (Quaker prison reformer), and Mary Seacole (pioneering nurse and heroine of the Crimean War).

Development of the Bid

From the point of view of the Home Office, there was a need for new accommodation as the existing estate was in poor condition. On the other hand, this project was a visible public project, so there was considerable interest from parliament. The story of the bidding can be shown in Figure 6-2, taken from the National Audit Office:

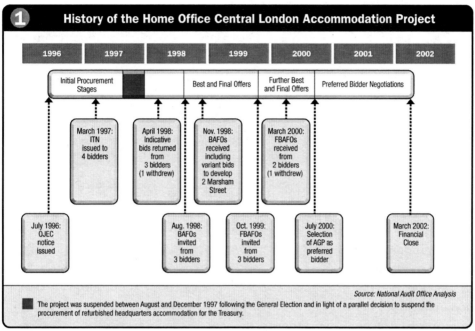

FIGURE 6-2.   HISTORY OF THE BIDDING PROCESS (National Audit Office, 2003).

In October 1999, three consortia were invited to submit bids based on development of the Marsham street site. However, only two bidders submitted further best and final offers (FBAFOs). There was a complex criteria-weighting system, similar to that employed in MoD building projects, and the bids were very close. The winning bid emerged as slightly cheaper, slightly faster, and offered more useable floor area. Both of the bidders suggested a bond (rather than a bank) financed solution. Extensive probing of the bid by the project team was undertaken, and the contract was awarded in March 2003.

It was proposed to carry out this contract under the UK Private Finance Initiative. This required evaluation of a public sector comparator (PSC), which is an assessment of the likely costs of hypothetical contracts to build and operate the building, including construction costs, life cycle capital expenditure, operating costs and in particular, an assessment of the risks associated with these costs. The risk-adjusted net present cost of the PSC was calculated as a total of £494 million, as compared to the same figure for the PFI option which was calculated as £460 million (£311 million for the payment scheme plus £149 million for costs which have been retained by the Home Office and included in the public sector comparator, thus added to the cost of the PFI solution to allow a like-for-like comparison). The decision-making process for agreeing PFI as the best route is described in the following.

The business case required that one of the key offices be vacated, the previous main location of the Home Office in Queen Anne's Gate, found a new tenant, and another government department did indeed take over that lease. The final business case and a side letter agreement with the developer provided for the possibility of an alternative solution for this office, although it was the case that the agreement for transferring the lease of Queen Anne's Gate to the other department existed in principle before the 2MS contract was signed.

It is perhaps also worth noting that there was a pre-existing separate PFI contract for Home Office information technology, which provided for relocation to 2MS. This was signed several years before the Marsham Street contract. This contract is not discussed in detail in this report.

Decision-Making Process

What were the driving objectives of the project? According to the National Audit Office Report (2003), the objective was a replacement for inadequate existing accommodation. Interestingly, the Marsham Street option actually required paying more money than using the existing estate.

The building was to support the business requirement to deliver an "up-to-date, flexible workplace, providing an efficient, effective IT platform and the range and quality of facilities expected of an employer of high calibre staff in central London." The scale of the project meant that treasury approval was needed to proceed. The rule is that contractual decisions are the responsibility of officials; accountability for decisions on the 2MS project rested with the department's permanent secretary. In view of the significance of the project and press/public interest, ministers including the home secretary were of course kept informed and gave guidance when needed, for example on the choice of acceptable location.

Other important issues driving the decision making included the following:

- The importance of time, and managing staff expectations. At an earlier stage of the project, staff had been told that a new accommodation would be provided by 2000. Some staff doubted whether this would happen, and the cultural change agenda underlined the need for a careful internal communications strategy that actively sought opportunities for staff involvement so as to encourage project ownership.
- Value-for-money and risk were the objectives in deciding the Marsham Street option over others. The business case demonstrated that an upgrade

of the existing estate was needed and would have cost more than the 2MS option, so an increase in costs was unavoidable. The 2MS PFI was shown by the business case to offer the best value out of all the options, although there were more risks.

- Given the choice of the Marsham Street option, price and risk were key determinants in deciding which bidder to use to build Marsham Street.
- The complex weighting criteria mentioned shows that technical quality and time were also important determinants.

An innovative aspect of the financing structure is that AGP has retained the risk associated with potential changes in the value of the property at the end of the contract term. To reduce the cost of the Home Office's annual repayment to AGP, the deal was constructed such that £100 million of debt is not repaid over the contract life. Instead it will either be paid off at the end of the contract if the Home Office chooses to buy the building (at the lower of market value or £137.5 million) or renewed if the Home Office does not take up this option. AGP are therefore retaining the risk that the market value of the site will not fall below £100 million in 29 years time and the Home Office has flexibility over its accommodation options at the end of the contract

From National Audit Office (2003)

The Project Planning Process

Because this is a PFI project, the authors did not have access to detailed time and cost estimates.

However, on submission of the FBAFO, the project team extensively probed the bid to look for reasonableness.

- They looked at the history of the company and previous similar projects. (The company supplied reference projects.)
- They revisited the risk (fundamentally, the cost risk lay with the contractor, but this risk was only in financial terms, clearly the risk of not having accommodation stayed with the Home Office).
- They had a detailed resourced program which could be probed.
- They could also probe the price. Quantity surveyors studied the price. The team was able to ask for more information where necessary to give them confidence.

Following the award of the contract, the project was run through the project board. The board met every 2 months and was presented with the latest version of the tools that were used, such as the risk register, project dashboard by the team (client, commercial, facilities management, and monitoring surveyor), and expenditure tracker. Cost and time ran roughly as planned during the project.

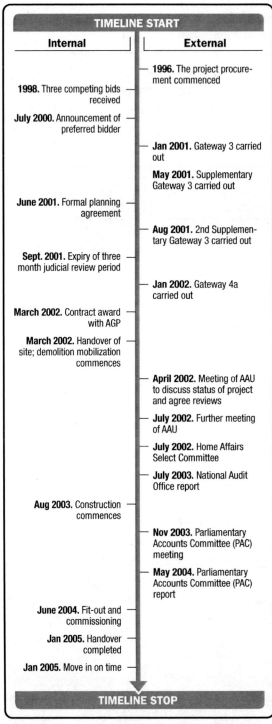

TIMELINE START

Internal	External
	1996. The project procurement commenced
1998. Three competing bids received	
July 2000. Announcement of preferred bidder	
	Jan 2001. Gateway 3 carried out
	May 2001. Supplementary Gateway 3 carried out
June 2001. Formal planning agreement	
	Aug 2001. 2nd Supplementary Gateway 3 carried out
Sept. 2001. Expiry of three month judicial review period	
	Jan 2002. Gateway 4a carried out
March 2002. Contract award with AGP	
March 2002. Handover of site; demolition mobilization commences	
	April 2002. Meeting of AAU to discuss status of project and agree reviews
	July 2002. Further meeting of AAU
	July 2002. Home Affairs Select Committee
	July 2003. National Audit Office report
Aug 2003. Construction commences	
	Nov 2003. Parliamentary Accounts Committee (PAC) meeting
	May 2004. Parliamentary Accounts Committee (PAC) report
June 2004. Fit-out and commissioning	
Jan 2005. Handover completed	
Jan 2005. Move in on time	

TIMELINE STOP

Figure 6-3.   **Timeline for the Home Office project**

As well as costs, benefits also need to be planned. However, the parliamentary governance process discussed in the following identified evidence of optimism bias: "There is evidence of optimism bias in PFI projects for departmental accommodation: departments have assumed much lower staff numbers than they have subsequently employed. The buildings have then not been large enough to hold everyone. Yet such projects are often justified in part, as in this case, by the advantages of bringing everyone under one roof. The Home Office assumed that staff numbers would be reduced due to outsourcing, efficiency gains, and changes in working practices. Instead, numbers increased dramatically between 1998 and 2003 as the Home Office took on new responsibilities, although the total increase is not fully explained by these new functions. Similar stories arose at GCHQ, the Ministry of Defence, and the former Department of Social Security" (House of Commons Committee of Public Accounts, 2004, p. 4).

Documentation

This project was carried out under the PFI contract. There are, therefore, no publicly available data on how the cost and schedule were developed by the bidders. The bids included details of capital programs and costs, and the contract documentation provides visibility about what service charges are based upon and the processes for making changes over time. All of the work carried out by the public sector was documented and stored. The business case is documented (see Figure 6-3), as is the public sector comparator showing the relative costs at a very high level for the public sector and PFI solutions. Copies of the Gateway Review reports are held. All correspondence with the parliamentary governance process is documented in the following.

The Impacts of the Governance Framework

Governance up to the contract award was handled through the project board. The project board met monthly, representing many parts of the Home Office and chaired by the SRO. The project director reported to the SRO, the project manager reported to the project director; there were various contractors reporting to the project manager. There were at this point no Gateways (although there was some element of the so-called Red Team Review).

Clearly, a major issue was the business case, and in particular, the question of whether the project would be undertaken under the private finance initiative. The files showed significant advice taken from consultants about the case for PFI. The files then showed correspondence with the National Audit Office particularly to obtain a view on whether the project would be regarded as on or off balance sheet, during which the NAO accepted the Home Office's accountants' analysis that the PFI contract would create an asset that did not need to go onto its balance sheet. (This process followed the practice at the time, as if the asset had to be recognized on the Home Office balance sheet, it would have counted against the Home Office's budget and would have presented issues on affordability). There is also benchmarking with other government contracts.

The first Gateway Review of the contract was a Gateway 3, in January 2001, in the lead up to placement of contract. The aim of the review, as should be for a Gateway 3, was (briefly) to confirm the business case and benefits plan in the light of the final tender information, confirm that the recommended decision, if properly executed, would deliver the specified outcomes and provide value for money, and ensure the various controls were in place and requirements had been carried out. The review team consisted of four from the Home Office and five external contractors (including a lawyer). A 10-page report was prepared, which was positive, although with a few detailed caveats. Since this review was a Gateway 3, cost and time estimates were not specifically revisited. Outstanding issues were looked at during a 1-day supplementary Gateway 3 in May 2001. Further issues later arose which led to the Home Office requesting further investigation, and a substantial report being prepared as a further supplementary Gateway 3 in August 2001, by a team consisting of two from the Home Office, one from the contractor, one government lawyer, and three outside lawyers.

Whether changes would have happened without these reviews is, of course, not known. However, it is clear that the project was entering a new phase, and the Home Office was starting on a relationship with the bidder; who was a very experienced, sophisticated company—having expert support from those experienced in dealing with such contractors must have been prudent for the project.

Following the contract award, the project was governed through a mixture of internal and external (that is, external to the project) processes. Internal governance was managed through the ongoing project board, who decided when Gateways were to be held. External assurance operated through the Audit and Assurance Unit (AAU) within the Home Office, and beyond the Home Office in the National Audit Office. Furthermore, the project was of considerable public interest, so there were many parliamentary enquiries about the project. All of these mechanisms will be covered.

The project board met every 2 months. Documentation from the project board showed the following:

- actions from the last meeting,
- progress reports, including 3–6 months look ahead,
- overall program status (classified as red, amber, or green),
- project dashboards and summaries from teams within the project, and
- a register of the main risks.

The minutes tracked the other main governance processes noted, namely Gateways, AAU reports, and parliamentary interest. Particularly, key risk areas or issues could be tracked here. For example, the exact numbers of staff actually going into the building took a long time to be finalized, which caused a number of issues, and this area was given particular attention. One particular cause of this was that a major organizational change occurred between 2002 and 2005, and a significant part of the prison service headquarters was transferred into the Home Office; this made the decisions on allocation more complicated, particularly as the total staff numbers had gone up well beyond the planned capacity of the building.

As is usual in projects, the effect of the project board is difficult to identify because the project went well. However, it appeared clear from the interviewees that had the project run away, the project board would have been an effective mechanism to identify this and contain the project.

It is interesting to note here that, while the specification of the project effectively stayed fairly constant, a new deputy undersecretary (DUS) joined the Home Office during the project, and this project reported to this person. Among other points, the DUS raised interest in cultural change (and thus change to business processes) within the Home Office, which had implications for the use of space within the building and thus for the project, interacting with the space-planning concern within the project.

A Gateway Review was held in January 2002 (the document states that it was a Gateway 4[a], because a Gateway 4 exercise had been carried out in February 2001), undertaken over 4 days by a three-person team from the Home Office, cabinet office, and OGC, respectively. The review had 15 specified purposes, including checking that the current phase of the contract was properly completed, verifying that the business case was still valid and unaffected by events, and looking at risks particularly. It acknowledged that this review was "being carried out 'slightly early' within the process at the request of Her Majesty's Treasury (HMT) (the finance department) and in agreement with the OGC." This process is interesting both because it shows flexibility in the system and the watching brief held by the treasury. The Gateway report was very positive (although it noted "resourcing and closing out of targets a challenge").

The AAU within the Home Office met on 25 April 2002 and July 2002 to discuss audit activity and the status of the project and agreed to conduct three short reviews in the following year (e.g., one on governance and document management). Various concerns were raised, including the question of whether the project was PRINCE2 compliant and whether it demonstrated the level of governance and transparency expected, and comments about the documentation were mentioned. Nevertheless, these were mostly audit-type operational issues.

The National Audit Office looked into the project, in particular the PFI deal that had been struck between the Home Office and the contractor and reported in July 2003, with an essentially entirely favorable report. Main recommendations from the report were to ensure the benefits were realized from the project.

The National Audit Office is there to scrutinize the public spending on behalf of Parliament and is totally independent of the government. This report was therefore taken up by the key Parliamentary Accounts Committee (PAC) of Parliament, a committee of 16 members of Parliament whose meetings are usually based on a published NAO (or Northern Ireland Audit Office) report. There was a PAC meeting on 12 November 2003, looking into value for money, including the running costs, financing, numbers of staff, and refinancing charges. The permanent secretary and deputy undersecretary at the Home Office, the most senior National Audit Office officers, a treasury officer, and the most senior representatives of the contractors: the CEO of AGP and the CEO of Bouygues Batiment and the Director at HSBC Infrastructure were questioned. The latter two organizations are the owners of AGP. The committee reported in House of Commons Committee of Public Accounts (2004). This report was by no means uncritical, the essential part of the report consisting of a terse nine pages, which had seven main conclusions and recommendations:

- The first finding was that "under-forecasting of staff numbers leads to bad decisions on accommodation. There is evidence of optimism bias in PFI projects for departmental accommodation" (p. 4). Given this first finding, there were three others about staff filling the space, whether officials needed to be in London, and in particular why the prison service HQ as a whole needed to be in London.
- Identification of wider business benefits from the move to the new building and a warning that these must be grasped.
- A question about a specific financing question (valuation of the right to share refinancing gains).
- A question about disposal of the existing estate from which staff were to move.

PAC reports are taken extremely seriously by the civil service, and these comments will have been acted upon by the project board. The authors did not have full access these reports, but the treasury did put detailed replies to the PAC before Parliament (HM Treasury, 2004). Among other items, this report explained further the sizing of the building, noting the uncertainties in forecasting of staff numbers and giving more details of which parts of the Home Office needed to be within London and referred to the integrated change program management board noted in the following.

This public project was visible, and there was considerable interest more generally within Parliament. There was a succession of parliamentary questions. Some of these were on fundamental issues in the project, such as the selection of preferred bidder (July 2000), progress on the building (March 2002), or the costs of new building (Sept. 2003 – to which the answer was that the Net Present Cost at contract signature in March 2002 was £311m, reflecting an initial annual cost of £30.3m. Many, though, were on much more detailed issues, such as the art in the building and its cost (July 2002) (there was also later a freedom of information request about offenses committed by prisoners whose art had also been chosen for display in the building, which led to a question during the Prime Minister's question time), the refrigerant used for air cooling (a whole succession of questions starting on October 2002), whether the timber for the building was legal and sustainable (again, a whole succession of questions, starting on October 2002), and transporting redundant concrete by water (Dec 2002).

On the other hand, at the Parliamentary Home Affairs Select Committee in July 2002, which looked into the performance on the Home Office as a whole, the permanent secretary, and some director generals of the Home Office were questioned and a comprehensive briefing was prepared on the building project for the attendees, but it is not clear whether the project was discussed.

A later (commercially sensitive) report by the OGC showed the building to be effective in multiple ways compared to government property benchmarks.

We noted previously that there was a separate PFI contract for the information technology provision in the building, whose operation was clearly linked to this contract. There was a separate team and program management board managing the integrated change program, covering not only the IT aspects but other projects such as electronic document management and changed financial management. It was not clear to the authors which governance processes (if any) looked at the integration of these with the building contract.

Our Analysis of This Case

This case is an example of a construction project carried out under the UK Private Finance Initiative (PFI). It was completed on time and with no increase in the agreed payment scheme. (There were design changes that were requested between 2003 and 2004, but these were accommodated by the developer and the project team without delaying the practical completion of the project.) Because of the PFI nature, much of the estimation of cost and schedule is not publicly available, but some observations can be made about the governance of the project.

The project came under the requirement to employ standard OGC Gateway Reviews. This requirement was not there at the start of the project, so the first Gateway was a Gateway 3, but this requirement does not seem to have diminished the effectiveness of the reviews. Although ongoing Gateway 0's were not employed, it was noticeable that Gateway Reviews included investigation of whether "the business case was still valid and unaffected by events." The flexibility (in what can appear a rigid process) was also clear. Gateway 3's and Gateway 4's could be carried out multiple times if there were outstanding issues; one gateway was carried out "slightly early" with the encouragement of OGC for particular reasons. It is not fully clear what effect the Gateway Reviews had, but at the Gateway 3 stage, having expert support from those experienced in dealing with sophisticated and experienced contractors appears to have been valuable. The project went well; however, if there had been problems, the governance in place should have meant that the project board was alerted early enough to take action.

The governance before Gateway 3 is less clear, which of course occurred only around 8 months after the foundation of OGC. It is likely that the structure offered by Gateways 0, 1, and 2 would have been useful and might have avoided questions that arose later.

What is also interesting in this visible public project is the identification of other governance processes. Key here is the National Audit Office, which scrutinizes public spending on behalf of Parliament (independent of the government), which was able to come in between contract signature and start of construction. Even more crucially, the key Parliamentary Accounts Committee (PAC) can take up NAO reports, and the PAC certainly took a good high-level view and identified important issues, including optimism bias in estimating staff numbers and issues about the wider business benefits of the project.

On the question of forecasting staff numbers, looking at the project now, it has to all intents and purposes achieved the provision of a single London headquarters for the Home Office. Staff numbers have been reduced generally but also around 1,500 staff were moved out of the Home Office into the Ministry of Justice. There is now almost no Home Office outside 2MS, and indeed 2MS currently continues to be shared with about 1,100 staff from the Ministry of Justice.

The parliamentary question process was also highly evident, although it is not clear what influence this actually had on the project. It is noticeable too that the treasury (or OGC) appears to have held a watching brief, since one Gateway was held "slightly early" at their request.

Finally, the governance mechanism appears to have been based on this single project, and the governance of linked projects, in particular, the integrated change program described previously, was not clear to the authors.

6.3 THE NETWORK ENABLED AIRSPACE DEFENCE AND SURVEILLANCE (NEADS) PROJECT OF THE UK MINISTRY OF DEFENCE

Ground-based air defence (GBAD) is an important defense against an increasing range of low-level airborne threats, such as attack helicopters, unmanned air vehicles, and cruise missiles (see Figure 6-4). In order to be effective, as well as a weapon, there needs to be the ability to take data from multiple sensors—ground-based, seaborne and airborne radars (Airborne Warning and Control System [AWACS])—and carry out data fusion to form a reliable picture of the situation, identification of the target (before it becomes a direct threat), and control to destroy the target. The requirement here is therefore not a single item of equipment, but a whole system.

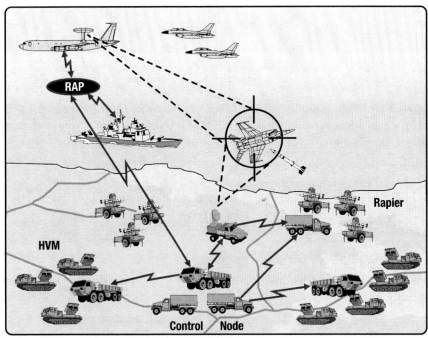

**FIGURE 6-4.   GROUND BASED AIR DEFENCE (GBAD). Source: http://www.armedforces.
co.uk/projects/raq3f574e9f26e72**

The UK defense currently has two ground-based air defense weapons in its armory: HVM and Rapier. Both are described in the following.

"The HVM system, commercially known as Starstreak, was designed, developed, and produced by Thales Air Defence Ltd (TADL) of Belfast - formally Shorts Missile Systems (SMS). It is a Very Short Range Ground Based Air Defence weapon system optimised for the attack of low flying armoured helicopters but with the capability to engage high performance aircraft. It is produced in three configurations, all of which employ a common missile: as a Shoulder Launched (SL) system, as a Lightweight Multiple Launcher (LML) on a tripod configuration and as a Self-Propelled (SP) system based on the Stormer vehicle.....HVM was declared as In Service on 1 September 1997." Source: http://www.armedforces.co.uk/projects/raq3f574e9f26e72

"Rapier FSC provides Low Level Air Defence over the battlefield for UK forces against enemy aircraft and cruise missiles. The system consists of a launcher with 8 ready-to-fire missiles and an electro-optical tracker, linked to accompanying radars. The combination of radar and EO trackers makes the system highly resistant to electronic countermeasures, and each fire unit group can cover an area of about 100 square km." Source: http://www.defenseindustrydaily.com/mbda-wins-through-life-maintenance-of-uks-rapier-sams-03802/

The project can be regarded for this chapter as having started in 1994 with a NATO-sponsored feasibility study (sponsored in the sense that it was for NATO; it was funded by all the nations, and managed by what was then the procurement arm of the UK Ministry of Defence, MoD(PE)). This project was called JPGC 28-30, for "Future close-in air defense." Twenty-eight industries were involved in eight countries (including both the UK and Norway). This reported in 1998 with a solution with an estimated price tag at around £8 billion/$16 billion (US) (which could be regarded as a full "gold-plated" solution). There were two approaches, one UK-led and one French-led. MoD(PE) (which later became the Defence Procurement Agency [DPA]) then drafted a NATO staff requirement.

A future GBAD, integrated project team, or IPT (upon which all projects are based, see Section 5.2.2) was set up within the MoD(PE). The funding line for the work was "endorsed" (see Figure 6-5). We can regard this point as the start of the project proper.

There were two stages to the project:

1.   The air-defense C3I (command, control, communication, and intelligence) under which extant UK air defense assets would be integrated with an advanced command and control system.
2.   A replacement weapon (i.e., the missile used in defense) and battle-space management C3I (including sensors and data-fusion) would be introduced.

The business case for (1), "GBAD Phase I," was prepared with a budget to develop (1) of approximately £1bn. The Initial Gate for this case was in 2001. This allowed the assessment phase for (1) and the concept phase for (2). The "Customer I" (i.e., the customer defining the requirement) was Director Equipment Capability (Theatre Airspace) (DEC(TA) (DefenceInternet, 2007).

However, in 2003 there was a general reduction in funding, revisiting previous decisions. DEC(TA) had to reduce the funding (while the authors have had no visibility of this, we presume that the resources and programs section of MoD will have required the customer to reduce funding). At that point, DEC(TA) had three programs within his remit: the Eurofighter Typhoon project, PAAMS (the weapon on the T45 destroyer), and GBADS (constituting a significant proportion of MoD future funding). While again, the authors have had no insight into the rationale of this decision, the first two of these programs were well forward in their program with a lot of money committed up-front—and the first at least was clearly politically very sensitive. In deciding how to apportion his funding, he decided to change the £1 billion/$2 billion for GBADS Phase 1 to £200 million/$400 million. The DEC(TA) effectively asked DPA what capability could be gained for £200 million and was told that he could be given limited situation awareness, but that operational analysis indicated that it had some value. An information note (a note that is generated by the sponsor/IPT to the Investment Appraisal Board via the scrutineers) was generated to formalize this process.

Thus, a very basic version of (1) became the Land Environment Air Picture Provision (LEAPP). It is mentioned in the 2006 Defence Statistics (compiled in March 2005) with a then forecast in-service date of 2010 and cost of £110 million/ $220 million (DASA, 2007, Table 1.15). This is now coming to the end of its second assessment phase and was schedule for a Main Gate around March 2008.

Network Enabled Air-Space Defence and Surveillance (NEADS) was then established as the capability in (2) plus the remaining capability in (1) (effectively, the difference between the £1 billion and £200 million programs). However, the budget was kept at the original sum that was just going to pay for (2). This part of the program is currently in the concept phase (which began October 2006) and is expecting to be in Initial Gate in 2009 and Main Gate in 2012. It has a Planning Assumption for Service Entry (PSAE) of 2020.

NEADS will consist of two main components:

1. A set of weapon systems (NEAD) (independent of the remainder of the system), and
2. Sensors, data-fusion, communications (NES).

Typically, possibly around 30% of the cost is in (1) and 70% is in (2). In 2002/2003, the team had been looking at technologies for the weapon. A company called MBDA[13] had been given a statement of requirements, with a cost limit placed by the DPA. This led to the development of a scheme for a common anti-air module missile (CAMM). MBDA was given a single-source development contract (this was before the DIS). From this series of technology demonstrator programs, a missile could be produced in 5 to 6 years (as opposed to the normal 12), and a guidance system at one quarter of the cost of equivalent systems. It also has open architectures (both because of obsolescence but also because the targets are getting harder).

When the funding was cut, there was a "cancellation charge" on the first phase (1), so industry had to be paid a charge or given something to do, so it funded the development of CAMM. It is planned that it will replace Rapier (and the marine point

---

13. "MBDA UK Ltd., the prime contractor for around half of our in-service inventory and that accounts for over 50% of the investment currently on contract." (Source: Defence Industrial Strategy [Secretary of State for Defence, 2005]).

defense weapon, Sea-Wolf, fitted in the Type 22 and Type 23 frigates). However, the key at this point is that MoD now has a candidate weapon to meet an anticipated user requirement, system requirement, capability gap analysis, a concept of employment, and so on; that is, the weapon specification is effectively completely out of sequence.

The concept stage of NEADS had £23 million/$46 million (US), which was also later cut in 2003/2004 by £10 million/$20 million (US). At the time of this writing, there has not been a lot of progress on (2). In December 2004, a technology demonstration program was placed into effect, which finishes shortly for CAMM. In late 2005 and early 2006, a concept stage was scoped to develop the parts that the previous paragraph noted were missing, and a technology watch for the whole system, which began in October 2006; this stage is now a third of the way through.

The Decision-Making Process

For the point of the view of the MoD, and the capability customer (DEC(TA)) particularly, the strategic need for this capability is clear. There are two weapons that will be going out of service, and the technology needed for ground defense has become much more sophisticated. The top-level statement from the Ministry of Defence in the "Defence Industry Strategy" (Secretary of State for Defence, 2005) says the following concerning "complex weapons" (defined as strategic and tactical weapons reliant upon guidance systems to achieve precision effects, "tactical" covering air-to-air; air defense (i.e., surface-to-air, including both land-based and maritime); air-to-surface, anti-ship/submarine (including torpedoes); and surface-to-surface):

Quote from Defence Industrial Strategy (Secretary of State for Defence, 2005, p. 100)

Complex weapons provide the UK armed forces with battle winning precision effects, which are able to achieve military advantage at a reduced level of asset use. The UK has over the past 10 years made a significant investment in the upgrade and development of complex weapons for the Armed Forces.....

Therefore, to maintain appropriate sovereignty, it is important that the UK can use, maintain and upgrade specific capabilities in its inventory, independent of other nations. To do this, the UK needs guaranteed access to the following key functions (p. 102) [inter alia – partial list only]

- Provide weapon systems design and performance expertise independently or as a leading player in collaboration with other nations.
- Understand threats from technology proliferation.
- Exploit emerging and novel technology
- Respond to UORs [Urgent Operational Requirements].
- Undertake national projects within the relevant legal and international frameworks
- Through-life capability management and support for the current weapon inventory.

The drivers to decision making here, therefore, appear at the first instance to be three-fold:

- The essential in-service date for the capability due to obsolescence of current equipment and to meet the increase in threat,
- The needs of the UK industrial base and the benefits from the science on other weapon-programmes that were coming to an end, and
- Cost restrictions, increasing during the course of the project so far.

These drivers affected the project process fundamentally. The first was the driver that caused the project to come into being in the first place; the second was also a contributory factor to the existence of the project—MoDs need to keep the UK defense-development industrial base employed; and the third in the multiple cuts in the budgets during the course of the project.

However, from the previous discussion, we can also see three other drivers coming into play:

- Political sensitivity,
- Opportunistic behavior, MoD's ability to react to opportunities, and
- The requirement to keep some UK sovereign aspects within the United Kingdom.

These latter drivers affected the project process: the first in the decision to cut the £1 billion program to £200 million; the second in MoD's ability to make use of the resource available to develop the weapon; and the third in the restriction of major parts of the project to the United Kingdom.

Current Technology and Current Contract

The description of the missile development has been given previously. A view of the Industrial Concept Study for the overall NEADS program can be seen in a website current at the time of writing (Advantage Business Solutions, 2007).

The Project Planning Process

This program already had a starting point in the NATO feasibility study, with a reasonably good whole-life cost model. This provided a cost of £8 billion which appeared reasonable to the (project) independent estimators (the project forecasting group, [PFG]), based on historic data, which is one of the estimating approaches used by this group.

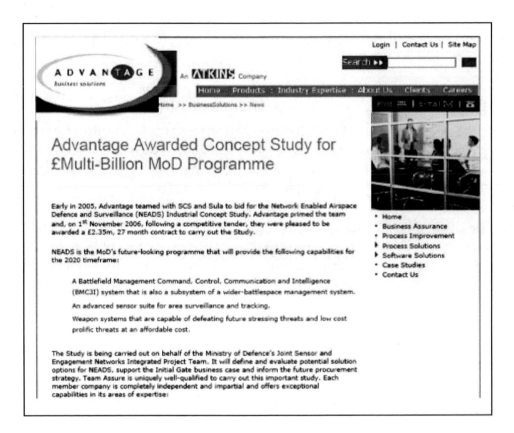

The funding line for the "future GBAD" was then *endorsed*, which means that it was accepted as a program (i.e., it appears in the long-term funding plans, but no gate has been gone through yet). PFG reviewed this funding line and vetted it (but did not change the numbers that industry had compiled).

The project planning was then revised due to outside requirements to cut the funding This revision required a new plan to be developed around the £200 million plan, and a new plan for the concept stage of NEADS.

Industry capacity became available unexpectedly due to rescoping of the program and so to retain critical expertise and avoid nugatory costs rapid replanning enabled new plans to be prepared for a weapon development program (CAMM). Because this was a single-source development contract, a missile was produced in 5 to 6 years rather than the usual 12, and a guidance system was produced at one quarter of the cost of equivalent missiles.

A missile is just one part of a missile system, and in late 2005/early 2006, a concept stage was scoped to develop the remainder of this system. The planning within this will again take a whole-life cost model framework set out by the PFG, and produce a whole-life cost model endorsed and monitored by the PFG.

The authors have had much less visibility of the time aspects of the planning to see how the various time to gates and planning assumptions for service entry have been estimated, other than that, they, too, are checked by the PFG. PFG is known to rely heavily on "parametric" cost- and time-estimating techniques, such as PRICE (2007) and HVR Consulting Services Ltd. (2007). This program is in an earlier stage than would be required for detailed cost and schedule development, so it is difficult to relate their work with (say) relevant PMI processes and inputs/tools.

Documentation

This project is in the early stages, and there was no documentation available on details about cost estimation or time schedules or work breakdown structures, etc., in documents to this study team (see Figure 6-5). The concept study is investigating potential architectures to meet the evolving requirements documents. Based on the architectures and technology selected for further evaluation, a whole life model is being developed to one-half order of magnitude based partially on a concurrent industry survey.

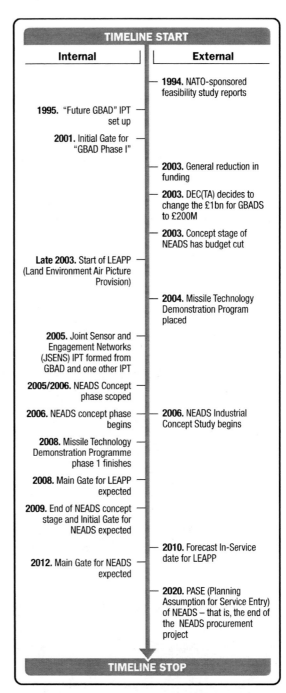

Figure 6-5.   **Timeline for the NEADS project**

The Impacts of the Governance Framework

In considering the impact of the MoD/DE&S governance framework on the project, there are two notable aspects of the NEADS project.

- The organization takes the appropriate interest in NEADS, bearing in mind that they are part of an IPT in which the other projects are nearer to gates. For governance of projects purposes, it is projects that are the unit of interest, as opposed to management of operating costs, in which IPTs are the unit managed.
- The project is in the early stages, where a project within DE&S perhaps finds it easier to minimize visibility and get the task done.

It was interesting to note that it was unclear who actually was the SRO for this project. The formation of the appropriate project board under through-life capability management will identify the right person for the role.

The NEADS project has so far been governed through a mixture of internal (to the IPT) and external assurance. Internal assurance is managed through a six weekly review by the team leader and IPT functional heads. This has reviewed project finance, top-level plans, and top risks and issues. The project team holds formal and informal team meetings to review the plan and address project risks. External assurance has been through DE&S's three monthly project review and assurance (PR&A) regime (AMS, 2007) using the standard project assurance template. PR&A assurance criteria are given in Project Review Dashboard Assurance Criteria Version 4.5 April 2007. Figure 5-8 gives a generic example of such a dashboard (not related to this project).

These quarterly reviews take place with the "Customer I" (representing MoD, requiring the capability), the Customer II (representing the user), the IPT team leader, the relevant 2* director within DE&S, and some of the other DE&S functions (e.g., Director General [DG] Finance, DG Commercial, DG Safety & Engineering, DG Joint Supply Chain, DG Human Resources, and those looking at interoperability). These look at customer agreements, and the PR&A criteria and key milestones. It is not clear how useful these reviews were, but clearly, they checked that appropriate processes were being followed.

NEADS has not undertaken any OGC Gateway Reviews so far (due to the origin of NEADS in the GBAD program and the fact that current work is under the existing GBAD approvals, no review such as a foundation review was undertaken). PR&A was checking processes, but the team appeared to feel that a review of the type of an OGC Gateway 0 or Gateway 1 would be useful as it would provide an independent review of the program. (As described in Section 5.5, the assurance regime is currently under review within the DE&S, and a major change instigated this year is for the project to be reviewed by the DE&S Investment Board prior to submission to the IAB, and this will apply to NEADS in the run-up to the Initial Gate expected in 2009).

The authors asked the team about their feeling on the governance burden upon them. They appeared to feel that their experience with the customer in this project had always been good, and that governance had led to useful early work. But the perception was that the burden seemed to be increasing (despite the Defence Industrial Strategy's statement that "We will take action to create a consistent and clearly defined operating framework for how we conduct, govern and control our projects. This framework will….reduce the burden of compliance and governance ….").

They also noted that currently, independence of thought only really comes from the IAB, and that only really comes at the two gates. We interpret this as an indication that an exercise such as an OGC Gateway, with thought independent at least of the project, would soon be appropriate.

Our Analysis of this Case

The NEADS project is an example of a complex defense development and procurement project. The case illustrates in a convincing way why emphasis is needed on the concept stage of such projects, as while there may be a clear understanding of the requirement, the best way to fulfil this requirement in a cost-constrained environment is a highly complex and changing decision. It illustrates both complexity and shifting assumptions/guidance and gives a practical example of why a governance framework is important and that it has to consider the kind of effects illustrated here.

The case perhaps illustrates the need for structured governance processes in the long period up to the MoD Initial Gate. The MoD rightly considers the project life cycle as extended both through the life of the equipment but also very much earlier than in many domains. However, this example shows the long and winding path that can be traveled between the idea of the capability and even the beginnings of its realization. We assume that the thought process for this project started after the NATO study, sometime in 1995. However, the first Main Gate for just a small part of the capability will not be around until 2012. An Initial Gate for the actual present project (i.e., NEADS) has not yet been carried out. This does raise the question of how long or how far a project idea should be allowed to develop before there has to be a gate of some sort, or at least some sort of independent assessment.

It also illustrates the difference between a straightforward statement of "the" governance process, and the actuality in projects operating over a number of years within an environment of changing political and cost priorities. This can be positive and negative, as the ability to make opportunistic use of the resource to develop the missile shows.

There are also issues illustrated in the division of a program into projects. Dividing projects into smaller sections so that they change criticality category should be avoided, but this was not relevant in this case. However, there are issues about the governance of the overall program (between the three subprograms: LEAPP, missile, and the remainder of the NEADS system). It is not clear whether the reviews and indeed the gates for these subprograms will look at the overall governance of the overall program (remembering that the missile also relates to other sub-programs outside NEADS), and what the mechanism is for ensuring this.

6.4   THE NEW BUILDING FOR THE DEPARTMENT OF INFORMATICS AT THE UNIVERSITY OF OSLO (IFI2)

The IFI2 project includes the construction of a new building for teaching, research, and ICT operations at the Department of Informatics at the University of Oslo (UiO) (see Figure 6-6). The building's planned gross area is 28,250 square meters (rounded). The current base estimate of the building is of 1.040 million (NOK) (price level 2006). The current total budget is 1.080 million (NOK)/$180 million (US) (price level 2006).

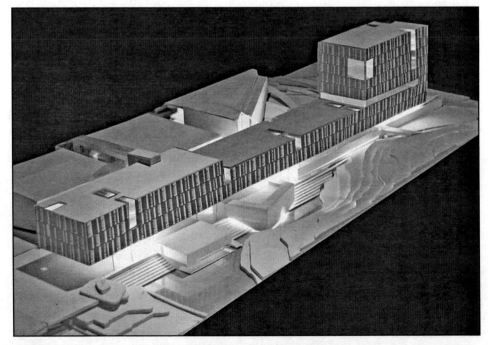

FIGURE 6-6.   MODEL OF THE IFI2 BUILDING. © Lund Hagem Arkitekter

The need for new facilities for the UiO Department of Informatics was explicitly mentioned in a government proposition to the Parliament in 1998 (Recommendation to Parliament No. 12 [1998–1999]). The driving forces seem to have been the UiO Department for Informatics' expressed needs for more space closely aligned with government strategies to strengthen research and higher education in ICT. The parliamentary committee urged to speed up the process to establish a new building, but no supplementary state funds were, at that time, allocated to the project. This urging was after a political debate, spanning almost the entire decade, about the state's role in the establishing of a national ICT cluster at Fornebu. This site is where the former international airport of Oslo was located and consisted of private businesses and also research and higher education in ICT. The outcome was that the state should not pursue a path where research and higher education would be integrated in the planned cluster, so after this ruling the University of Oslo looked around for other means to house the Department for Informatics and the growing number of students.

In 1999, the Research Council of Norway (NRC) ordered a design proposition for a new building which was presented in 2000. The initial plans included a 10,000 square meter extension of an existing building in Gaustadbekkdalen, Oslo, Norway, and financed by the NRC. The new facilities would then be rented by the University of Oslo. In 2001, however, Parliament decided to put the new building on the list of prioritized state building projects, which meant there would be 100% state funding of the new building (Recommendation to Parliament No. 12 [2001-2002]).

We have not found the exact explanation why the initial alternative was abandoned, but studies of written parliamentary sources (Oral Question Period [2000–2001]) suggests that there were discussions concerning the expected size of the annual rent for the new building. The Ministry of Education and Research estimated an annual rent of 40–50 million (NOK), some two times higher than the rent estimated by the NRC and Statsbygg. The Ministry, therefore, viewed the project to have such budgetary impact for the University of Oslo that it wanted Parliament to look into the matter in connection with the handling of the state budget. Parliament did this in 2001 on its own initiative, instructing the government to execute the IFI2-project as a state building project executed by Statsbygg (Recommendation to Parliament No. 12 [2001-2002]).[14] It is perhaps also worth noting that in Norway, the four major universities (of which the University of Oslo is the largest) are responsible for property management of their own buildings, unlike regional universities and most other state institutions which are managed by Statsbygg (The Directorate of Public Construction

---

14. It should be noted that, at this stage of the IFI2-project, Statsbygg acted as the government's advisor in property affairs.

and Property). This may have added some tension to this discussion, but we lack data to elaborate further on this issue. The unconventional outsourced model was replaced by a more traditional/standard state-funded project, planned and executed by Statsbygg.

The project thus went into a new planning phase, and in 2002 Statsbygg, the Directorate of Public Construction and Property, launched a design contest for the IFI2-building. The preproject was completed in February 2004, but the project remained on the list of state prioritized building projects, awaiting funding, until the parliamentary decision to finance and execute the project was made in May 2005.

The new building will, according to the current schedule, be completed in 2010.

Basic Organization of the Project

The Ministry of Education and Research is involved in the project as the sectoral ministry. This Ministry can be described as the project owner in traditional project management terms.

The University of Oslo represents the users and is very actively involved.

Responsible for the planning, organizing, and execution of the project is Statsbygg, the Directorate of Public Construction and Property. This directorate is a subordinate of the Ministry of Government Administration and Reform, which makes this ministry involved as well as administratively responsible.

Responsible representatives of the two ministries, the directorate, and the university make up the group having coordination meetings[15]—this model is traditional for coordination between multiple owners in Norwegian public projects.

Statsbygg acts on behalf of the Norwegian government as property manager and advisor in construction and property affairs. It is responsible for organizing, planning, and completing building projects within set framework for budgets, time limits, and quality.

Statsbygg is an administrative body, responsible to the Ministry of Government Administration and Reform and operates in accordance with standard business principles. However, achievements in accordance with government objectives take precedence over Statsbygg's own business interests.

Statsbygg, as an organization, consists of the head office in Oslo and five regional offices. Three hundred of the 670 employees are based at the head office, and 300 are engaged in the operation and maintenance of Statsbygg's properties.

---

15. Currently there is a discussion in Norway about the owner role and the future role of this coordination arena. Earlier this meeting made strategic decisions, but this may change in the near future; the current mandate seems somewhat unclear.

The Project Planning Process

The IFI2 project is planned and managed according to the procedures, routines, and decision processes adopted by Statsbygg. These procedures are established in correspondence with directives for economic control within the Norwegian government, and their project management methods are basically standard according to international practice. They have their own experience-based methods and tools for estimation and documentation of building projects. Statsbygg uses standard project management tools like Oracle and Artemis for economic control and Microsoft® Project for monitoring progress in this project.

In this report, the authors put the most emphasis on describing the quality of project planning at the stage when the external quality assurance assessment was initiated. The quality assurance assignment was executed between mid-July and mid-August 2004—a short time span compared to the normal procedure.

The basis for the assessment was: the project mandate (2003), project management plan (2004), and preproject documents (2004).

The external consultants' assessment of specific relevant areas was contract strategy.

Statsbygg had chosen parallel prime contracts as their contract strategy for this project (Statsbygg, 2004). This model was well-known and preferred for many years. This model keeps much of the coordination responsibility on the hands of the commissioning party (delegated to the project manager on behalf of the owner). The project management emphasized using a relatively small number of contracts to reduce the number of interfaces. They assumed that this would contribute to fewer coordination conflicts and thereby a reduced risk for Statsbygg as responsible for execution (commissioning party). They also expected that few contracts would prevent possible "pulverization" of responsibility for inadequate execution of activities.

The external QA consultants did a review of the chosen strategy based on several issues such as Statsbygg's project organization, design, and engineering, complexity of the building, risks, etc. The QA consultant stated in a report dated August 2004 (Metier Scandinavia AS, 2004) that Statsbygg has extensive experience with the chosen strategy, the complexity of the building is limited, and the involved risks are known and manageable. It was concluded that the chosen strategy was appropriate.

Project Management Plan

The quality assurance team stated that the project management plan (the steering document as it is often referred to in Norway) was adequate for the present project phase and would with some adjustments make an excellent basis for execution of the project. Furthermore, it was recommended what measures could be implemented before the execution phase of the project. The recommended measures were based on "best practice" industry standards from PMI and the Construction Industry Institute (CII) (Metier Scandinavia AS, 2004).

Uncertainty Analysis of Costs and Schedule

The cost estimate presented by the project organization before the quality assurance process had been subjected to an internal quality assurance by Statsbygg. The Statsbygg's method for cost estimation includes multiplying the separate cost items presented by the project engineering team with a factor that is supposed to account for expected cost additions up to the stage of tendering. This step is labeled completion 1. The next step, completion 2, involves multiplying the separate cost item with another factor which represents expected cost additions during execution. The size of the factors varies between 0% and 12% and is based on historical experience data from completed Statsbygg projects. The Statsbygg method is completed by an additional mark-up for uncertainty connected to the present project.

TABLE 6-1.   THE ESTIMATES (1–3) PRESENTED BY STATSBYGG PRIOR TO THE QA. (1) IS THE EXPECTED DETERMINISTIC COST ESTIMATE, (2) AND (3) REFER TO DIFFERENT LEVELS OF PROBABILITY FOR NOT OVERSPENDING FROM THE UNCERTAINTY ANALYSIS. NUMBERS IN NOK MILLION (FIXED PRICES [2006]).

		Evaluation Estimate 1	Sketch project Estimate 2	Pre-project Estimate 3	QA2 Estimate 4	Approved budget	Revised budget
(1)	Basis cost	896	903	871	875	n/a	n/a
(2)	P50	928	934	901	899	901	1040
(3)	P85	1015	989	979	975	979	1080

As shown in Table 6-1, there was no significant difference between the results of the QA consultant's independent analysis and Statsbygg's own analysis at the time. The project also shows a remarkable stable cost level over time in these early phases of development. It should be noted that the IFI2-project is rather atypical in the sense that it is the only project under Statsbygg (according to a complete review of the 11 Statsbygg projects from 2001 to 2007 subjected to external QA) where the external consultant recommends a budget on the exact same level. The IFI2 is actually a rather exceptional case. Possible explanations for this will be discussed in more detail below.

The Impacts of the Governance Framework; Quality Assurance QA2

The QA team verified the cost uncertainty through a multiple-stage analysis based on estimate 3 in Table 6-1. The QA team started by characterizing the Statsbygg method as "necessary and good" as long as the judgment involves "normalized" markups[16] (Metier Scandinavia AS, 2004, p. 36).

The point of departure of the external consultants' independent analysis was a qualitative analysis to identify and describe internal and external factors which may influence the basis cost. In the following quantitative analysis, the expected cost impact of the internal and external factors were estimated. The analysis was completed by an analysis to estimate effects of external events. The results are shown in the table above (estimate 4).

As can easily be verified from Metier Scandinavia AS, (2004), differences between the proposed estimate and the consultant's independent analysis are insignificant. The market situation in the building and construction industry was seen as the most important element (accounted for 41 % of the uncertainty) in the overall cost uncertainty profile, followed by project management/project planning and control (14%) and contractual issues (11%).

It is a specified part of the QA assignment to recommend a cost-reduction list (a list of elements which can be excluded if the project fails to meet the budget). The QA team did produce a list of possible savings, but concluded that the total size of the identified elements was rather small, i.e., the ability to introduce cost-reduction measures were at this stage estimated to be limited (Metier Scandinavia AS, 2004). The size of realistic cost-reduction measures were consequently not included in the budget recommended by the external consultants.

The review of the proposed schedule based on the CPM method did not result in other conclusions than those proposed by the project.

The QA team concluded that the project so far has demonstrated well-developed routines, high awareness, and knowledge concerning project uncertainty management (Metier Scandinavia AS, 2004).

The QA Team's Assessment of the Project

The QA consultant reported that the project seemed thoroughly prepared, in fact above average, at this stage. The project organization is described as competent and well prepared to undertake the task (Metier Scandinavia AS, 2004).

---

16. It should be noted that the method for cost estimation used by Statsbygg has been challenged. In a subsequent QA assignment, done by one of the other prequalified consultancy firms, final report dated September 2005, the QA team suggests that Statsbygg's method introduces bias in the result of the cost analysis, allegedly because the same uncertainty factors are included several times by Statsbygg's use of completion factors.

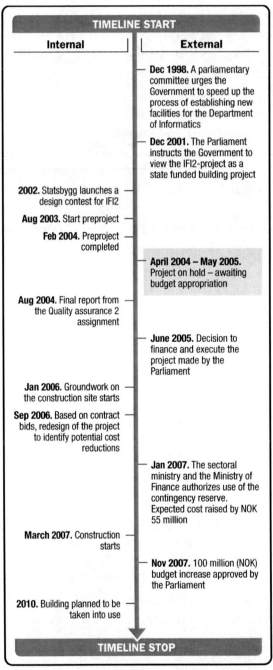

Figure 6-7. **TIMELINE FOR THE IFI2 PROJECT**

In June 2005, the Parliament decided to finance and execute the project. Budget: 979 million (NOK). Base estimate: 901 million (NOK) (see Table 6-1) (Proposition to Parliament No. 65 [2004–2005]) (see Figure 6-7).

Current status and important events in the detailed engineering and execution phase:

During the following detailed engineering phase and the review of tenders, it was discovered that market prices were substantially higher than anticipated. In January 2007, the expected cost was raised by 55 million (NOK)/$9.2 million (US). This needed to be done after the bids had been put in September 2006.

Contract bids were, supposedly due to construction market pressure, significantly higher than anticipated. The project organization approached, after heavy redesign of the project to reduce costs (without reducing size or functionality), the Ministry of Education and Research with a request for more resources. The matter was brought to the Ministry of Finance and use of the contingency reserve was authorized.

The construction of the new building commenced in March 2007, and shortly thereafter, a Statsbygg/project team cost uncertainty analysis, based on offers on the remaining construction work, showed that the existing budget was too low. The deviation allegedly stemmed from price increases in the construction market (Proposition to Parliament No. 90 [2006–2007]).

Statsbygg is authorized to adjust the budget and base estimate by a factor determined by the so-called SBED index, a joint index for price level adjustment in Statsbygg's projects, calculated by Statistics Norway.[17] The Ministry underlined in its proposal to Parliament, (Proposition to Parliament No. 90 [2006–2007]), that the index did not capture the actual price increase in the construction market. The difference between actual and compensated price changes amounted in the IFI2 project to 100 million (NOK)/$16.7 million (US).

A change in the upper financial level should, according to procedures established in connection with the quality assurance scheme, be decided by the Parliament. In November 2007, the Parliament endorsed a 100 million (NOK) budget change. New budget: 1.080 million (NOK)/$80 million (US). New base estimate: 1 040 million (NOK) (see Table 6-1).

Impacts of the Framework

The project manager, at the time when QA took place, viewed the external QA as a process to verify whether the project planning and control at all stages is most satisfactory or not. Efforts were thus put into the process of documenting how the key areas economy, schedule, and quality were followed up. It was further stated that his impression was that the QA team was highly skilled in these types of projects. The dialogue between the project team and the QA team was described as excellent.

The interviewee of the QA team underlined that their general approach was that the "expertise is present in the project," and saw their role as facilitators to get facts on the table. They also saw Statsbygg as a professional developer and saw the project documentation as a reflection of this. He also underlined that the process and impacts of the QA must be judged from the scope of the assignment.

No distinct preparations, other than those normal for a project of this size, were done by the project team prior to the external QA. Adjusting the approach in this project as a response to an upcoming QA was seen as an inadequate strategy. The project manager and the project team focused on utilizing the existing procedures and planning and control systems in Statsbygg.

The project had prepared and repeated a complete cost analysis according to Statsbygg's procedures three times before QA2 took place. A great deal of effort was put into documenting the proposed cost. The project manager at that time worked with

---

17. A central body responsible for collecting, analyzing, and disseminating official statistics, organized under the Ministry of Finance.

cost estimation techniques in Statsbygg and was also involved in the cost estimation process in the new Opera House project.[18] He also had highly relevant experience from another recently completed 39,000 square meter university building project. This could of course be one factor explaining why the external review of cost did not raise any specific issues.

According to the project manager, the QA team did not conduct an independent cost analysis from scratch. There were only small differences between the budget proposed by Statsbygg and the budget recommended by the external consultant, but the results were discussed thoroughly. This is supported by statements made by an interviewee from the QA team. The uncertainty analysis of costs made by the QA team cannot be described as independent in the sense that it relied upon Statsbygg's estimated basis cost. He also noted that a completely independent uncertainty analysis of costs would not be possible to establish within the scope of the QA assignment. The interviewee also pointed to the cost estimating skills of the project manager and the fact that up-to-date experience data from the project manager's prior assignment in Statsbygg were available.

There were otherwise no particular areas where heavy discussions took place. On a more general level, it was noted that the QA consultants advocated a stronger focus on a theoretical approach, to some extent to an exaggerated level, as described by an interviewee from the project team. The project manager expressed he has learned a great deal on a general level about the management of large projects through the process.

Our Analysis of this Case

The selection of cases presented in this report span across different traditional categories such as project type, size, and complexity. Some would describe this project as "a walk in the park" compared to the complex technologies and contracts involved in the defense projects described in this report, and in many instances impossible to analyze under a joint framework. Seen from an overall perspective, however, there are many similarities in the way these projects are planned and managed. First of all we observe that generally the same approaches are used, the same methods and principles, and it should be noted that the quality assurance assignment has the same aim and content, even if a multibillion defense project or a, at least in monetary terms, smaller and supposedly uncomplicated building project is dealt with.

The early stages of development shows that issues concerning the execution model and funding sparked some discussion, but there seems to have been no disagreement of the basic need for the project.

---

18. The planning and construction of a new 3.3 billion (NOK)/$0.55 billion (US) Opera House in Bjørvika, Oslo.

It is evident that the budget of the project has been raised, first by authorization to use the contingency reserve and later by a regular budget increase, and it was raised mainly due to price increase in the construction market. The cost focus is prevalent in the QA2 analysis. The uncertainty analyses of cost are supposed to factor in uncertainty associated with the market. In this project, the market situation was even placed on top of the list of identified uncertainty elements. Should the successfulness of the QA be judged from the ability to predict accurately costs or just from the ability to identify this as the most important risk?

The project has not been completed, so the accuracy of the cost estimate remains to be seen. Some would also argue, on a more basic level, that comparing budgets with actual outcomes would be a too simplistic approach if the aim is to measure the real cost efficiency. This is, of course, a highly relevant issue, but we do not elaborate further on it in this report. In this project, the cost analyses presented by the project organization and the QA team showed insignificant differences and the market uncertainty was identified as the major threat. The impact of the market is seen as the most difficult aspect to account for. It should also be noted that, in this project the QA assessment was completed in August 2004, in time for the government to present the project to the Parliament in connection with the national budget in October the same year, which is common for such projects. The project was, however, not prioritized in the national budget and the decision to finance and execute the project was done in May 2005 in connection with the revised national budget. As a result, the project came to market roughly a year later than what was assumed. One interviewee stated that the cost uncertainty analyses should be regarded as "fresh produce" and that the impact of the postponement of the decision to finance and execute the project on the further cost development should not be underestimated. A project cost estimate cannot be regarded as valid and relevant without continuous updates. This should have been acknowledged by the decision makers as it is one of the most important prerequisites for the external analyst's review of costs. The project faced a totally different market situation when the decision to finance and execute the project was made, and the uncertainty analysis had not been updated.

There is little doubt that the control focus is prevalent in the QA2 assignment. The main argument is that there should be a review of cost, schedule, and other key areas before the decision to finance and execute large public projects is taken. It is observed that the subordinate agency generally does not oppose this, but their assessment of QA and its output in this project is that it is redundant and cost consuming. In this case, the QA did not lead to budget changes or other direct changes to the decision basis. This is perhaps the reason for one of the interviewees from the project to suggest that: "The QA is done more to relieve the Ministry of Finance than to help Statsbygg."

There seems to be a great deal of consensus on how the process itself should be described. Interviewees from the project organization and the QA team described the exchange of information as excellent and the interaction between the involved parties as very good.

On the question of output of the process, we observe that the project organization expects a bit more than a "scratch in the surface" of project documents. The QA2 cost focus is described as important by interviewees from the project organization, but the control of cost should also include an assessment of technical solutions and their cost effectiveness. This would require another focus in the analysis, from control of numbers to evaluation of technical solutions, and, thus, more technical skills from those responsible for conducting the analyses.

6.5 THE SKJOLD CLASS FAST PATROL BOAT (FPB) PROJECT OF THE NORWEGIAN DEFENSE

The Skjold class fast patrol boat (FPB) project (hereinafter the Skjold project) encompasses the construction of new Skjold class FPBs (see Figure 6-8). Weapon systems, personnel training and logistics, and support are also included. The pre-series vessel, P960 HNoMS Skjold, was completed in 1999, as a separate project terminated at the time of commission of the new ship. Immediately after the

FIGURE 6-8.   THE SKJOLD CLASS
(Photo: Umoe Mandal)

commission of the P960 HNoMS Skjold in 1999, preparations for a subsequent delivery of a series of ships were initiated. A planned ship technical upgrade and reconstruction of the P960 HNoMS Skjold is, however, also a part of the delivery of the series of new vessels.

In June 2001, the Norwegian Parliament made the principal decision that six Skjold class vessels (five new vessels plus the P960 HNoMS Skjold) should be phased-in as a part of the operational structure of the Royal Norwegian Navy (Recommendation to Parliament No. 342 [2000–2001]). In October 2003, the final decision to build and finance the vessels was made. The budget was as follows: (upper financial limit) 4.675 million (NOK)/ $779 million (US) (price level 2003) (Proposition to Parliament No. 82 [2002–2003], Recommendation No. 11 [2003–2004]). The contract was signed in November 2003 with Skjold

Prime Consortium (SPC), an umbrella organization for the companies responsible for the design and production of the vessels. The series of ships are currently being constructed at the Umoe shipyard in Mandal, Norway. The weapon system will be delivered by the French Armaris and the Norwegian Kongsberg Defence and Aerospace. The Norwegian Defence Logistics Organisation (NDLO) is responsible for the execution of the Skjold project. The main tasks of the NDLO is to deliver logistics according to military needs, including procurement, investment, support, supply, and maintenance of all weapon systems and military materiel in times of peace, crisis, and war (The Ministry of Defence, 2007; Proposition to Parliament No. 42 [2003–2004]).

The Skjold project is planned to be terminated (delivery completed) in 2009. Ships and planned delivery (planned to enter service):

- P961 HNoMS Storm: April 2008,
- P962 HNoMS Skudd: August 2008,
- P963 HNoMS Steil: December 2008,
- P964 HNoMS Glimt: April 2009,
- P965 HNoMS Gnist: June 2009, and
- P960 HNoMS Skjold*: September 2009.

*Upgraded version of the ship delivered in 1999.

From an overall perspective, the Skjold project is currently on budget and schedule. It should be noted that none of the vessels have been delivered to the end user, but the construction phase goes on as planned.

The project is an example of a complex defense procurement project. It is complex in many dimensions: the decision-making process, the technology, and the contract.

The Decision-Making Process
The basic need for the project was not an issue in the QA assessment, and could thus be characterized as irrelevant in terms of an analysis of the impact of the QA at the time.[19] There was, however, a discussion on the political level before the principal decision about whether the project should be prioritized or not, which calls for a short description of the main characteristics of the political process. We believe an overview is needed to understand the shaping of the project.

---

19. QA1 was introduced later, making this a main point of quality assurance in the Norwegian governance framework.

FACTS OF THE SKJOLD CLASS VESSELS. Source: http://www.mandal.umoe.no

---

Air Cushion Catamaran Fast Attack Craft

Umoe Mandal and its Partners Armaris and Kongsberg Defence & Aerospace received a contract for the delivery of 6 Skjold class Fast Attack Crafts, including a complete weapon suit in November 2003. The vessels are primarily designed for antiinvasion, fast attack operations and patrolling purposes. The vessel are planned to be delivered in the period 2008 to 2009.

This is the first vessel where it has been possible to integrate Radar Absorbing Materials into the load carrying structures itself. Specific attention has also been made to the design and development of special doors and hatches in support of the low signature concept. Two trainable missile launchers have been developed and integrated in the aft part of the vessels.

This state of the art design is based on the Air Cushion Catamaran principles. Water-jets and 2 x 4000 kW plus 2x2000 kW gas turbines in mother /daughter COGAG configurations provide propulsion. Diesel engines provide power for the two lift fans and the electric power production.

The Fast Attack Crafts will be armed with 8 new Kongsberg developed Naval Strike Missiles (NSM). A 76 mm Oto Melara gun with stealth shield will be installed on the fore deck along with a chaff/decoy system. The weapon system will be characterised by high flexibility and a close integration with the different sub elements. This is essential due to a limited crew. Only 7 operators are dedicated for all warfare tasks and 2 operators for navigation of the ship. A limited number of the crew will have support tasks inflicting on the tactical operation of the ship.

The Weapon System consists of:

- Above water sensors system, including 3D surveillance radar, Fire Control radar, Electro Optical Sensor and ESM
- Above water weapons system, including NSM, 76 mm MPG, Mistral (man pad)
- Communication system, including Link 11 and Link 16
- Combat management system, including 6 work stations
- Navigation system, including a fully integrated "joy stick" operated bridge system

The Platform system has the following main features:

- Length 47 m
- Beam 13.5 m
- Displacement 270 t
- Speed at SS3 45 knots
- Speed at SS0 60 knots
- Draft on cushion 1 m
- Range 500 nautical miles
- Crew 20+

The principal decision to establish the Skjold class FPBs as a part of the Norwegian Navy was resolved in a broad political compromise. In 2001, the recommendation from the Ministry of Defence was *not* to pursue the Skjold project further (Proposition to Parliament No. 45 [2000–2001]). The Chief of Defence, in the recent Defence Study 2000, concluded that the investment and operating costs of the proposed fleet of FPBs should not be prioritized, considering other investments[20] and current liabilities of the Norwegian Defence. An appeal by the Chief of Defence to the Ministry of Defence that the decision should be postponed until the handling of the long-term plan for the armed forces coming up the following year, did not make any difference. In October 2003, the political compromise from the principal decision was sustained and the Parliament authorized the start-up of the project (Recommendation No. 11 [2003–2004]). The contract with the supplier followed shortly thereafter.

The political majority in favor of the project saw the fleet of FPBs as a strengthening of the capacity to national sovereignty enforcement, territorial security, and civil operations support in the Norwegian maritime zones (Recommendation No. 11 [2003–2004]). There is, however, little doubt that also regional politics played a major role in the political decision process. There was a desire among politicians on the local and the central level to secure employment in the troubled (at that time) shipyard industry. Repurchase contracts for the Norwegian defense industry worth 1 billion (NOK)/ £90 million were also established as a direct result of the Skjold project.

It was stated previously that an assessment of the basic need for the project was not part of the QA assignment. From a narrow project-oriented perspective, the principal discussion on the political level could be seen as irrelevant as long as the decision to build and finance has been made, and the project has a clear assignment. Seen in a wider perspective, the output of the top-level political and military debate determines the ultimate fate of the project, so the continually recurring discussion on the Norwegian Defence's need for new FPBs requires an updated description.

In the Defence Study 2007 published in November 2007, the Chief of Defence proposes termination of the Skjold project before completion (see the text-box). Upon presenting the study, which represents the comprehensive and professional military advice for the Minister of Defence and the Government in the area of Defence, the Chief of Defence underlined that three successive defense studies have advised against the acquisition of the new FPBs. The purchase was, according to the Chief of Defence, pushed through by parliamentary politicians in 2003 and has later not been accompanied by budgets adequate for acquisition and operation of the new FPB fleet. The defense study was backed by a parliamentary appointed defense policy committee, who reached the same conclusion on this issue (Norwegian Official Reports [NOU] 2007, p. 15).

---

20. It should be noted that the Norwegian Parliament in May 2000 decided upon the largest Norwegian defense investment ever; a 21 billion (NOK)/$3.5 billion (US) program consisting of the delivery of five new multipurpose frigates to the Royal Norwegian Navy. The delivery schedule calls for one new frigate each year from the second quarter of 2006.

The Defence Study 2007 on the FBP Skjold class (p. 21):

The FBP weapon Skjold class is developed primarily to operate near the coast in an anti-invasion role by being able to sink large surface vessels using long-range sea-target missiles. Combat force against surface vehicles can however be delivered by the new frigates too with sea-target missiles (Naval Strike Missile, NSM) and by submarines with torpedoes. Today's fighter planes have a moderate ability to combat such vessels, whereas the new fighters* will have good ability to combat surface targets. The recommended structure's capacity to combat surface vessels is considered to be good. FBP Skjold does not supply any significant new capacity which is not already included in the recommended structure. Based on a consideration of this capacity against other structural elements, the operational need and the economic limits, the recommendation is not to continue the FPB Skjold class.

Translated into English by the authors
*At this point the authors of this report make the remark that buying these new fighters is not yet approved by Parliament.

It should be noted that the proposals from both the chief of defence and the defence policy committee serve as input to the parliament's handling of the long-term plan for the armed forces in early 2008. Therefore, it remains to be seen whether the project will be terminated before completion or not. The outcome of the decision is truly a difficult political issue.

THE MAST OF THE SKJOLD CLASS VESSELS
(Photo; Umoe Mandal)

The Technology

A central characteristic of defense procurement projects in general is high technological complexity. The complexity can be described in many dimensions. First of all the system or platform itself can be complex and demand development of new technology, thus introducing a great number of uncertainties. The need for integration of a system with other systems is correspondingly high, and there seems to be a shift of paradigm in the defense sector, especially with respect to information processing systems. The FPB vessel is in itself a platform for integrated command, surveillance, and weapon systems.

In this case, the project involves development and construction of a new class of catamaran design vessels built in composite material. There is no need to go into the technical details other than pointing to the fact that the Skjold class vessels with their jet propulsion system will be among the world's fastest warships. It is constructed in composite material to reduce weight and designed to maintain stealth capabilities. See additional details in fact-box above.

The Contract

The defense market can be described as asymmetrical when compared to free, open civilian markets. The assymmetry in the defense market is typically characterized by the situation that a customer, typically a nation's armed forces, frequently faces a single or a few dominating suppliers or contractors qualified to deliver defense systems. The technical information is not equally distributed at both sides of this relationship. The systems are, as noted previously, often highly complex, and there is a high demand for integration with other systems. A single procurement will typically also involve long-term contracts covering aspects of operation, maintenance, and support of the system. The case described here is no exception in this matter.

The NDLO, responsible for execution of the project, chose the strategy to start negotiations with a prime contractor candidate, equal to the small group of contractors who performed the engineering work and physical production of the pre-series vessel. Therefore, in practice there are no other alternative contractors to build the series of vessels. Although the customer in this case can be said to face a classical monopoly situation and no competitive bidding took place, it should be noted that it is also viewed as an advantage that the competence and experiences gained by the contractors from the pre-series vessel can be pursued in the series production. This was part of the chosen strategy. There is, however, no doubt that the sole supplier situation was regarded as an important matter in the quality assurance assessment of the project.

The contract can be described as a fixed-price contract subject to adjustment for price and currency changes. The project organization initially wanted the small group of contractors to bear the complete system responsibility including the responsibility for integration of all systems and components in accordance with functional requirements, i.e., act as one supplier, a prime contractor, with joint and several liabilities for the delivery. The contract negotiations showed that it was not possible to reach an agreement on this issue. No clauses on complete system responsibility or joint and several liabilities were achieved. Instead, a "guarantee of completeness" was introduced in the contract. It is supposed to secure that the work shares of the three contractors, the Umoe Mandal shipyard, KDA, and Armaris, equal the total work scope of the contract. The division of work is, however, seen as a clear risk because this could easily lead to a narrow focus on the separate works shares instead of on the total work scope.

The Project Planning Process

The Skjold project is planned and managed according to the procedures, routines and decision processes described in the Norwegian defense's project management handbook at the time, the so-called Prinsix (Prinsix, 1999). Prinsix corresponds with the principles and methods described in *PMBOK® Guide*. The definition from the Prinsix project management system is as follows (translated by the authors):

"Through PRINSIX the Defence has described principles and methods used in most projects, in accordance with the most common principles and methods used in Norwegian industry, but also the international project standard Project Management Body of Knowledge (PMBOK® Guide)."

(Prinsix, 2008)

We have not been able to obtain the original documents documenting the use of Prinsix procedures, methods, and tools.

Steering documents, the most important planning and decision documents, in defense projects are as described in Prinsix[21] as follows:

- The Goal Document contains a description of operative, functional, and financial goals. (In this project, this document was dated 1993 including plans to upgrade the old Hauk class and introducing the new Skjold class.)
- Functional requirements for the project are being settled in a formal Functional Requirement Document. The link between the desired effect and expected costs should also be described. (This document for the Skjold class was dated 1996.)
- The Overall Project Document describes the totality of the system or solution and serves as an integrated principal plan for the realization of goals and functional requirements. It describes consequences and uncertainties attached to the planning and management of the project. It is the most influential document with respect to budgetary appropriation. (In this case, this document was a preliminary version with a planned finish date February 2002 (see also Figure 6-9).)

There was no project control basis established for the execution phase at the time of the initial QA2 (March 2002). Consequently, no information on details about cost estimation or time schedules, work breakdown structures, etc., appeared in these documents.

The Impact of the Governance Framework

The Skjold project was subjected to quality assurance 2 (QA2) in October 2001 (final report March 2002, Terramar, [2002]). QA2 supplementary analyses (regarding contractual issues and updated uncertainty analyses of costs), prior to the final decision to finance and execute the project, were performed from May to June 2003 (Terramar, 2003).

---

21. Prinsix, originally from 1996, is expanded and upgraded gradually. A new generation was turned into a complete framework for acquisition about 2004–2005. The definitions and names of documents have later changed accordingly.

QA2 October 2001 – March 2002:

At the time of the initial QA2, the negotiations between NDLO and the supplier were not completed. The QA2 was based on earlier (detailed) option contracts and the first-target-prize (FTP) from the supplier. The QA consultants made their first cost assessment on this basis.

After the first meeting between the QA consultants and the Skjold project organization on 31 October 2001, focus was put on the review of the project's steering documentation—identified by the external consultant as consisting of the *goal document*, the *functional requirement document*, and the *overall project document*.

The main conclusions of this first QA2 report (TerraMar, 2002, p. 3) was as follows (translated into English by the authors):

The project seems to be well prepared and competent to execute an acquisition of this size. Especially the experience from the contracts of Skjold pre-series and Hauk is valuable

Figure 6-9.   **TIMELINE FOR THE SKJOLD PROJECT**

for this contract. The project is mainly satisfactorily defined and limited.

The management documentation produced according to Prinsix appears thoroughly worked through, but [the QA consultant] recommends the following changes and supplements: Effect goals for the project and requirements for control in the execution phase (especially supplier follow-up, change control, and project organization and management).

The contract strategy, based on a single system contract, seems reasonable and well argued and is mainly based on the experience from the pre-series contract and Hauk. [The QA consultant] points out the following for special clarification: the supplier's system responsibility and other unsolved judicial terms in the contract with the "prime contractor."

Important success factors/pitfalls to succeed with the preparation and execution of the project are connected to 'prime contractor' and the system contract, integration of weapon-systems, and continuity and competence in the project organization.

In the final report (TerraMar, 2003, p. 5), the earlier analysis and report were summed up as follows (translated to English by the authors):

There would normally be presented a budget/cost estimation schema from the project as a basis for the uncertainty analysis. Because of the special situation with only one supplier and because a binding offer was not planned until June 2002, the 2002 analysis was developed on a different basis.

1. The project had earlier detailed option contracts with the supplier consortium
2. The project received 08.02.02 a "First-Target-Prize" (FTP) from the supplier consortium, characterized by the supplier as a "price not to exceed." The total sum was 3.600 million (NOK).
3. FTP had to be revised on a few points:
    *   Some systems which did not comply with key requirements had to be updated. This gave a cost increase of 157 million (NOK).
    *   Some guarantees from the supplier had to be included/expanded.
    *   The total effect of these changes gave a revised FTP of 3.800 million (NOK).
4. By quantifying some single elements (estimation uncertainty) in the uncertainty analysis, the earlier option prizes were assumed to form a lower/optimistic limit, whereas the prizes in FTP represented an upper/pessimistic limit.

A large share of the total uncertainty for the project was connected to the process of reaching a final contract. [The QA consultant] recommended in this analysis a total cost limit of 4.200 million (NOK) included the project's own costs, equivalent to a probability level of 90%.

The point of departure for the external risk assessment in the Skjold project was a specific offer from the supplier. Normally, the basis would be some estimated price

---

22. This means 90% probability of the cost limit not being exceeded, according to the cost uncertainty analysis. The general level of probability accepted was later decided to be 85%—as shown in supplementary analysis.

based on experience, so in this respect this project is a case not representative for normal QA practice.

In addition, based on the experiences from the pre-series vessel, there was a great deal of highly relevant experience data to build upon. The Skjold project organization did a risk assessment early in 2002 based on the "first target price" from the prime contractor candidate. The external risk assessment was heavily based on the internal risk assessment although some new risk elements were identified, the analysis was systematized in another manner (division of before and after contract), and a dynamic correlation model was introduced. As shown, expected cost rose from NOK 3.600 million to NOK 3.800 million (5.5%) during this process, and the recommended cost limit was NOK 4.200 million/ $700 million (US) (probability level 90%[22]).

Supplementary Analyses May–June 2003:

The negotiations with the supplier took more time than anticipated and did not conclude until June 2003. The updated external risk assessment report is based on the result of the negotiation. Due to the ongoing negotiations, the QA consultant was not allowed to discuss with the supplier in this period.

The cost analysis does not include costs prior to 2002 (sunk costs) and covers only the investment, not life cycle costs. The cost of the other defense organizations' cost is not included. These cost estimate assumptions are representative for the practice at the time. This has later changed into taking all costs and life cycle into consideration. Systematic risk due to currency rates and inflation was not included (agreed by the Ministry of Defence). Some adjustments concerning interface with other projects removed 30 million (NOK) from this project. The new expected cost was 4.150 million (NOK) and recommended cost limit 4.330 million (NOK)/$722 million (US) (probability level 85%). The expected cost rose another 9.2%. Recommended cost limit rose by 3%.

Interviews indicate that the parties involved in the quality assurance process generally agree on the main characteristics of the process itself. It was characterized by fair and open discussion, they cooperated well, and the exchange of information was excellent.

Members of the project organization stated in interviews that 90% of the mindset in the quality assurance report was based on their judgment. The project organization held nothing against the QA2, it was stated in interviews that they actually welcomed it. An objective assessment by third-party experts in project management was seen as a learning opportunity. The report itself is in no way judged to be inadequate or faulty. Still, the project organization's learning from it is characterized as limited. The reason for this was stated to be the particular characteristics of the project in terms of complex technology and contract. The project organization had experience from the

Skjold pre-series (the vessel was delivered in 1999) and an upgrade of the existing FPB fleet, the Hauk class, was completed some years ahead.

The QA assessment was conducted at a point in time when the contractor had placed a "price not to exceed" and consisted mainly of uncertainty analysis of costs and risk assessment based on input from the project organization. The initial cost estimate from the project organization, based on background experience from the pre-series vessel completed in 1999 and the Hauk class upgrade, was raised as a response to the result of the uncertainty analysis of costs. The project schedule was not revised as a result of the QA. There was a good deal of attention concerning the costs of the project, but the increased budget sparked little discussion. It was merely stated as a fact, and the budget recommended from the external consultants was subsequently used as a basis for the decision to finance the project.

Our Analysis of this Case

The Skjold project is an example of a complex defense procurement project. The complexity of the decision-making process, the technology and the contractual arrangements proved to be a challenge for the quality assurance in this case. The process described here seems to uncover some weaknesses in the quality assurance at the time.

Indications:

- An assessment of the basic need of the project is not part of the QA assignment. The value perspective was not present in the QA analysis. This was not introduced until later as a part of QA1 in 2005.

- One main focus was performing a cost uncertainty analysis. No independent cost estimation was done. The analysis was based only on the projects own cost data, primarily the first-target-prize from the supplier consortium. This is not a critique against the specific QA2 analysis, it was according to the prevailing interpretation of the framework contract at the time. There was no better alternative since this basis represented the best available knowledge of the project and alternative sources of relevant cost data were not available.

- Another main focus was controlling the documents describing the project. The QA2 report (March 2002) comments that the documents produced at the time was of good quality up to the stage of entering a contract, but was not prepared to enter the execution phase (p. 9). There was no project control plan established at the time of the QA2, therefore this was not controlled (p. 10). This raises the question why the project was allowed to go on, given there was a clear requirement to produce a basis for management of the next phase. This was, however, in an early phase of the Norwegian QA scheme and the practical procedures were not yet established as a common basis (this happened later in 2003). There was some reluctance to be very strict until these common procedures were established and the governance framework had found its form and place.

* Due to ongoing negotiations, the QA consultants were not allowed to access the supplier's personnel. This cut them off from a prime source of information and questions the timing of the QA2 itself.

These weaknesses were due to the governance framework being less than mature and the special situation analyzing a unique highly complex project. No relevant reference data were available for independent cost estimation. The quality assurance documented here is representative for the time it was executed.

Turning to the question of the impact of the quality assurance, some of the weaknesses identified imply the amount of cost and time information available in this case is limited. The QA2 reports are the only source available with specific cost and time data. It is limited to the uncertainty analysis and does not show details of the underlying cost estimate or time plans.

The impact of the QA2 was less significant in this case. No significant changes to cost estimates or schedule were made. The project organization did not develop or produce any new or specially adapted documents. However, the process of QA2 gave reassurance that the project was well planned. As shown previously, the project goes on according to plan, so there is no sign to indicate this was not a good conclusion.

The potential impact was not produced in this case—from reasons mentioned above. Going through the descriptions of the decision-making process and the quality assurance reports is like reading about two totally different projects (see the timeline illustration). The most important aspect illustrated by this case is that no matter how clear professional advice is for or against the project and whatever the result of extensive use of rational methods, the final decision is a political one. This decision is not altered by QA2 or any other control instrument. It is anchored deep is the democratic system and the governance framework, and that is how it should be.

6.6 ANALYSIS OF THE CASES AND FRAMEWORK PRACTICES

The cases presented here illustrate several interesting issues concerning the impact of governance measures and the practical performance of reviews. In hindsight, some of the initial research questions (see Section 1.3) cannot be answered due to lack of relevant information in these cases. This lack of information is unfortunate, but does not imply the case study was unsuccessful. Even though the cases were not optimal, they tell many interesting stories about governance of projects.

In this chapter, we summarize the cases and analyze them to identify the major learnings from each case and in the end a comparison and analysis of the cases and their links to the framework used in each case.

Home Office Case

This case illustrates flexible use of a complex governance framework. The project does not seem to be a technical challenge, but the complicated contract arrangement in this private financing initiative was a challenge to handle within the common framework. The PFI also leaves detailed cost and time data not available for us.

Important findings by the Parliamentary Accounts Committee not highlighted by the Gateway Review illustrates the importance of the "status" of the framework and what organizational level the review challenges (the Parliamentary Accounts Committee having a stronger position and challenged a higher level of the organization). This finding points towards other important governance measures than the ones installed in this framework.

Although a political decision, this case documents substantial influence by rational decision making. The building was delivered in 2005 on time and without rise in the service charge. It is considered a success story in the project perspective. Hopefully it is also considered a success in the strategic perspective, as indicated by the home secretary upon moving into the new building.

NEADS Case

An extremely complex development and procurement project illustrating the need for governance in early phases of a system development, the case gives a practical example of why a governance framework is important. It also illustrates how assumptions change over time and the degree of change to be faced during the initiation and development of a complex defense system. The initiation phase has gone on for many years, but the project has still not reached a formal Initial Gate. This raises a question about how long the development should be allowed to continue before an external review is called for.

This project illustrates why governance in early phases are vital to the success of a project. It is still in a very early phase and there is no way of telling whether this will be a success or not in the strategic or project perspective.

IFI2 Case

In this building project, the contract arrangements had special focus, following a discussion about the fundamental concept of the project. Early direct interventions by the Ministry of Education and Research that were based on the cost being too high sparked this focus. Although a political decision, this case documents substantial influence by rational decision making. Although there are no indications of large impact of the quality assurance to the project, there was obviously reassurance in having an independent review. The role of the QA in legitimizing projects should not be underestimated.

One interesting aspect of this case is the question raised about how to evaluate the performance of a review. Is it the ability to identify the risks that are important—or the ability to predict the exact cost? In this case, history after QA2 tells us the identified market risk has had considerable consequence on the cost and the project had to have an increased budget for completion. Does this imply a successful performance of QA2 or not? No clear criteria for this are established.

Skjold Case

The Skjold case illustrates in a very convincing way why it was of great importance for the Norwegian government to expand the QA scheme to include QA1—introducing the value focus in the early stages of development. The strategic perspective, obviously critical from the decision-making point of view, is not present in the QA2 quality assurance reports. However, in this case a QA1 performed at the time of the reported QA2 would probably not have made any difference. The lack of support by the defense organization was well known to the decision makers. A QA1 intervention would have to be performed much earlier to be effective. Ultimately, this political decision was obviously about something totally different—securing jobs at the shipyard in Mandal. The shipbuilding industry in Norway faced severe problems at the time because it had too little work. For the politicians this seems to have been more important than whether this was the right project. Similar situations may occur no matter what expert opinion is presented and independent of which governance framework is installed in a democracy.

The performance of QA2 had weaknesses due to the situation and time it was performed. It was in an early phase where the rules of practice within the framework were not yet established. Thus, the impact of quality assurance in this case was not big. Reassurance was the benefit gained from it.

TABLE 6-2.   COMPARISON OF CASES IN THIS REPORT BASED ON PROJECT SOURCES

Project name	Home Office	NEADS	IFI2	Skjold
Sector	Civil	Defense	Civil	Defense
Object type	Building	Weapon system	Building	Vessel
Project type	PFI	Development & Commissioning	Design & Build	Commissioning
Decision making	Political/ Rational	Political	Political/ Rational	Political
Framework	UK OGC	UK MoD	Norway	Norway
Number of gateways passed (which)	2 (OGC3 & OGC4)	1 (MoD1 – only a part of the project)	1 (QA2)	1 (QA2)
Nature of gateway	Friendly	Critical	Critical	Friendly
Mode of operating the framework	Flexible	Flexible	Flexible/Rigid	Flexible
Framework strictly followed	No	No	No	No
Deviations	Several Gateway 3's and 4's. Early Gateway 4.	Initial Gate for a previous sub-project only	Time & scope restrictions. Accept having no Project Management Plan.	No independent cost estimate.
Key findings in review	Confirming business case and contract	Not relevant	Confirming cost, risk and contract	Confirming cost and risk
Overall project performance according to review	Excellent	One part of project passed gate	Good	Good
Influence of review on project	No	No	No	No
Actual performance as of today	Completed on time and budget	In accordance with current plan	In accordance with plan, expanded budget	In accordance with plan

The project perspective shows a well-defined and well-prepared project. The execution of the project also seems to be progressing excellently. Still, judged by the current signals from the defense study and chief of defence, this project is doomed to be a failure. The failure was publicly proclaimed by high-level officials long before the project was started.

Comparison and Cross-Analysis of Cases

In Table 6-2, facts about the four cases extracted from project sources (interviews and document studies) are compared.

Table 6-2 seems to question both the choice of cases for this study and the performance of the reviews/operation of the frameworks. Compared to the descriptions in Chapter 5, there are quite a few deviations. Performance of friendly gateways in the early period of the Norwegian framework is an example. All cases show deviations from the rules defined by the framework at the time of the review. The UK frameworks were described in Chapter 5 as rigid but were executed flexibly in practical life. All deviations are explained by situational causes, and as such these deviations are noted as positive. The frameworks are flexible and can be adapted to a wide range of situations. There is also individual considerations taken as to how strong the scrutiny should be, depending on the established (or lack of such) practice.

It is more worrisome that none of the cases show any sign of the framework actually having any direct effect on the project activities. This lack of effect may be a consequence of the fact that all cases are judged very positive at the time of review and are still at current performing well. It might be a result of how these cases were chosen. Another aspect is the general experience that the projects always have to spend a substantial amount of time and resources to prepare for review. Obviously it influences the project activities one way or another. The sources probably have limited their answers to the time of the review and after. Anyway, the conclusions drawn on this very limited sample cannot be very strong. We will only use them as illustrations, not proof.[23]

To find out more, we looked at a selection of interesting aspects including both good performances and potential for improving the projects based on the material in these cases. Table 6-3 summarizes some observations.

The cases did not allow access to as many details about the cost and time elements of the management systems as expected up front in this study. However, following our initial hypothesis, while we were not able to look at the particular aspects of time and cost estimation as much as expected, we were able to concentrate at a higher level on

---

23. Flyvbjerg (2006) (p 224): "Look carefully at individual cases—not in the hope of proving anything, but rather in the hope of learning something!"

TABLE 6-3.　　SELECTED ASPECTS FROM THE CASES

Project name	Home Office	NEADS	IFI2	Skjold
Governance in early phases	Ad hoc	Governance unclear	Direct intervention	Ad hoc.
Organizational issues	Unclear scope (staff numbers) at an early stage.	Industry integration. IPT is monitored, not the project.	Statsbygg procedures not adapted to current case	Need for more clear definition of roles in defense organization.
Portfolio/program links identified	Yes – dependency on property development	Yes – a program in itself.	Only concerning cost/execution	Only concerning cost/execution
Contract issues	Gateway 4 all judicial. See also complexity.	Partnership contract	Contract strategy – market adaptation	Single supplier
Dealing with powerful suppliers	Service contract	Partnership	Direct control	Delivery contract
Cost & time issues	Scrutiny and validation	Project-independent cost estimate by PFG	Statsbygg methodology flawed?	No alternative source of data
Cost & time system elements identified	No	No	No	No
Complexity issues	Risk sharing major contract issue	Complexity inhibiting the governance process.	Independent uncertainty analysis	Independent uncertainty analysis
Project managers experience from the process	Information not available	Would have increased emphasis on external view.	Learned a lot about executing large projects	An opportunity to learn

the overall effect of the governance framework upon the projects and take a broad look at a number of important aspects.

Table 6-3 contains a mix of information from the project documents, interviews, and review reports. No attempt has been done to represent the complete situation in any of the cases. Only a few highlights are chosen to look for patterns.

The table can be read horizontally—it gives an impression of the multitude of issues that can arise from reviews of different cases, exemplified by the row showing how each project deals with powerful suppliers. The means chosen span from partnership to direct control, with service contract and delivery contract as intermediate solutions. None of the cases has chosen similar solutions to this issue. Another example is the governance in the early phases, before any review was performed (remember development of these cases started before the frameworks investigated in this report was established). The NEADS case appears to show insufficient governance at this early stage and the Home Office and Skjold shows what we choose to call an "ad hoc" governance, whereas IFI2 was subject to direct intervention by its owner. An example of observations confirming previous description (Chapter 5) is the portfolio/program links identified in reviews. QA2 in the Norwegian framework only looks for interfaces to other projects as long as it affects the cost or execution of the project analyzed. The UK frameworks, on the other hand, have an explicit focus on program level.

Table 6-3 can also be read vertically. Doing so, a story about each case emerges. Look, for example, at the NEADS case: The project is overly complex and was seemingly inhibited by an apparent lack of governance in the earliest stages. The partnership strategy is chosen to handle the situation, supplemented by support by project independent cost estimation expertise. The project manager expresses a wish for more emphasis on external scrutiny, a third party view. The story of IFI2 is also interesting. In this case many of the observations indicate a strong owner and customer position. Direct intervention and direct control is typical for the governance and management strategy in this case. The review questions the degree of adaptation to the current situation and questions the method used for cost estimation. This method has no direct consequence for the project but the project manager expresses he has learned a lot on a general level about the management of large projects. The Home Office case shows a development emerging from a complex situation with many dependencies and ad hoc governance. The framework was established and supported with gateways giving scrutiny and validation, leading up to a well-defined contract and a successful project execution. Reading the Skjold story is more difficult from Table 6-3 due to its fragmented observations documented in the table. The challenges are obvious: unclear roles and a complex project (as we have seen earlier) overruled by a decision-making process with a different objective. The opportunity to learn was evident to the project manager, but this was not the case where this potential was to be released.

Table 6-3 shows that there is considerable potential for learning for the individuals and organizations involved, which is illustrated in documents and stated by the interviewees.

Table 6-4 shows our interpretation of these cases and their links to the governance frameworks.

All cases document the importance of governance frameworks, each in its own way. The Home Office illustrates the need to support governance officials with professional advice in matters in which they may be naive or have insufficient competence.

TABLE 6-4.   CASES AND GOVERNANCE FRAMEWORKS

Project name	Home Office	NEADS	IFI2	Skjold
Documents the importance of governance frameworks	Yes	Yes	Yes	Yes
Achieved value* of review	Reassurance	Review for part of project: legitimization	Reassurance and legitimization	Reassurance and legitimization
Potential improvements to framework at the time of review	Need for early reviews (G0 - 1 - 2)	Need for early reviews (before MoD1)	Need for early review (QA1)	Need for early review (QA1)
Information issues	Info dependent on who asks and who is asked	No information issues known (everything kept within MoD)	All information was available	Supplier not available for reviewers.
Potential improvements to current frameworks	Wider perspective of reviews	Stronger governance in early phases	Need to update analysis regularly Stronger technical focus	No
Other governance mechanisms identified	NAO/ Parliamentary Accounts Committee	No	No	No

*Value for whom: Reassurance for owner, legitimization for the project organization.

NEADS illustrates the need for stronger governance in early stages of complex system developments. IFI2 documents the need of the owner and government in general to have validation of the basis for decisions and legitimating of the use of resources. Skjold, despite the notion that no added information at the point of intervention shown here would have made any difference, shows why it is so important to raise the big questions early in the process and to put the development on the right track before the snowball rolls by its own weight or is driven by other forces.

The potential improvements at the time of the review (compared to the framework as it was defined at the time) are well-known. Most of these are already established in later versions of the frameworks. This indicates the developments of these governance frameworks are targeted and efficient. The identified problems faced in some of the reviews (information issues) are just pointed out as general reminders of points to be learned. For the Home Office, the review did not identify the planning optimism later discovered by PAC by asking other, more highly ranked people in the system, also indicating the position of the one who asks is important. This is addressed in current transitions of the OGC framework. The IFI2 case shows all information was available. The review identified the decisive risk to be market. Still the project was started 1 year later (delayed) without renewing the analysis, resulting in the need for an expanded budget due to market changes later. The QA report gave a clear message for those able to read it. In the Skjold case, a major source of information was not available to the reviewers due to contract negotiations. This questions the timing of the review. Good timing is important.

Even today's frameworks have potential for improvement based on these cases: Stronger governance in the very early stages of development, the wider perspective of reviews, the need for a stronger technical focus in reviews and the need to renew the analysis regularly to make them stay relevant to the decision is noted here.

The Home Office case in addition reminds us that there are other governance mechanisms available (and highly relevant) than the ones defined to be part of the frameworks discussed here.

7 Theoretical Analysis

Earlier in this report, we described the political and economic setting in the two countries (the United Kingdom and Norway) and found many similarities. The frameworks too have many things in common. Most notably, they were all established for a similar purpose. They are all instruments to improve the performance of public projects, hence the weight put on the instrumental-structural perspective. Further, the frameworks have the same aims, high-level political anchoring and were introduced more or less at the same time. Still we found many differences in structure and form, as well as in the way the initiative is organized and supported within government. The previous section concluded that the three different frameworks could be described like this: The UK OGC framework is the complex, complete, and detailed approach. The UK MoD framework is a high-level approach combined with linking to concrete guidelines. The Norwegian framework represents a simplistic approach. The embedded governance principles are however quite similar.

In this chapter, we will use some of the theories described earlier to analyze the Norwegian and UK frameworks. Section 2.5 gives literature references and brief descriptions of the theories. The purpose is to find potential theoretical explanations for how these frameworks are designed and work. These findings will add to the practical observations in interviews, documents, and case studies, completing the study of the frameworks in this report. More weight is put on the practical side to this report. Consequently, this theoretical analysis will be limited in detail.

In this chapter, we will point out indications of how and how much the different theoretical models can explain the differences between the frameworks and how much emphasis seems to be put on each of the chosen theories. The issues relevant to the design and implementation of governance frameworks are very complex and multi-faceted. Consequently, we need to use several perspectives and different theoretical models in our analysis. We have chosen to use the following perspectives and theories:

1. The instrumental-structural perspective is dominant; it is close to the actual perspective of the government entity establishing it. We look at:

    a.   Principal-agent theory
    b.   Public choice theory
    c.   Bureau-shaping perspective
    d.   Theory of economic analysis/analysis of political behavior
    e.   Theory of transaction cost economics

2. The cultural-institutional perspective: the importance of organizational values and traditions.

3. The environmental perspective is used to explain important sides of the way these frameworks are working within its context.

4. The network perspective is the last main direction used in this analysis, looking at the different actors as interconnected in a network.

In this section, we will try to point to possible and probable explanations for these differences and their consequences. We do so by assessing each framework against the characteristics of each theory and put marks on how strong indications there are to the implied use of this specific theory in the framework. When putting marks using adjectives like "strong" and "weak" in the following analysis, we do not imply good or bad, but put more or less emphasis on the specific characteristic solutions typical for each theoretical perspective. We use "moderate" for the position between the extremes, and "mixed" when the indications go both ways. The reference for comparison is the theory and the three frameworks studied in this report. No standard is used for reference.

The purpose of the theoretical analysis is not to point out which framework is the best. They are all adapted to its specific environment. Any attempt to create a new governance framework should start with defining and describing the context or environment in which it is supposed to work. Having knowledge about theoretical and practical models (framework elements and principles), the design of an adequate framework is achievable.

The development of governance frameworks may be seen as a consequence of two successive lines of development: first came the new public management (NPM) movement in the 1980s with the philosophy to "let the managers manage"—increasing their freedom to act within their area of responsibility and to measure their effort by results. This freedom, based on a contract to deliver results, has to be balanced by control efforts. This contradictory tendency has over time grown more visible and is the core of the next wave of development in public governance: the post-NPM reforms. The post-NPM reforms include measures to reinstate a more central political and administrative control. Compared to the NPM reforms the post-NPM reforms are generally more about cultural than structural features (Christensen, 2007, p. 37). We will look for indications of these trends in our further analysis, although we do not analyze the broader trends comprised in these reforms. These trends in governance show the shifting focus in governance, and are a consequence of the evolving science and art of organization theory. For a deeper analysis of the Norwegian framework in the light of NPM and post-NPM, see Christensen (2007). For an excellent analysis of the general organizational perspectives in the public sector, see Christensen et al. (2007). Here we choose to go down into each theory within the chosen broader perspectives.

7.1   INSTRUMENTAL-STRUCTURAL PERSPECTIVE

In Section 2.5, this perspective is described as a close relative to the rational perspective. The main difference is accepting the bounded rationality and putting emphasis on structure and the logic of consequence. This perspective focuses on the reasons behind problems of control. This means that if we are able to understand the causes of our decision making and control problems, we are also able to design structures and instruments to support better decision making and control. This rationale is vital to all planning and governance.

The basic assumptions in this perspective frequently criticized and discussed by scholars are the assumptions of rationality, causality, and control. We accept these assumptions are not perfect, and will use other perspectives to identify and analyze problems related to them. Our basic assumption is still that the actors are dominantly rational, able to see beyond their own personal goals and thus willing to act according to a decision-making framework (which includes both motivational and control elements). The decision-making problems in question are highly complex and information is limited and basically uncertain. The administrative system is put in place to support the political decision making and implement political decisions, not to make the decisions. It follows that it is not possible or desirable to standardize decisions or reduce them to mathematical formulae. Instead, the solution is to clarify and improve the decision-making process and structure with its roles, regulations, and professional standards.

There are many stakeholders, since the major public investment projects have important influence on people's physical surroundings, business opportunities, and quality of life. Since taxpayer's money pay for much of it, we are all legitimate interested parties. Therefore, a large number of perspectives and theories are needed to cover the important issues in this discussion.

The system we analyze is the administrative hierarchical organization that defines, plans, and executes major public projects. The organizational entities and individuals in this system are agents on different levels to the state. The most important actors are mentioned briefly:

- The political decision makers elected to make decisions on behalf of the voters, ultimately the whole population of the country.
- The owner, representing the society at large—ultimately its citizens. This role is multifaceted and would be worth studying on its own. Financing, commissioning, operating, and administering are among the important functions.
- The professional decision makers, responsible civil servants in government agencies. Representing the state as responsible for supporting and implementing decisions, responsible for execution of political decision, customer for private sector suppliers, in some cases also an institutional representative for the users.
- The public planners, increasingly recognized as project planners. Traditionally civil servants in a government agency, lately more frequently outsourced to private sector.
- The program and project managers. Usually civil servants in government agencies, but this role is also frequently outsourced (in which case the interface—the division of responsibility—between this role and the corresponding responsible decision maker in the agency has to be adjusted).
- The project evaluators—the independent reviewers performing controls and assessments as part of the governance framework. These can be external (private sector) or internal (civil servants).

According to **principal-agent theory**, each of these parties has its own own position with specific motivations, competence, and availability to information, etc. The agents are supposed to act according to the instructions, enforcing powers transferred by the principal. The principal-agent theory is important in understanding the function of governance frameworks. Obviously, there are major concerns about information asymmetry and opportunistic behavior when agents are performing their specialized tasks on behalf of the principal (the owner, in this case the responsible ministry).

This quickly leads to the control aspects of the frameworks. The three different frameworks are genuinely different in this aspect.

- The Norwegian framework is clearly a control measure throughout. The position of scrutiny is very strong and the gateways are "critical," meaning you have to meet professional standards to pass them and be able to continue.

* The UK MoD framework includes control measures. The position of scrutiny is less independent than in the Norwegian framework, the assessment is more on the hands of the decision makers themselves (which in this case is more professional) and the gateways are critical.

* The UK OGC framework is not a control measure, but it uses independent professionals to tease out hidden facts. The gateways are "friendly" meaning the assessment and good advice of the expert may be followed or not, the professional standards may be met or not, but the projects are still continuing.

In a control perspective, the Norwegian framework seems the strongest initiative and UK OGC the weakest. This perspective is balanced by a starting position where the tradition for government to make and enforce detailed regulations and procedures seems stronger in the United Kingdom than in Norway. The UK MoD framework is also strong in control perspective—there are multiple layers of multiple-discipline scrutiny before the decision basis reaches the decision makers (the IAB). Independence in scrutiny is not strong, but this is compensated by lifting more of the assessment to the (professional) decision makers. This is possible when limited to one sector like the defense. It is hard to imagine it working as a general framework covering many sectors like the Norwegian and UK OGC. This would create need for a large administrative decision making body or a multiprofessional "super-body." The capacity of single decision makers to process information would otherwise go to overflow. Initiatives to strengthen both the UK frameworks have been taken in 2007–2008 (MoD introducing the DE&S Investment Board and OGC by turning mandatory).

We have not documented the consequences of these differences in detail. One possible consequence might be that the frameworks with stronger control measures may give stronger signals to improve professionalism and may be better able to stop projects not meeting standards. A deeper study going into more cases and looking for trends over time would be needed to establish proof of such development.

The principal-agent relationship is also regulated by incentives. It is not easy to find indications of incentives being used actively in the Norwegian and UK MoD frameworks. There are incentives in the consequence of working in accordance to the framework (rapid progress, having a favorable decision, getting the project financed, etc.), but we see these as consequences of the control aspect. There is no strong indication that the frameworks have given the projects and their promoters economic or other incentives by adapting well to the framework. There have been claims in Norway that including contingency in project approvals gives the projects more money to spend, but this is highly questionable and not in any way intended as an incentive. The UK OGC framework does not include economic incentives either, but strongly promotes the idea of professionalizing staff through education and certification. This is the strongest position in this perspective. Similar ideas are indicated in the UK MoD framework, but they are not as strongly promoted and give a "moderate" position.

Another use of the principal-agent theory is to look at the information aspect. The basic assumption in this theory is that information is not equally distributed among principals and agents (there is asymmetry). In these systems, there are many organizational layers implying distance and there could be very different information for instance at cabinet level compared to within a single project. This influences the decision making and control. Gathering more information is one of the powerful ways of reducing information asymmetry and opportunistic behavior.

In this aspect, the three frameworks choose different ways, but information is obviously important in all frameworks. In Norway, this difference is obvious through the use of all external (private sector) consultant companies with a wide array of experiences from different sectors and project types, performing independent cost estimates and reference checks on cost estimates, and by distributing the QA reports to all levels of government. In the UK MoD case, it is done by gathering all available information, including the scrutiny report, in the decision-making dossier available for the decision makers. Distribution of the dossier is limited. MoD also puts high demands on the decision makers' competence. In the UK OGC framework, experienced external experts are used to perform scrutiny of the projects. This obviously increases the access to information about best practices and the projects. It is not widely distributed though, so we assume there are other strategies to handle this, like other incentives (PPP/PFI) and introduction of "reference class forecasting," which are not a part of this study. In this perspective, the Norwegian and UK MoD framework is the strongest, whereas the UK OGC framework has weaker emphasis on this perspective. It has a moderate level.

The **public choice theory** may be used to explain why there are different choices of assessors in different frameworks. This theory is based on skepticism to the professional bureaucrats and public planners because of strong belief in individual incentives. It gives an argument to choose external assessors to balance out the influence of these internal professionals. The arguments used by our interviewees are access to competence and capacity (Norway), additional third party views (UK), but also independence (both countries). The cost of external assessments is also mentioned as an element in this choice. Even if skepticism towards planners' incentives is not used as an argument by our interviewees, it may be an element in the explanation, at least theoretically. The emphasis on this theory seems strong in the Norwegian framework, moderate in the UK OGC framework, and weak in the UK MoD framework.

Using public choice arguments, one could say that the framework should not be used as an argument to build up a large public entity to maintain and support the framework: It is better to keep it out of the hands of the professional bureaucrats. One could argue in this perspective that planning and assessment should be completely outsourced. Taking it even further, some would stretch the argument to say there should not be such a framework at all—let people choose freely how to reach decisions. As mentioned earlier, we do not follow this line of argument. A structured decision-making process and control framework are important. However, let us look at the organization supporting the frameworks.

The degree of "lean" choices in organizing may give indications to the emphasis on this theory. In Norway, where there is no such support organization, the arguments used are the lack of resources available to build up such an organization, and that there is no need as long as the framework is kept simple enough. The situation in the UK OGC is very different: OGC has built up a large support organization (with a wide specter of tasks—following up the governance framework is only one of these—the organization is currently being reduced to a leaner ideal. See Section 5.5). An important part of the total capacity is external consultants offering competence and capacity to be used in supporting the major public projects. In the UK MoD case, the framework is institutionalized and internal resources do most of the job. Consequently, in this perspective, the Norwegian framework is the strongest, UK OGC is moderate, and the UK MoD framework has weak characteristics in this perspective.

This theory underlines the need for increased transparency and insight into vested interests and competition bias, clearer definition in contracts of rights, and duties for public and private actors. These elements are clearly a part of the development in both countries. Increasing transparency is explicitly stated to be a main aspect of the Norwegian framework. All documents from assessments, not containing commercial or defense secrets, are available to the public and all decision makers. There are strict instructions not to include sensitive information when not necessary. The emphasis on transparency is obviously strong. The UK MoD framework is in a position where limitations to transparency can be viewed as natural, given the sensitive nature of defense business. As the Norwegian framework shows, this does not necessarily mean no transparency is possible. At least all decision makers have full insight into the basis (although a limited group of people), which is a moderate position. The UK OGC framework is in a weaker position because review reports are not distributed. They are often just available to the OGC and the SRO and project management. The wide distribution of guidelines and methods within the OGC are not perceived in this study as a question of transparency, and also outside the framework.

Another way of using the public choice theory in explaining the development of these frameworks is focusing on the contracts. Contracts are used internally within the public organization (in the NPM meaning of the word; objective- and results-oriented contracts regulating government bodies in relatively free positions within the state) and externally (commercial) towards suppliers. In both countries, the initiative is clearly connected to strengthening acquisition functions. This puts the commercial contracts in focus. This is evident in all the frameworks, although more clearly explicit in the United Kingdom than in Norway. The UK MoD framework is presented under the name Acquisition Operating Framework and the UK OGC framework is operated by the Office of Government Commerce. In Norway, contract strategy is one of several focus areas within the control tasks. The focus is clearly on the project itself, not on the acquisition function of the public entities. By elevating these issues to the coordination arena on a department level as done in Norway, the same effect is possible in the longer time perspective. In this perspective, the UK frameworks are strong and the Norwegian one is weak.

The **bureau-shaping perspective** suggests that bureaucrats and their institutions benefit from the decisions made and the structures designed. One outcome might be, for example, that autonomous public units, like regulatory agencies or public entities, begin to set their own standards rather than those formulated by the legislature and the political executive. This theory is highly relevant to the development of governance frameworks. An important part of the assessments done in these frameworks is checking that the documents of the project are still in keeping with the purpose, objectives and priorities expressed by the decision makers, and according to professional standards defined by government or other professional entities (examples are industry standards, professional associations and universities). This goes for all the frameworks discussed here. The choice of external assessors increases the importance of this theory since one would expect this to introduce a benchmark of the professional standards within and outside the agencies.

As shown previously, all frameworks include this, although in slightly different ways and levels of attention. This is explicitly an important part of the Norwegian framework, although the official reason for establishing it is not low professional standards. The external consultants are explicitly called to make their own estimates in which they do a reference check (benchmark) towards other standards; the same is true when it comes to professional standards for use of methods and tools, etc. It gives a strong characteristic in this perspective. The UK OGC framework has got the same explicit call for high professional standards and uses external experts with knowledge of the best practices in other projects etc. However, the advice given is not shared with a wide range of users, only the program/project management and OGC, which reduces the strength in this perspective to moderate. UK MoD is a difficult case to assess in this perspective. In the defense sector it is always difficult to find benchmarks to hold up against, so this aspect is expected to be weak. On best practices and use of methods, etc., it is expected to be strong. This gives a mixed status.

Plurality in methods and approaches is one potential consequence in this theory. When every organization develops its own identity and standards, they have a tendency to end up with their own language, definitions, and descriptions of methods and tools. They may be based on international and generally acknowledged standards, but still it is important to each organization to develop their own variant. The Norwegian framework acknowledges this and does not tell how the tasks of the project management should be done, only what to achieve. It sets the professional standard but does not limit plurality in approaches. It is a strong position in this perspective (in the sense defined at the start of the chapter, indicating a strong emphasis on the specific characteristic solutions typical for this theoretical perspective). The UK frameworks both prescribe certain methods and tools as part of the attached toolboxes to the framework. The purpose is to help projects and responsible personnel perform better. This good intention limits plurality, which in this perspective is a weak position. The MoD framework is legitimate in doing so since it works only within one organization. This position is mixed.

The **theory of economic analysis/analysis of political behavior** suggests (among other things) that special interests and interest groups are trying to pursue their own interests into the decision-making processes and influence the outcome. It is a well-known fact in political decision making that this happens (Altshuler & Luberoff, 2003). It would be more important to us if we analyzed the political decision making. There is a difference between the political decision-making process and the administrative process: Influence may not be as easy in the professional system due to the fact that planners and administrative decision makers do have their professional standards. On the other hand, looking at professional parties interested in specific outcomes, it is expected they will also use any opportunity to try to influence the design of the plans in the first place before it reaches the decision makers. Some of them will have competence, position, and power to do so. Positioning in favor of one preferred solution over the other or in favor of exploiting a monopoly situation is realistic in some cases.

How well the planners and professional decision makers apply their professional standard is not a part of this study. However, this theory gives arguments to have governance frameworks in the first place, to make sure the decisions are not influenced too strongly or in a negative way.

If we look at the framework as a bulwark against unwanted or illegitimate influence, it is a question whether the framework clarifies the decision-making process and makes it clearer at what stage in the process a specific party has legitimate influence on the outcome. This is highly regulated by planning legislation in Norway and the United Kingdom for buildings and infrastructure. Specifically, the planning legislation designates the legitimate participants in the process and when they are able to interact with the planning and decision making processes. This does not apply to other projects, undoubtedly leaving a need for a clear and structured decision-making process to reject unwanted influence. The political process is not included here. The general public is mostly interested in the political process. Users and neighbors/directly influenced stakeholders are involved in the planning process at a local level and thus could be influenced by the framework. The introduction of QA1 raised this question in Norway and the conclusion was that nothing really changed (the right to influence according to planning legislation is still intact). Still, by introducing a framework that makes the roles and processes more clear and outspoken adds an external assessment of what is relevant and legitimate certainly adds to the bulwark against illegitimate influence to the planning process. The signals are mixed for all the frameworks in this study.

Using this perspective to look at the new position established by these frameworks, the evaluator role may be interesting: Obviously, a quality assurance consultant in the Norwegian governance framework or a review team leader in the UK OGC framework is in a position to influence the decision, not directly, but by influencing the basis for decision. It works either because the responsible project manager takes the good advice from the reviewer, or because the decision makers actually use the report in their decision making. The effect is more direct in Norway since the QA report is available for the decision makers. The assumption that review reports influence decisions are based on evidence that the reports are credible and has actually been influential (Magnussen & Olsson, 2006). In this perspective, it is a strong position. The effect on decisions is less obvious in the United Kingdom, but it is also strong in the MoD case, since reports are directly available for the decision makers in the dossier. In the UK OGC case, the position is weak since the report is not distributed, leaving only the effect of good advice on the plans.

Independence has been an important issue in discussions in Norway, and the Ministry of Finance has made it very clear that the QA consultants cannot have any commercial interest in the projects they assess before or after the quality assurance. Similar considerations are relevant for the review team leaders in UK OGC, but are not expressed as explicitly. The use of "intervention" as a measure for improving the projects shows a situation where this perspective is set aside in the UK OGC framework. In the UK MoD case, the assessors are mostly internal, excluding this discussion; on the other hand, the monopoly situation is expected to be quite usual, pointing towards a stronger emphasis on lack of independence. This is possibly one explanation for the design choice of combining a high-level approach with concrete guidelines for the acquisition functions. Since the assessors are internal, they can handle instructions that are more detailed and their own position is expected to be more in line with the organization. The strict regulations and guidelines combined with the critical gateways acts as a bulwark towards the monopoly supplier's power. In this perspective, the Norwegian framework seems to have strong characteristics, the UK MoD framework has weak characteristics, and the UK OGC has mixed characteristics.

Theory of transaction cost economics may explain some aspects of the frameworks.

The theory of transaction cost economics is an analytical tool mostly used where asset specificity plays the key role, as mentioned in Section 2.5. Asset specificity concerns to what degree the asset is specific to that particular contract (thus distort normal competition), so is clearly particularly appropriate for projects which develop unique one-off items. The theory is particularly appropriate to MoD, as the assets being developed are highly specific. The position of the OGC and the Norwegian frameworks are mixed as they both have to handle both low and high degree of asset specificity.

The transaction costs are shown to have an increasing importance compared to the production costs, and thus this aspect has an increasing focus (Encycogov, 2007). Transaction cost economics relies on competition to sort out the inefficient modes of organization. Looking at competition as an indication of strong weight on this theoretical perspective, we would say that OGC has the strong position here, whereas Norway has the weak position. This position is in accordance with the traditional modes of operation in the two countries. MoD seems to have a somewhat mixed position, between a market mode of operation and a defense market with clearly limited competition.

Organization theorists find this theory preoccupied with decreasing insecurity and costs in transactions between the parties involved. Most of the tasks in planning and execution of projects may be seen as either information transactions or transactions of other resources. Given its position as representative for the whole society, the Government is supposed to create the programs and policies (and thus the projects) that citizens want. It is not able to do this, however, without involvement of the people or their representatives. Herein lie the reasons why these transactions are necessary at all levels. Different measures can be put in place to increase or reduce the transaction costs involved when different parties try to influence decisions (Sager, 2006). The processes integrated in the frameworks are an important part of such a perspective. Inviting parties to involve and supply information reduces transaction costs, while defining a process that gathers alternative information, or control measures which make it more difficult to influence decisions increase them. The framework decides who can legitimately influence the decisions and who cannot. This is basic in all the studied frameworks. See also the paragraph on economic analysis/political behavior.

By introducing a more professional planning process and a more central decision making that is typical for the post-NPM reforms, the transaction costs naturally increase for all stakeholders. This is also one of the main arguments behind them; there is a will to centralize these functions after having experienced the fragmentation effect of earlier NPM reforms.

The tendency to centralize decisions increases the transaction costs for all parties with an interest in the outcome. They all have a longer way to go to influence the decision. This has (in this perspective) to be viewed as a cost to achieve better quality (more consistent decisions). The degree of centralization is used as a measure of position in this perspective. The Norwegian framework has a strong centralization effect in QA1 but introduces no change in QA2, which is centralized in the first place. This characteristic is strong. The UK MoD framework centralizes the relevant decisions to the investment appraisal board—also a strong position. The UK OGC is directed towards the projects performance and not towards the decision as such. In this perspective, this position is weak.

Note that the intended effect is not to shut out the users and public from these decisions, but to guide the involvement to the appropriate point in the development process. The increased clarity in the roles and decision-making process should help reduce the transaction costs in the appropriate places.

The Norwegian and the UK OGC frameworks are general frameworks applied to a wide array of different sectors. The UK MoD framework stands out as different because it works in a more restricted field limited to the defense sector. Alternative sources of information are normally scarce; the project involves technically complex solutions with few suppliers available. The traditional control measures and information gathering are weaker tools in this situation than in a functional market. This aspect is more hidden, but well known, also in the Norwegian framework when it comes to the defense sector. Instead of staking everything on control, MoD has chosen to go for strategies of closer cooperation (partnership, etc.), in order to reduce the transaction costs. This choice is a part of the values defined as a basis for the framework. There are strong arguments for similar developments within the Norwegian defense sector (Warberg, 2007). This aspect does not give the answer for the general frameworks. UK MoD is strong whereas UK OGC and the Norwegian framework are weak.

Using this theory to look at the expert role may be interesting as well. Two roles extracted from this theory may explain the roles of the experts and planners; the "broker" and the "steward" (Turner and Keegan 2001). Since the decision makers cannot have all relevant and correct information (limitations in knowledge), the experts and planners have to be the ones gathering and presenting the correct and relevant information for the decision makers. When acting as a judge of what information is relevant and correct, the expert is a broker. When supporting the decision makers with information supporting the desired development, the expert is a steward. Having a combination of primarily internal experts/planners and external consultants giving third party judgment will strengthen both these functions. The external view primarily strengthens the role as broker and controls this function. When used to obtain information otherwise not available in the internal environment, the steward role is strengthened. The internal planner/expert role is normally expected to be a stronger steward role than the outsourced one, but even the independent evaluator may be found in this role in given situations.

Again, the UK MoD framework is slightly different due to its more limited sector and more professional decision makers. The expert here is more steward than broker. The position towards this perspective is weak. The Norwegian framework and the UK OGC frameworks both build on the combination of internal experts/planners and external evaluators. This position is strong towards this perspective.

The theory of transaction costs can be used to explain a number of other, more detailed, effects. In this report, the theoretical perspective is less important than the practical observations. Therefore, we choose to stop here.

Some Additional Instrumental Perspectives Disconnected from Specific Theory

The previously mentioned theories are all versions of the economic-rational perspective. We believe the instrumental-structural perspective is the best perspective to describe the core of governance frameworks. One reason is explained as follows: "What is important for that selection is the formal structure, i.e. the position and tasks the individual actors have will pre-select most of the decision-making premises, in other words, one's structural position governs how one thinks and acts" (Christensen, 2007, p. 15). This awareness is what makes the choice of introducing or enhancing a governance framework an obvious one.

In this report, the limitations to rationality are accepted and furthermore we acknowledge the limitations to causality and control. Sometimes people act irrationally, and sometimes initiatives do not have the intended effect. Partly because we do not have the complete and correct understanding of the causality involved, because different parties value differently and other times because personal goals and ambitions obstruct the logic.

In this position, the importance of the processes and structures becomes clear, as shown above. The weaknesses in basic assumptions may be used to argue the need for a framework, the testing of assumptions, and the need to tease out the hidden facts. It also delivers arguments for enhanced control. The basis for this line of thinking is the "logic of consequence." This logic makes the basic concepts of control, incentives, and information work. All frameworks have this as a basic assumption and are thus strong in this perspective.

A different aspect of the instrumental perspective is the need for clear definition of roles and responsibilities (the clarity of the positions). In this perspective, the frameworks in Norway and the United Kingdom are different—more in expression than in reality. The UK frameworks are both very clear and explicit on all roles and responsibilities—a strong position. The Norwegian framework defines only the role of the QA consultant (assessor) and takes the other roles for granted. From the initiator's side, there is a great awareness about the roles and responsibility, but it is all implicit in the framework. In this perspective, this position is weak.

Objectives are one of the most common means in the instrumental perspective. Defining, formulating, and communicating objectives, following up with goal-oriented actions bringing the development closer to the preferred state expressed through the objectives is a basic idea. The objectives, often developed into more operational goals and targets, are an important instrument in all public planning and project execution. All the frameworks in this study put a great deal of emphasis on objectives. They all have strong indications of this.

The natural extension of the objectives-concept is measuring the development/movement towards the goals. This result-oriented approach is found more or less equally in all frameworks as well. Measuring performance is taking it even further towards an instrument of managing the process. When looking at performance, one should notice the difference between the two countries is the societal/judicial position: In Norway the state is the responsible entity. Only the state can be sued, not the individual. Bad performance has little consequence. In the United Kingdom, there is much more a culture of individual responsibility. With it also comes blame; "it is your fault," and the potential consequences for the individual and its organization become more severe.

In the United Kingdom, performance has consequences and performance measurement is a natural thing. In Norway, measurement of performance is not very common and there is great reluctance to publish any results of measurements (both in judicial and social perspectives). This may explain some differences between the frameworks as well: In the Norwegian one there is little emphasis on measurement (the only clear measurement initiative is in the hands of a harmless research program)—a weak position. In the UK frameworks, there is much emphasis on measurement—a strong position. The measurements are meant for improvement based on larger trends, not for identifying "scapegoats" or culprits.

This 'instrumental' analysis has to be supplemented by other perspectives for a more complete view, including perspectives critical to the basic assumptions of the instrumental-structural perspective. It is certainly questionable whether the assumption of rationality, causality, and control is a good one in each case. Examples illustrating flaws in these assumptions are not hard to find. Therefore, we choose to look at the governance frameworks in a few additional perspectives in the following sections.

7.2 THE CULTURAL-INSTITUTIONAL PERSPECTIVE

The reality of the different organizational structures and cultures in Norway and the United Kingdom is also a part of the explanation of differences between the governance frameworks. The frameworks obviously have to adapt to the already established structures of the organization (ministries, agencies, directorates, etc.) and to work together with established structures.

Frameworks have to adapt to the current structures as they have been shaped over time. The cultural-institutional perspective suggests public organizations develop gradually and are not possible to design and control. Informal norms and values are supposed to be more important for the thoughts and actions of public actors than formal norms, and they influence the development of formal structures. When people act inside public institutions, they act according to logic of appropriateness, not according to logic of consequence. We follow the logic of this theory up to a certain point. Norms and values are undoubtedly important (these are also influenced but it takes more time, and it is not always clear what are the effective sources of influence). Organizations are, however, designed and controlled (at least their processes and structures, which is the issue in this report).

Our interviewees made the point clear that people act in the logic of appropriateness, and that this is important for the effect of the frameworks. Our Norwegian interviewee called it the "principle of expectancy management." The function of the frameworks is to clarify better the roles and what are the appropriate actions and professional standards. When everyone knows what the appropriate thing to do is, it costs more to deviate. When people know what is expected of them, they tend to act accordingly (especially in combination with some instrumental influences like incentives and control). This theory then gives one of the explanations why the governance frameworks actually work. Based on the strength of arguments used, the Norwegian framework seems to have strong emphasis on this theory. The defense culture and the adaptation to a specific sector also put the UK MoD framework in a strong position. The UK OGC framework covers a wide range of sectors and cultures and consequently seems to put moderate emphasis on this perspective. However, with the UK tendency to a "blame culture" this will only be a nuance.

When are the logic of appropriateness and the logic of consequence in conflict? When the logic of appropriateness makes people act not in accordance with the framework (with its mandatory status—the framework will arguably define the formally right thing to do). The logic of appropriateness will naturally lead to diversity in approaches, whereas the logic of consequence could be seen as striving towards a position where there is one correct approach. We looked at this duality in the bureau-shaping perspective.

There is also a historical perspective in culture. Frameworks are more or less built on the result of previously developed processes, structures, and systems. These are developed over time and have a strong or weak position in the professional communities influenced by the framework. Here the frameworks analyzed are seemingly very different: The UK MoD framework is explicitly based on findings published back in the late 1960s and the developments that followed over time after that. The current framework is being installed as a result of consultant work defining a new and better structure for government. The UK OGC framework shares some of this history, of course, but it also has a more explicit history connected to procurement work over time (interestingly enough also from the defense sector) leading up to an "internal revolution" in 2000 based on existing "best practice" guidelines and systems. Both UK frameworks have strong positions in this perspective. In Norway, the explicit story of the framework is much shorter, starting with the Ministry of Finance questioning the performance of major investment projects in the late 1990s. Norway, being a small country and consequently a small administration, created a new concept and introduced it over a remarkably short period. This position is a weak position in this perspective.

The development story of the Norwegian framework is more like a "joint effort of all good forces" than a revolution. The responsible ministries, the users, and the QA consultants took part in the development. There has been a strong focus on developing and establishing the framework as such, more or less free from the weight of history. The Norwegian framework is stated to be a brand new concept, and actually, it is. There is no toolbox attached that is filled up with history. This does not totally exclude history to be a part of its basis. All the participants in the development (ministries, consultants, researchers) brought with them their experience and history to the table. The new thinking, however, was mainly on the hands (in the head) of the Ministry of Finance. All in all, the focus on the framework as such is very clear. This marks a strong position in this perspective. In the United Kingdom, the frameworks seem to be more designed by experts. The historical elements are included in the frameworks as a part of the framework elements and principles, and attached as part of toolboxes to the framework. In the MoD case, a consultancy company was important in finding its current form. In the OGC case, a prominent expert from the industry defined the basis from the beginning based on his experience. These frameworks are of course also open to feedback and adjustments from the practical use. The focus of the UK development seems more directed towards the toolbox side than the framework, especially in the OGC case. MoD seems to develop a framework with supporting tools. Looking at the clarity of the framework focus among the active parties developing and supporting it, the Norwegian framework seems to have the strong position together with the UK MoD, while the UK OGC has a weaker position.

The toolboxes and the framework have a strong connection. This is underlined in the UK OGC case by the active "branding" of the OGC name and the different parts of the framework and toolboxes as products in a commercial market. We believe there is not a strong awareness among the users about what is part of the framework and what is not. For example, many users know the PRINCE2 management system better and associate it more with the UK OGC framework than the actual framework, specifically the OGC Gateway™ Process. All in all the focus on the framework as such is weak among users. When looking at the users' awareness, we have found that the pattern is the same as the focus within the organization, with mixed indications on part of the UK OGC framework.

7.3   THE ENVIRONMENTAL PERSPECTIVE

The environmental perspective determines whether the system (organization, or in this case the framework) is dependent on its technical and institutional environment. It is focusing on how the environment influences the organization, and how the organization adapts to its environment. In this perspective, the technical environment is the structures discussed previously. The institutional environment above has more of the cultural and juridical perspectives in it. Much was already covered in the previous section.

There is an important difference between Nordic/Scandinavian social welfare tradition and the Anglo/American strong market orientation. These tendencies are clearly visible in the corporate governance in the two countries: The United Kingdom has a shareholder value model, whereas Norway has a communitarian model. As a result, the frameworks have more emphasis on the market in the United Kingdom and more towards the responsibility of the state in Norway. In the United Kingdom, there is a strong public administration tradition. There is a large influential civil service program. In Norway, on the other hand, the civil service has a weaker position and to a larger extent has to bargain its way through difficult decision-making processes where other interests (i.e., local government, private sector, and the public) are in strong positions. This position probably explains the large degree of flexibility built into the Norwegian framework, whereas the UK frameworks can be more decisive, and define the premises for the decision making. This is even more characteristic for the UK MoD framework which works within a single sector and a military, disciplinary culture. This position is strong with a large degree of adaptation to its environment. In this perspective, the Norwegian framework is in a weak position (not focusing on environmental adaptation but instead on flexibility to handle the multiplicity). The UK OGC position seems moderate in this perspective. It is not specifically adapted to any sector, but adapted to the wider UK business culture.

The performance culture perspective may partly explain the strong focus on control in Norway versus the use of advice in the UK OGC framework. In a culture allowing bad performance to have little consequence, strong control measures have to be put in place. In a culture with strong individual responsibility, everyone has to take the blame themselves; they choose whether or not they want to listen to the expert's advice. This is an indication of frameworks adapting to the characteristics of its established environment. All frameworks show strong indications of adaptation to its performance culture context.

Flexibility, the garbage can perspective, suggests that collective rationality and instrumentality is low. The decision-making process is ambiguous, shifting, and unpredictable (like the contents of a garbage can), and the decision-making situation is flexible and subject to change. This perspective, like the one before, explains why flexibility is important. This aspect points towards one of the strong positions of the Norwegian framework. The UK frameworks are described with less flexibility/more detailed instructions and are in a weaker position towards this perspective.

The garbage-can model suggests that in certain situations the solutions seem to seek problems instead of the opposite; the opposite being the instrumental ideal of developing a solution to each problem. We have not identified any specific indications of this happening, but from a theoretical point of view, any established tool may be put in this position. The Norwegian framework may be seen as having strong emphasis but it does not offer any solutions. It only tells the users what to achieve, not how to achieve it. Consequently, there cannot be any seeking of problems to use it for. The UK MoD framework does prescribe solutions, and it is in a legitimate position to do so, since it is established by the responsible owner of the sector it is used in. The indication is a mixed position. The UK OGC framework has a more risky approach in this theoretical perspective, since the toolboxes are actively marketed as general tools to an open market. This position has a weak emphasis on this theory.

7.4   THE NETWORK PERSPECTIVE

Using a network perspective, the relations between different actors within the framework processes comes into focus. It explains how and why the actors interact (see also transaction cost theory). Networks are naturally a preassumption for the development of the frameworks and a part of their environment. To understand this perspective, the different sizes and business structures of the two countries come in handy.

Norway is small, in population more than geographically. People tend to know each other within the different sectors and industries. Networks are tight and relatively stable. There are a limited number of actors to choose from when establishing or maintaining networks. As mentioned earlier, the tendency is that low performance has no consequence. The culture is communitarian pointing to each one's responsibility for supporting the society's interests. The United Kingdom, on the other hand, has a large population and an over complex company structure; the actors have to make their way into and perform well to keep their position in the networks. The market-orientation and performance culture in the United Kingdom underpins this situation.

The situation in Norway, with small, tight networks, gives stability, and professional standards travel fast and efficiently. However, it is not easy to eliminate unwanted elements. Contractual arrangements make it possible to exclude members not living up to the standard, but it takes a lot in practice.[24] Still, the position in this perspective is rather strong. The UK position is also strong, but for the opposite reason: networks are potentially large, and it is easy to exchange elements not working up to standard. The downside is the size and rapid changes making the professional standards harder to spread. The UK OGC compensates by offering lots of support.

Due to acquisitions and mergers, restructuring the different market segments the patterns of interaction changes.[25] This is most notably in the defense sector and it influences the UK MoD framework. The framework is explicitly based on establishing trust and close relations to the suppliers. To a large extent, the same could be said about the UK OGC framework. OGC also seems to put much emphasis on PPP/PFI/ Partnership models for project execution. In Norway, these strategies are not a central part of the government policy, although three pilot projects were being evaluated in 2007. Several large actors in the Norwegian building and construction sector argue that the PPP strategy offers little new. Due to the small, tight, and stable networks

---

24. The same EU regulations on tendering and non-discriminating competition are applied in both countries.

25. The same effects are also happening in Norway, but less notably because of the small scale. As in the UK, the effect is more evident in the defense sector.

in Norway, they argue they are operating in partnerships for all practical purposes. Some public entities embrace the partnering idea very strongly, but certainly not the Ministry of Finance. In this perspective, the Norwegian position is mixed, and the UK position is strong.

In a network perspective, the time horizon, legitimacy, and power determine which types of interaction processes occur in projects (Larsson & Wikström, 2007) and are appropriate. The parties' positions are clearly relevant. The state administration's position has already been mentioned as weaker in Norway than in the United Kingdom. This indicates differences also concerning the frameworks. In Scandinavian countries, the culture tends towards seeking solutions based on consensus, whereas in the United Kingdom, the solution may well be found as the civil service on its own decides how the problem should be solved. In Norway, the governance framework with its elements and principles, as well as demands for professional standards are discussed (negotiated) in coordination arenas where all-important stakeholders participate to find a solution with broad support. This indicates strong emphasis on the network perspective. In the United Kingdom, the solution is designed, decided, and introduced from the top. This solution marks a weak position in a network perspective.

7.5   CONCLUDING REMARKS ON THEORY

Going through documentation of the three governance frameworks and interviewing key people, we believe we have a quite good picture of how the frameworks are structured and designed, how they are enforced and how the support is working in a practical sense. The practical sides of the frameworks are documented in Chapters 5 and 6. This chapter fills the need for a closer look at the theoretical platform. It links back to Chapter 2. This study into the world of governance of projects is a new area of work and as such, there is not much literature to build on. We had to go "back to basics" and draw on the rich literature on organizations and governance to find a theoretical basis.

The theoretical findings are shown as a summary in Table 7.1. The marks "strong" means "puts much emphasis on" the theory in question, and "weak" means "puts little emphasis on," accordingly. There is a "moderate" position in between the two extremes, and a "mixed" position where the indications go both ways. It is not a characteristic of the quality of the framework or how well it is able to secure success in major public projects. These marks are not nuanced, and we refer to the previous text to have a more precise impression of the actual differences.

It is important to understand that this analysis only builds on comparison of the existing frameworks as they were mid-2007, compared to a selection of theoretical perspectives. We have tried to highlight their characteristics through different sets of theoretical glasses. The indications we find are only representing the end result of how the frameworks have been developed. It is not a documentation or speculation into how the actual thinking has been during the actual development process. We have no basis to form opinions on that.

On the contrary, we know the thinking was not primarily focused on these theories. The following is an example from Norway: We find indications, using the public choice theory, suggesting it could be argued there should not be a large public organization operating the framework. In Norway, there is no large public organization supporting the framework. This is an indication that this specific theory could have had strong emphasis in the development. Consequently, in Table 7-1 the Norwegian framework has the mark "strong" on lean organization. We do not suggest this is how the Norwegian government actually came to the conclusion not to have a large supporting organization. On the contrary, our interviewee gives a very different (practical) argument for this choice; it was because resources were not available and the simplicity of the framework made it redundant.

This chapter and Table 7-1 in particular offer theoretical support to design of governance frameworks. It could potentially be further developed into a theoretical framework for design of governance frameworks. An indication of how this could work is found when looking at some examples of current changes (see Chapter 5.5):

UK OGC:

- Reviews becoming mandatory: This process can indicate a stronger emphasis on control (principal-agent theory).
- Leaner organization: This can indicate a stronger emphasis on public choice theory.

UK MoD:

- Reorganize with a stronger emphasis on clear roles and closer involvement. This practice can indicate a stronger emphasis on the expert role (transaction cost economics) and trust and close relations (network perspective)
- Improved systems for reward and recognition. This may indicate a stronger emphasis on principal-agent theory.

Norway:

- Developing new guidelines. This may indicate a stronger emphasis on professional standards (network perspective).

As mentioned, other explanations for these changes are certainly possible, as well as highly probable. The development towards a useful theoretical framework for design of governance frameworks are not pursued further here. The summary of our findings is shown in Table 7-1.

7.6 PRACTICAL IMPLICATIONS

Having compared the frameworks to several theoretical ideas and lines of thought, we believe we have unravelled some aspects of establishing governance frameworks, which could be supported by theory. We have shown a set of different perspectives and theories which can be helpful in the design process. We believe readers will have a better understanding and awareness after reading this. The theories may help make findings transferable to countries other than the two studied here. We believe the theories presented here can be of help to those working with governance of major public projects.

The field of governance of projects is also subject to change. The frameworks studied here are frequently changed and improved. The status reported here is the one corresponding to the third quarter of 2007. The content of this analysis of the actual frameworks has a limited lifetime, and the result would look different had the analysis been made at a different time. The theories are more stable over time and if they can work as a reference, the result could be of help over a longer span of time.

As already mentioned, the real reasons for designing the frameworks the way we have in Chapter 5 are not these theories. Therefore, a comparison with findings from the case studies is interesting to see if we can observe indications supporting or denying the theoretical findings in Table 7-1. Here are some observations based on Chapter 6.

Governance frameworks as a means of control (principal-agent theory): The Norwegian framework shows strong emphasis on this. The IFI2 case confirms this with its critical gateway and control focus in review, although not strongly indicated due to the case being well planned and executed. The Skjold case, on the other hand, seems to indicate the position is less strong performing a friendly gateway review and allowing the project to continue despite lacking a project management plan for the execution phase. The NEADS case seems to confirm the MoD frameworks control emphasis with continuing internal scrutiny. In the Home Office case, the reviews contain general comments and good advice to the SRO concerning the project. Some formulations indicate a "control" state of mind, but the OGC framework does not implicate the recommendations have to be followed. This indicates the weak emphasis on this theory is correct.

TABLE 7-1. SUMMARY OF THEORETICAL FINDINGS—EMPHASIS ON THEORETICAL ASPECTS

Perspective/Theory	Aspect	Norway	UK-MoD	UK-OGC
Instrumental-Structural Perspective				
Principal-Agent Theory	Control Incentive Information	Strong Weak Strong	Strong Moderate Strong	Weak Strong Moderate
Public Choice Theory	Internal skepticism/External review Lean organization Transparency Acquisition support	Strong Strong Strong Weak	Weak Weak Moderate Strong	Moderate Moderate Weak Strong
Bureau-Shaping Perspective	Benchmarking professional standards Supporting plurality	Strong Strong	Mixed Mixed	Moderate Weak
Theory of Economic Analysis / Analysis of Political Behavior	Bulwark against illegitimate influence Influencing decisions Independent evaluator role	Mixed Strong Strong	Mixed Strong Weak	Mixed Weak Mixed
Theory of Transaction Cost Economics	Asset specificity Competition Centralization of decision making Lower transaction costs by cooperation Expert role	Mixed Weak Strong Weak Strong	Strong Mixed Strong Strong Weak	Mixed Strong Weak Weak Strong
General Instrumental Perspectives	Logic of consequence Clarity of roles and responsibilities Objectives Measurement	Strong Weak Strong Weak	Strong Strong Strong Strong	Strong Strong Strong Strong
Cultural-Institutional Perspective	Logic of appropriateness Historical anchoring Clear framework focus Awareness among users	Strong Weak Strong Strong	Strong Strong Strong Strong	Moderate Strong Weak Mixed
Environmental Perspective	Adaptation to environment Adaptation to performance culture Flexibility Problem seeking	Weak Strong Strong Strong	Strong Strong Weak Mixed	Moderate Strong Weak Weak
Network Perspective	Professional standards Trust and close relations Negotiation	Strong Mixed Strong	Strong Strong Weak	Strong Strong Weak

Transparency in governance frameworks (public choice theory): The Norwegian framework shows strong emphasis. Both Skjold and IFI2 cases confirm this emphasis. There is great openness at all levels and the QA reports are available to decision makers at the time of making the decision, and after being processed in Parliament, they are also open to the public. The only indication pointing in the other direction is the fact that suppliers were not available for the reviewers in the Skjold case (this was due to commercial aspects). The MoD framework has moderate emphasis on transparency. Supplier information is somewhat more available. Review information is available to the project; however, it is limited to within MoD as is normal in the defense sector; NEADS shows these aspects. In the OGC framework, the emphasis on transparency seems weak. The reviews are only available for the SRO and the OGC. The Home Office however gives an interesting additional slant; in this case the Parliamentary Accounts Committee (and NAO) show intimate interest in the project, making information open to the general public. At the other end of the scale, being a PFI leaves some aspects of the project unavailable to other than the executing party.

Plurality in methods and approaches (bureau-shaping perspective): Again, the Norwegian framework shows strong emphasis. Skjold and IFI2 confirm this emphasis by the use of different approaches in managing the projects. The Prinsix method used in Skjold is considered appropriate in the Skjold case, and the Statsbygg method used in the IFI2 case is facing some criticism but is still being accepted. The MoD framework limits the plurality by imposing the MoD method as a common quality system within its organization. We do not know from the NEADS case how strong this indication is here, but there is no indication in any other direction. The OGC framework limits plurality by requiring conforming to the principles or spirit of PRINCE2, although in fact it was the audit and assurance unit governance process that made this requirement in the Home Office case. This seems to support the theoretical analysis.

Competition (theory of transaction cost economics): In this perspective, the OGC framework is in the strong position. Competition is a major issue to the UK government and this market mode is one of the main pillars of OGC. The Home Office case confirms this statement to some extent by the reviews (No. 4) having a strong contract emphasis following a competition where two bids for accommodation were considered. However, the position does not seem very strong judged on the basis of this case. The MoD position is mixed: on one hand the UK market mode, on the other hand the severely limited defense market. The NEADS case illustrates this well showing a partnership between the customer and its dominating supplier. The Norwegian position is weak, having more emphasis on responsibility of the state, than on competition. This result is in line with the Skjold case, where the political decision is to help the shipyard stay in business by giving them a large contract (the general characteristics of the defense sector in Norway is equal to the UK one). The IFI2 case shows a very different picture. The strategy of Statsbygg was to divide the delivery into many contracts to increase competition – clearly a strong emphasis on competition. The procurement regulations in Norway, based on EU regulations, point in the same direction. Nondiscriminating competition is an important aspect and this strengthens the emphasis on competition in practice compared to theory.

Flexibility (environmental perspective): In this perspective, the Norwegian framework has strong emphasis. The Skjold case illustrates this very well by the obviously flexible handling of this project's special situation and the consequences of the difficult timing of the review. The IFI2 case illustrates both flexibility and rigidity at the same time, bringing nuances into the picture. From a theoretical point of view, both the MoD and OGC frameworks have little emphasis on flexibility, giving detailed instructions on how things should be. The impression from the practical case is different. The Home Office case shows clear signs of flexibility—having several Gateway 3's and 4's—one of which was performed early on the request of the treasury. The NEADS case also shows the necessary flexibility to cope with an extremely complex problem in a changing environment.

Other elements of Table 7-1 could be commented on in a similar way, but most of them are self-explaining to a degree that this would not bring in anything the reader would not easily see by studying Table 7-1 with the frameworks in Chapter 5 and the cases in Chapter 6 in mind.

Many of the elements in Table 7-1 also focus on the framework itself; aspects to which the cases give no indication. These aspects are already covered in Sections 7.1–7.4.

8 Conclusion

We are now at the conclusion of this investigation, and we should return to the original intentions and review the journey followed over the study.

In Chapter 2, we reviewed the literature in the area of what has been called project governance and found it to be an ill-defined term. Therefore, we had to define carefully the concepts of governance *through* projects and governance *of* projects, which we are looking at together in this report (and not governance *within* a project). Then we could define a governance framework for investment projects as comprising the processes and rules established to ensure the project meets its purpose. Along the way to this definition, we established various theoretical perspectives for looking at projects, which help us later ground our work in good theory.

The literature also points us to the important characteristics of a governance framework, and Table 4-1 provides a useful checklist for anyone looking at a particular framework and thinking about its essential nature: we look at the background (why and how the framework came to be), the explicitly stated purpose of the framework, its current status and how the framework is maintained and developed, the underlying governance principles, and the current framework structure. In our particular study, we were interested in framework elements concerning cost estimation and time planning and the governance of transactions. While these are generally especially important anyway, the particular needs of an investigation will dictate where the focus is here.

This generic framework enabled us in Chapter 5 to study in detail the frameworks set up in Norway and the United Kingdom—in the latter case, one generic and the MoD framework. These are continuously changing even as these chapters are being written, but taking a structured view of the frameworks as they are at the time of study (mid-2007) gives us an interesting comparison (and note current developments in the following).

We saw that the aims of the frameworks are similar, but the process of developing those frameworks and the focus of the frameworks are genuinely different—to some extent mirroring the administrative culture in the two countries, and the military culture in MoD. The underlying governance principles are similar and derived from common western thinking about business, but again there are real differences coming from the different administrative cultures in the two countries and MoD. The outward manifestations of the frameworks appear obviously different, but in fact there is probably more that makes them similar, than what makes them different; they all specify the "rules of the game" supporting the decision-making process and planning and execution of successful projects. Differences were found, however, in the roles of gatekeeper and decision makers, means of coordination vertically and horizontally, use of resources to perform reviews, and so on, as well as in the particular governance elements addressing cost and time.

Apart from information about possible choices in developing frameworks, this analysis provided (perhaps slightly more subjective) indications of issues in designing new frameworks or improving existing frameworks in other situations. These are summarized in Table 5-10. This could be a counter-weight to the common practice of standardization and simply transferring framework elements and methods between sectors, countries, and regions regardless of the new situation.

This comparison and analysis give us the foundation of our main results and enable us in a structured way to describe how governance frameworks differ. However, our original research topic was to look at how these differences actually play out in practice. The structure developed in the analysis was therefore taken and used to look at four case studies. Clearly, there were issues in the cases that were provided for the researchers to study, which limited not only the findings, but also the generalizability of those findings. Chapter 6 gives detail of these case studies, each with their own story of the actuality of the framework in practice: generally following but always a little different from the framework as espoused by the authorities; Chapter 6 then gives an analysis of each case giving lessons for the use of each framework. Table 6-4 shows our interpretation of some of the aspects and their links to the governance frameworks across all the cases. All of the cases documented the importance of governance frameworks. In all of the cases, reassurance and/or legitimization of the project were important. They all highlighted the need for governance in the early stages in the project—three of the projects began before their relevant full frameworks were in place, so that certainly underlines the need for elements such as QA1 and early OGC Gateways, while raising the question whether more, earlier governance is needed. Some possible improvements to all three current frameworks were identified. In one case, other governance mechanisms proved particularly important.

Our initial research questions in the research proposal were threefold. First, we aimed to see what fundamentally characterizes an institutional framework and how frameworks differ, which we have done. We saw areas in which these particular frameworks do well and where they could perhaps be strengthened. Second, we aimed to look at how the frameworks worked out in practice and what effect the framework had on a project; while we have done the former, we found surprisingly little impact on the projects, perhaps more an indication of the type of project we were given to study than the typical effect (so for example we had no "red traffic lights" to use the OGC term). We had disappointingly little visibility of cost and time estimation to help our third research question, so we were unable to see much effect of governance frameworks here, which is perhaps instructive in itself; however, we were able to see in three of the cases the mechanisms operating (the fourth was a PFI project), and to see the strength of the governance here relative between the frameworks.

All of the study described so far was pragmatic. But as we said previously, the literature provided various theoretical perspectives for looking at projects, and these allowed us to look at the governance frameworks through the lens of the dominant instrumental-structural perspective, looking at principal-agent theory, public choice theory, the bureau-shaping perspective, theory of economic analysis and transaction cost economics, but also through the lens of the cultural-institutional, environmental, and network perspectives. The aim of this was not to claim which framework is the "best," or even which perspective is "best," rather it was to try to understand the differences between the frameworks and to explain the behaviors we have been studying.

Table 7-1 attempts to explain where the current (mid-2007) frameworks lie looked at from these various perspectives. This might be useful in looking at how to place a framework in a new situation. It is also instructive in looking at current developments (late 2007 and 2008) in the frameworks, and Section 7.5 looks at these based on the theoretical analysis. Table 7-1 is based on a theoretical analysis of the espoused frameworks, but this chapter goes on to look at the outworkings of the frameworks in the case studies, and sees how these theoretical perspectives actually are seen in practice. We also look at the current developments in the frameworks, in the light of the theoretical analysis.

Obviously, this research is just one small step in this area. We could think of extending this work, for example by seeking:

- A wider understanding of the influence between frameworks and their context by studying more frameworks in more different contexts.
- A better/deeper understanding of the effect on projects by studying more cases, or going deeper into cases to reveal the specific effect on cost and time.
- A better understanding of the effect of frameworks by studying other sides of the cases—sustainability, contractual issues, organizational structures, risk management, and so on.

- A better understanding of the link between frameworks and projects by including the portfolio and programme levels of management.

What do we conclude, then? Our study sought a better understanding of how governance frameworks work and how they interact with the projects they seek to govern. Let us return then to our three initial research questions given in Chapter 1, to see what messages we can offer.

- The first was, "What fundamentally characterizes an institutional framework and how do frameworks differ?" We looked at this question in Chapter 4, which describes the characteristics, and Chapter 5, which describes the differences between these three frameworks. We have given an insight into what underlies the frameworks, how they are constructed, how they tie in to the motivations and organization of the public sector and the administrative culture of the country. In this way, we showed in particular how frameworks were dependent on their purpose and context.

- The second question was, "How do the frameworks work out in practice; what effect does the framework have on a project, and how well does that agree with the intended effects? And does this suggest any improvements to the frameworks?" We answered this question in Chapter 6. We found that the potential effect was large, but that the cases we have studied did not show the full potential. We found that a key benefit of the frameworks was legitimization for the project and reassurance for the project owner. We also found that the flexibility in the frameworks was very important. And we saw the importance of governance, particularly in the early stages of projects where concepts are established.

- The third question was, "To what extent does the framework guard against under-estimation in time and cost; and does it allow overrun to be exposed, reduced and for cost control to be effective?" We tried to look at this in Chapter 6. We saw that governance of cost, time, and benefits estimation was important, and we saw important principles, but we were unable to see much of this in the case studies. This question is difficult and calls upon more research.

Finally, we have tried to put our findings into a theoretical context, to ground them and help in the transfer of them to other situations.

Overall, we believe that this study has provided some useful insights and some practical tools for others to appreciate the studied frameworks and to use when devising new or improving current frameworks in other situations. We could summarize our main message as being that governance is important—and that governance frameworks are the way to make governance of projects effective—so governance frameworks are very important. Understanding them is vital to all successful project owners and project managers.

References

Abbott, K. W., & Snidal, D. (2001). International standards and international governance [Special issue]. *Journal of European Public Policy, 8*(3), 345–370.

Advantage Business Solutions. (2005). http://businesssolutions.advantage-business.co.uk/news/article/0/114.

Acquisition Management System. (2007). http://ams.mod.uk/content/topics/3309.htm.

Acquisition Operation Framework. (2008). http://www.aof.mod.uk/index.htm.

Altshuler, A. A., & Luberoff, D. (2003). *Mega-projects: The changing politics of urban public investment.* Washington, DC and Cambridge, MA: Brookings Institution Press and Lincoln Institute of Land Policy.

Amin, A., & Hausner, J. (1997). *Beyond market and hierarchy: Interactive governance and social complexity.* Edward Elgar Publishing.

Anguera, R. (2006). The Channel Tunnel – An ex post economic evaluation. *Transportation Research Part A, 40,* 291–315.

Artto, K. A., & Dietrich, P. H. (2004). Strategic business management through multiple projects. In P. W. G. Morris & J. K. Pinto (Eds.), *The Wiley guide to managing projects* (pp. 144–176). New York: Wiley.

Artto, K. A., Dietrich, P. H., & Nurminen, M. I. (2004). Strategy implementation by projects. In D. P. Slevin, D. I. Cleland, & J. K. Pinto (Eds.), *Innovations: Project management research* 2004, (pp. 103–122). Newtown Square, PA: Project Management Institute.

Artto, K. A., Kujala, J., Dietrich, P. H., & Martinsuo, P. (2007). *What is project strategy?* Paper presented at the EURAM 2007 Conference, Paris, France.

Association for Project Management. (2002). *Directing change: A guide to governance of project management.* London: Association of Project Managers.

Association for Project Management. (2007). *Co-directing change; A guide to governance of multi-owned projects.* London: Association of Project Managers.

Aubry, M., Hobbs, B., & Thuillier, D. (2008). Organisational project management: A historical approach to the study of PMOs. *International Journal of Project Management, 26,* 38–43.

Bemelmans-Videc, M. L., Rist, R. C., & Vedung, E. (1998). *Carrots, sticks and sermons. Policy instruments and their evaluation.* New Brunswick, NJ: Transaction Publishers.

Berg P., et al. (1999). Styring av statlige investeringer. Sluttrapport fra styringsgruppen for prosjektet for styring av statlige investeringer. Finansdepartementet.

Berger, P. L., & Neuhaus, R. J. (1977). *To empower people: The role of mediating structures in public policy.* Washington, DC: American Enterprise Institute.

Brunetto, Y., & Farr-Wharton, R. (2003). The impact of government practice on the ability of project managers to manage. *International Journal of Project Management, 21*(2), 125–133.

Burgelman, R. A. (1983). A model of the interaction of strategic behavior, corporate context, and the concept of strategy. *Academy of Management Review, 8*(1), 61–70.

Bush, T., Johnsen, E., Klausen, K. K., & Vanebo, J. O. (2005). *Modernisering av offentlig sektor; Utfordringer, metoder og dilemmaer* (2 ed.). Oslo: Universitetsforlaget.

Cabinet Office (2000) *Successful IT: Modernising Government in Action* London: Stationery Office.

Carver, J. (2001). *A theory of corporate governance: Finding a new balance for boards and their CEOs.*

Clarke, T. (2004). Introduction: Theories of governance – reconceptualizing corporate governance theory after the Enron experience. In T. Clarke, (Ed.), *Theories of corporate governance: The philosophical foundations of corporate governance* (pp. 1-30). Abingdon, Oxon, UK: Routledge.

Chelimsky, E. (1997). The political environment of evaluation and what it means for the development of the field. In E. Chelimsky & W. R. Shadish (Eds.), *Evaluation for the 21st century: A handbook* (pp. 53–71). Thousand Oaks, CA: Sage.

Christensen, T., & Lægreid, P. (2001). *New public management. The transformation of ideas and practice.* Aldershot, Hampshire, England: Ashgate.

Christensen, T. (2007). The Norwegian front-end governance regime of major public investment projects – A theoretically based analysis and evaluation. Preliminary version of report to the Concept Research Programme.

Christensen, T., Lægreid, P., Roness, P. G., & Røvik, K. A. (2007). *Organization theory and the public sector: Instrument, culture and myth.* London: Routledge.

Cleland, D. I. (2004). Strategic management: The project linkages. In P. W. G. Morris & J.K. Pinto (Eds.), *The Wiley guide to managing projects* (pp. 206–222). New York: Wiley.

Collinridge, D. (1992). *The management of scale: Big organizations, big decisions, big mistakes.* London: Routledge.

Committee on Standards in Public Life. (1995). *Standards in public life: First report of the Committee on Standards in Public Life.* London: Committee on Standards in Public Life.

Committee on Standards in Public Life. (2005). *Survey of public attitudes towards standards of conduct in public life report.* London: Committee on Standards in Public Life.

Committee on Standards in Public Life. (2007). *Review of the Electoral Commission. Committee.* London: Committee on Standards in Public Life.

Committee on Standards in Public Life. (2009) Web pages: www.public-standards. gov.uk/about.html. Last approached 28.1.2009.

The Concept Program. (2006). *Principles of governance for major investment projects* [Brochure]. Available from http://www.concept.ntnu.no//index_engelsk.htm.

Condon, E. (2006). *Project game: Strategic estimating on major projects.* Unpublished doctoral thesis, University of Calgary.

Cooper, R. G., Edgett, S. J., & Kleinschmidt, E. J. (2002a). Optimizing the stage-gate process: What best-practice companies do – Part 1. *Research Technology, 45,* 21–27.

Cooper, R. G., Edgett, S. J., & Kleinschmidt, E. J. (2002b). Optimizing the stage-gate process: What best-practice companies do – Part 2. *Research Technology, 45,* 43–49.

Defence Analytical Services Agency. (2007). UK defence statistics 2006. Retrieved from http://www.dasa.mod.uk/natstats/ukds/2006/c1/table115.html.

DefenceInternet. (2007). Key stakeholders.

Detomasi, D. A. (2006). International regimes: The case of western corporate governance. *International Studies Review, 8,* 225–251.

Downey. W. G. (1969). *Report of the steering group on development dost engineering (The Downey report).* London: Ministry of Technology.

Driessen, P. P. J. (2005). Restructuring the Dutch countryside: Limits of a governance strategy. *Planning, Practice & Research, 20*(1), 69–77.

Easterby-Smith, M., Thorpe, R., & Lowe, A. (1991). *Management research: An introduction.* London: Sage.

Eden, C., Ackermann, F., & Williams, T. (2005). The amoebic growth of project costs. *Project Management Journal, 36*(2), 15–27.

Eden, C., & Huxham, C. (2006). Researching organizations using action research. In S. Clegg, C. Hardy, W. Nord, & T. Lawrence (Eds.). *Handbook of organization studies* (2nd ed.). Thousand Oaks, CA: Sage

Eikeland, P. T. (2001). Teoretisk Analyse av Byggeprosesser, Samspill i byggeprosessen, prosjektnr 10602 [Theoretical Analysis of the Construction Process].

Eisenhardt, K. M. (1989). Building theories from case study research. *Academy of Management Research, 14*(4), 532–550.

Encycogov. (2007). The encyclopedia about corporate governance. Retrieved from http://encycogov.com/B11TransactionCostEconomics.asp.

Engwall, M. (2002). The futile dream of the perfect goal. In K. Sahil-Andersson & A. Soderholm (Eds.), *Beyond project management: New perspectives on the temporary-permanent dilemma* (pp. 261–277). Malmo, Sweden: Libe Ekonomi, Copenhagen Business School Press.

Eskerod, P., Blickfeldt, B. S., & Toft, A. S. (2004). *Questioning the rational assumption underlying decision-making within project portfolio management literature.* Paper presented at the PMI Research Conference 2004, London, England.

Fainstein, N. I., & Fainstein, S. S. (1983). Regime strategies, communal resistance, and economic forces. In S. S. Fainstein & N.I. Fainstein (Eds.), *Restructuring the city: The political economy of urban development* (pp.). Harlow, Essex, United Kingdom: Longman.

Finansdepartementet. (1999) Ministry of Finance. Budget Proposal for 2000. [St.prp. nr. 1 (1999-2000)], Available at; http://www.regjeringen.no/nb/dep/fin/dok/regpubl/stprp/1999-2000/Stprp-nr-1-1999-2000-.html?id=137216

Finansdepartementet. (2004) Ministry of Finance. Budget Proposal for 2005 [St.prp. nr. 1 (2004-2005)], Available at; http://www.regjeringen.no/nb/dep/fin/dok/regpubl/stprp/20042005/Stprp-nr-1-2004-2005--2.html?id=138734

Finansdepartementet. (2004). Invitation to tender. [Ref.jnr. 04/1267C Anbudsinnbydelse – Rammeavtale om konsulenttjeneste vedrørende kvalitetssikring av konseptvalg, samt styringsunderlag og kostnadsoverslag for valgt prosjektalternativ]. Ministry of Finance.

Finansdepartementet, (2008a) Guideline No. 1 Steering Document, [Veileder nr. 1 Det sentrale styringsdokument], Available at www.concept.ntnu.no (in Norwegian).

Finansdepartementet, (2008b) Guideline No. 2 Common terms in QA2, [Veileder nr. 2 Felles begrepsapparat KS2], Available at www.concept.ntnu.no (in Norwegian).

Finansdepartementet, (2008c) Guideline No. 6 Cost Estimation, [Veileder nr. 6 Kostnadsestimering]. Available at www.concept.ntnu.no (in Norwegian).

Fiscal Budget 2008: Underpinning Macroeconomic Stability. Press release 60/2007 [5.10.2007] from the Norwegian Ministry of Finance. Available at: http://www.regjeringen.no/en/dep/fin/press-center/Press-releases/2007/Fiscal-Budget-2008-Underpinning-Macroeco.html?id=484802.

Flyvbjerg, B., Bruzelius, N., & Rothengatter, W. (2003). *Megaprojects and risk: An anatomy of ambition.* Cambridge, UK: Cambridge University Press.

Flyvbjerg, B. (2006). Five misunderstandings about case-study research. *Qualitative Inquiry, 12*(2), 219–245.

Foss, K., & Foss, N. J. (1999). Understanding ownership: Residual rights of control and appropriable control rights. DRUID working papers 99-4. Copenhagen: Copenhagen Business School, Department of Industrial Economics and Strategy/Aalborg University.

Gareis, R. (1990). Management by projects. *Proceedings of the IPMA World Congress 1990*, Vienna.

Gershon, P. (1999). *Review of civil procurement in central government.* London: HM Treasury.

Gershon, P. (2004). *Releasing resources to the front line: Independent review of public sector efficiency.* London: The Stationery Office.

Glaser, B. (1992). *Basics of grounded theory analysis.* Mill Valley, CA: Sociology Press.

Grünfeldt, L. A., & Jakobsen, E. W. (2006). Hvem eier Norge? Eierskap og verdiskapning I et grenseløst næringsliv.Oslo: Universitetsforlaget.

Hall, P. (1981). *Great planning disasters.* Harmondsworth, Hillingdon, UK: Penguin Books.

Hardie, J. (2005). *Transparency, accountability and rationality, discussion paper series DP74/05.* London: LSE's Centre for Philosophy of Natural and Social Science.

Harpham, A., & Kippenberger, T. (2005). Staking a lot on programme and project management. Paper at the 19. IPMA World conference 2005. New Delhi, India.

Heap, D., Hicks, S., Livesey, D., & Walling, A. (2005) Public Sector Employment Trends 2005. Downloaded from http://www.statistics.gov.uk/cci/article.asp?ID=1293 January 2008.

HM Treasury. (2002). 2002 Spending Review Public Service agreements July 2002. Chapter 9: Ministry of Defence. Available on http://www.archive2.official-documents.co.uk/document/cm55/5571/5571-09.htm.

HM Treasury. (2003). *The green book: Appraisal and government, treasury guidance.* London: The Stationery Office.

HM Treasury. (2004). *Treasury Minutes on the Fourteenth, Fifteenth, Eighteenth, and Nineteenth Reports from the Committee of Public Accounts 2003-04 (Cm 6244).* Presented to Parliament by the Financial Secretary to the Treasury by Command of Her Majesty.

HM Treasury (2007a) "Budget 2007: Building Britain's Long-term Future: Prosperity and Fairness for Families – HC 342". TSO (The Stationery Office): London.

HM Treasury. (2007b). *Transforming government procurement.* London: HM Treasury. Retrieved from http://www.hm-treasury.gov.uk.

House of Commons Committee of Public Accounts. (2004). *PFI: The New Headquarters for the Home Office. Eighteenth Report of Session 2003–04.* London: The Stationery Office.

Howard, C. (2007). *Experiences of implementing gateway reviews.* Paper presentation at the Project Controls EVA 12 Annual Conference of the APM Special Interest Group on Earned Value Management, London, England.

HVR Consulting Services Ltd. (2007). *Product and marketing strategy.* Retrieved from http://www.hvr-csl.co.uk/DecisionSupport/HTMLS/ProductMarket Strategy.htm

ISO 9000. (2005). Quality management systems; Fundamentals and vocabulary. Standard Norge.

Ive, G. (2004). Private finance initiative and the management of projects. In, P. W. G. Morris & J. K. Pinto (Eds.), *The Wiley guide to managing projects* (pp. 249–381). New York: Wiley.

Jacoby, S. (2005). Corporate governance and society. *Challenge, 48*(4), pp 69-87.

Jessop, B. (1997). The governance of complexity and the complexity of governance: Preliminary remarks on some problems and limits of economic guidance. In A. Amin & J. Hausner, J. (Eds.), Beyond market and hierarchy (pp. 95–128). Cheltenham, UK: Edward Elgar.

Johnson, G., & Scholes, K. (1993). Exploring corporate strategy: text and cases. Toronto: Prentice-Hall.

Jones, C., Heserly, W. S., Borgatti, S. P. (1997). A general theory of network governance: Exchange conditions and social mechanisms. *Academy of Management Review, 22*(4), 911–945.

Kaufmann, D., & Vicente, P. C. (2005). *Legal corruption.* Retrieved from http://siteresources.worldbank.org/INTWBIGOVANTCOR/Resources/2-l_Governance_and_Corruption_Kaufmann.pdf. Last approached October 2007.

Kaufmann, D., & Kraay, A. (2008). *Governance indicators: Where are we, where should we be going?* Oxford: Oxford University Press and retrieved from http://web.worldbank.org.

Keohane, R. O., & Nye., J. S. (1977). *Power and interdependence.* Boston: Little Brown.

Kerzner, H. (2000). *Applied project management: Best practices on implementation.* New York: Wiley.

Klakegg, O. J. (2004). Målformulering i store statlige investeringsprosjekt [Formulation of objectives in major public investment projects]. (In Norwegian with English summary). Concept Report No. 6.

Klakegg, O. J., Samset, K., & Magnussen, O. M. (2005). *Improving success in public investment projects. Lessons from a government initiative in Norway to improve quality at entry.* Paper presented at the IPMA World Conference 2005, New Delhi, India.

Klakegg, O. J. (undated). *Improving performance in decision making on public investment projects: An industrial ecology perspective on the Norwegian quality-at-entry regime.* Manuscript submitted for publication.

Klakegg, O. J. (2006). A new trend in project management? *The Measurable News.* Spring.

Koch, C., & Buser, M. (2006). Emerging metagovernance as an institutional framework for public private partnership networks in Denmark. *International Journal of Project Management, 24,* 548–556.

Kooiman, J., & Van Vliet, M. (1993). Governance and public management. In K. Eliassen and J. Kooiman (Eds.), *Managing Public Organisations* (2nd ed.). London: Sage.

Krasner, S. D. (1983) Structural Causes and Regime Consequences: Regimes as Intervening Variables. In S. D. Krasner, (Ed.) *International Regimes*. Ithaca: Cornell University Press.

Lægreid, P. (2006). Reguleringsreformer og fristilling i staten. Presentation at the seminar Fag og beslutninger 23. Concept Research Programme (in Norwegian).

Larson, M., & Wikstrøm, E. (2007). Relational interaction processes in project networks: The consent and negotiation perspectives. *Scandinavian Journal of Management, 23,* 327–352.

Linehan, C., & Kavanagh, D. (2004). *From project ontologies to communities of virtue.* Paper presented at the Second International Workshop of Making Projects Critical, University of Western England, UK.

Lundin, R. A. (1995). Editorial: temporary organizations and project management. *Scandinavian Journal of Management, 11,* 315–317.

Magnussen, O. M., & Samset, K. (2005). *Successful megaprojects: Ensuring quality at entry.* Paper presented at the Euram 2005 Conference in Munich, Germany.

Magnussen, O. M., & Olsson, N. O. E. (2006). Comparative analysis of cost estimates of major public investment projects. *International Journal of Project Management, 24*(4), 281–288.

Malgrati, A., & Damiani, M. (2002). Rethinking the new project management framework: New epistemology, new insights. *Proceedings of the PMI Research Conference,* 371–380.

March, J. G., & Simon, H. A. (1958). *Organizations.* New York: John Wiley & Sons.

Metier Scandinavia AS. (2004). Kvalitetssikring av kostnadsoverslag - P10258 Nybygg for informatikkmiljøene ved UiO, IFI2 [Quality assurance of cost estimate P10258 new building for the Department of Informatics at the University of Oslo IFI2]. Oslo: Metier Scandinavia AS.

Michaud, P., & Lessard, D. (2000). Transforming institutions. In Miller & Lessard (Eds.). *The strategic management of large engineering projects: Shaping institutions, risks and governance.* Cambridge, Mass.: MIT Press.

Miller, R., & Hobbs, B. (2005). Governance regimes for large complex projects. *Project Management Journal, 36*(3), pp 42–50.

Miller, R. & Lessard D. R. (2000). *The strategic management of large engineering projects: Shaping institutions, risks and governance.* Cambridge, MA: MIT Press.

Ministry of Defence. (2006). *Enabling acquisition change: An examination of the Ministry of Defence's ability to undertake through life capability management.* A report by the Enabling Acquisition Change Team Leader (the McKane Report). London: Ministry of Defence.

Ministry of Defence (2008) Aqcuisition Operating Framework. http://www.aof.mod.uk/index.htm version 2.0.8 - December 2008.

Mintzberg, H., & Quinn, J. B. (1996). *The strategy process: Concepts, contexts and cases.* Upper Saddle River, NJ: Prentice-Hall.

Mitchell, C., Carew, A. L., & Clift, R. (2004). The role of the professional engineer and scientist in sustainable development. In A. Azapagic, S. Perdan, & R. Clift (Eds.), *Sustainable Development in Practice*. New York: John Wiley & Sons.

MoD. (2007). Acquisition Operating Framework. Retrieved from http://www.aof. mod.uk/index.htm.

Monks, R. A. G., & Minow, N. (2004). *Corporate governance*. Oxford: Blackwell & Sullivan.

Morris, P. W. G., & Hough, G. H. (1987). *The Anatomy of major projects. A study of the reality of project management*. Chichester, UK: John Wiley & Sons.

Morris, P. W. G., & Jamieson, A. (2004). Translating corporate strategy into project strategy: Realizing corporate strategy through project management. Newtown Square, PA: Project Management Institute.

Müller, R., & Turner, R. J. (2005). The impact of principal-agent relationship and contract type on communication between project owner and manager. *International Journal of Project Management*, 23, 398–403.

Næss, P., Flyvbjerg, B., & Buhl, S. (2006). Do road planners produce more "honest numbers" than rail planners? An analysis of accuracy in road-traffic forecasts in cities vs. peripheral regions. *Transport Reviews*, 26(5), 537–555.

Næss, P. (2004). Prediction, regressions and critical realism. Journal of Critical Realism, 3(1), 133–164.

National Accounts of OECD Countries, volume 1 (2006). More information: http:// www.oecd.org/ and http://www.ssb.no/ppp_en/.

National Audit Office. (2003). *PFI: The new headquarters for the Home Office*. Report by the Comptroller and Auditor and Auditor General HC 954 Session 2002–2003.

National Audit Office. (2006). *Ministry of Defence: Major projects report 2006*. Report by the Comptroller and Auditor and Auditor General.

National Budget for 2004–2007 (Norwegian Ministry of Finance). Available at; http://www.regjeringen.no/en/dep/fin.html?id=216.

Nohria, N. & Eccles R.G. (eds) (1992) Networks and Organisations. Harvard Business School Press. Boston, MA.

Norwegian Official Reports. (2007). *Et styrket forsvar [A strengthened defence]*. Oslo, Norway: The Norwegian Ministry of Defence.

Norwegian Official Reports. (1999). Analyse av investeringsutviklingen på kontinentalsokkelen [Analysis of the development in investment on the continental shelf]. Ministry of petroleum and energy. Statens forvaltningstjeneste, Statens trykning.

OECD (2004). *OECD Principles of Corporate Governance*. Organisation for Economic Co-operation and Development. Retrieved from www.oecd.org. http://www. oecd.org/document/49/0,3343,en_2649_34813_31530865_1_1_1_1,00. html.

OECD (2005). *Modernising government, the way forward.* Organisation for Economic Co-operation and Development.

OECD Factbook 2007: Economic, Environmental, and Social Statistics - ISBN 92-64-02946-X. available at http://titania.sourceoecd.org Last approached October 2007. http://lysander.sourceoecd.org/vl=475071/cl=12/nw=1/rpsv/factbook/02-04-01.htm. Last approached October 2007.

Office of Government Commerce. (1999). Managing successful programmes. Office of Government Commerce. Norwich, UK: The Stationery Office.

Office of Government Commerce. (undated). "A manager's checklist," Retrieved from http://www.ogc.gov.uk/documents/cp0001-Gateway_Manager_Checklist.pdf.

Office of Government Commerce. (2002a). *Managing Successful Projects with PRINCE2™ (PRINCE Guidance).* London: The Stationery Office.

Office of Government Commerce. (2002b). *Prince2™ project management method.* Retrieved from http://www.ogc.gov.uk/methods_prince_2.asp.

Office of Government Commerce. (2004). *The OGC Gateway™ process: Gateway to success.* OGC Best Practice Leaflet ref CP0002/12/04. London: Office of Government Commerce.

Office of Government Commerce. (2005). *Common causes of project failure. OGC Best Practice.* London: Office of Government Commerce.

Office of Government Commerce. (2006). *2005 and 2006: OGC: Key achievements, releasing resources to the front line.* London: Office of Government Commerce.

Office of Government Commerce. (2007). OGC Gateway™ Process. Review 2: Delivery strategy OGC Best Practice – Gateway to success. London: Office of Government Commerce.

Olsson, N. O. E., Johansen, A., Langlo, J. A., & Torp, O. (2007). Project ownership: Implications on success measurement. (Forthcoming in *Measuring Business Excellence*). Trondheim, Norway: Norwegian Centre of Project Management. The white paper "Who owns a project" on which this paper is based is available at http://www.concept.ntnu.no/Publikasjoner/Publikasjoner.htm.

Olsson, N. O. E., & Samset, K. (2006). *Front-end management, flexibility and project success.* Paper presented at the PMI Research Conference, Montreal.

Oral Question Period. (2000–2001). Question no. 24 to the Minister of Research and Education [Stortingets spørretime 14.2.2001]. Oslo: The Norwegian Parliament.

O'Sullivan, M. (2000). *Contests for corporate control: Corporate governance and economic performance in the United States and Germany.* Oxford: Oxford University Press.

O'Sullivan, M. (2003). The political economy of comparative corporate governance. *Review of International Political Economy, 10*(1), 23–72.

Packendorff, J. (1995). Inquiring into the temporary organization: New directions for project management research. *Scandinavian Journal of Management, 11,* 319–333.

Partington, D. (2000). Implementing strategy through programmes of projects. In Turner, J. R., & Simister, S. J. (2000). *Gower handbook of project management.* Aldershot, UK: Gower.

Patel, D. (2007). Why executives should care about project governance: What your peers are doing about it. *PM World Today, 4*(4).

Peters, P. B. G., & Pierre, J. (1998). Governance without government? Rethinking public administration. *Journal of Public Administration and Theory, 8*(2), 223–243.

Pollitt, C., & Bouckaert, G. (2000). *Public management reform: A comparative analysis.* Oxford: Oxford University Press.

PRICE. (2007). Retrieved from http://www.pricesystems.com.

Prinsix. (1999). Prosjekthåndbok for Forsvaret [The Norwegian Defence Project Handbook]. Oslo: the Norwegian Supreme Command of the Armed Forces.

Prinsix. (2008). Hva er Prinsix? [What is Prinsix?]. The Norwegian Education Command/ The Norwegian Defence Logistic Organisation. Retrieved February 7, 2007, from http://www.prinsix.no/prinsix/prosjektportal/prinsix/om_prinsix.

Project Management Institute. (2004). *A guide to the project management body of knowledge (PMBOK® Guide)* (3rd ed.). Newtown Square, PA: Project Management Institute.

Proposition to Parliament No. 45. (2000–2001). The restructuring of the Armed Forces in the period 2002–2005 [St.prp. nr. 45 (2000–2001) Omleggingen av Forsvaret i perioden 2002–2005]. 2001. Oslo, Norway: The Ministry of Defence.

Proposition to Parliament No. 82. (2002–2003). The building of Skjold class fast patrol boats [St.prp. nr. 82 (2002–2003) Bygging av Skjold-klasse missiltorpedobåter]. 2003. Oslo: The Norwegian Ministry of Defence.

Proposition to Parliament No. 42. (2003–2004). The further modernisation of the Norwegian armed forces 2005–2008 - Short English version. 2003. Oslo, Norway: The Norwegian Ministry of Defence.

Proposition to Parliament No. 65. (2004–2005). Supplementary appropriations and reassignment of priorities in the state budget including the national insurance 2005 [St.prp. nr. 65 (2004–2005) Tilleggsbevilgninger og omprioriteringer i statsbudsjettet medregnet folketrygden 2005]. 2005. Oslo, Norway: The Norwegian Ministry of Finance.

Proposition to Parliament No. 90. (2006–2007) The new building for the Department of Informatics at the University of Oslo (IFI2) [St.prp. nr 90 (2006-2007) Om nytt informatikkbygg ved Universitetet i Oslo (IFI2)]. 2007. Oslo, Norway: The Ministry of government administration and reform.

Pryke, S. D. (2005). Towards a social network theory of project governance. *Construction Management and Economics*, *23*(9), 927–939.

Putnam, R. D. (1993). *Making democracy work. Civic traditions in modern Italy.* Princeton, NJ: Princeton University Press.

Recommendation to Parliament No. 12. (1998–1999). [Innst. S. nr. 12 (1998–1999)]. 1998. Oslo, Norway: The Norwegian Parliament.

Recommendation to Parliament No. 342. (2000–2001). Recommendation from the Standing Committee on Defence on the restructuring of the Armed Forces in the period 2002–2005 [Innst.S.nr.342 (2000–2001) Innstilling fra forsvarskomiteen om omleggingen av Forsvaret i perioden 2002–2005]. 2001. Oslo, Norway: The Norwegian Parliament.

Recommendation to Parliament No. 12. (2001–2002). Recommendation from The Standing Committee on Education, Research and Church Affairs [Innst. S. nr. 112 (2001–2002) Innstilling fra kirke-, utdannings- og forskningskomiteen om bevilgninger på statsbudsjettet for 2002 vedkommende Utdannings- og forskningsdepartementet, Kultur- og kirkedepartementet, Nærings- og handelsdepartementet, Fiskeridepartementet og Landbruksdepartementet]. 2001. Oslo, Norway: The Norwegian Parliament.

Recommendation No. 11. (2003–2004). Recommendation from the standing committee on defence on the construction of Skjold class fast patrol boats [Innst.S. nr. 11 (2003–2004) Innstilling fra forsvarskomiteen om bygging av Skjold-klasse missiltorpedobåter] 2003. Oslo, Norway: The Norwegian Parliament.

Rhodes, R. A. W. (1996). The new governance: Governing without government. *Political Studies*, *44*, 652–667.

Rhodes, R. A. W. (1997). *Understanding governance: Policy networks, governance, reflexivity and accountability.* Buckingham, UK: Open University Press.

Rietiker, S. (2006). Der neunte Schlüssel – Vom Projektmanagment zum projektbewussten Management. Bern: Haupt.

Sager, T. (2006). The logic of critical communicative planning: Transaction cost alteration. Planning theory. Thousand Oaks, CA: Sage Publications.

Samset, K. (2003). *Project evaluation; Making investments succeed.* Tronheim, Norway: Tapir Academic Press.

Samset, K., Berg, P., & Klakegg, O. J. (2006). *Front-end Governance of Major Public Projects.* Paper presented at the EURAM 2006 Conference, Oslo, Norway.

Schmidtlein, F. A. (2004). Assumptions commonly underlying government quality assessment practices. *Tertiary Education and Management*, 10, 263–285.

Secretary of State for Defence. (2005). *Defence White Paper: Defence Industrial Strategy.* Cm 6697.

Seider, R. (2006). Optimizing project portfolios: Engineering productivity and effectiveness can be improved applying the theory of constraints. *Research Technology Management*, *49*(5), 43.

Shenhar, A. J., Dvir, D., Lehler, T., & Poli, M. (2002). One size does not fit all – True for projects – True for frameworks. *Proceedings of PMI Research Conference 2002.* Newtown Square, PA: Project Management Institute.

Shenhar, A. J., Dvir, D., Guth, W., Lechler, T., Patanacul, P., Poli, M., & Stefanovic, J. (2005). Project strategy: the missing link. *Paper presented at the 2005 Annual Meeting of the Academy of Management in the 21st Century, Honolulu, Hawaii.*

Simon, H. A. (1957). *Administrative Behavior.* New York: Macmillan.

Simons, R. (1995). *Control in an age of empowerment.* Harvard Business Review, March.

Slevin, D. P., & Pinto, J. K. (1989). Balancing strategy and tactics in project implementation. *Sloan Management Review*, Fall, 31–41.

Statistics Norway (2007) Available at http://www.ssb.no/english/ Last approached October 2007.

Statsbygg. (2004). Project Management Plan for the new building for the Department of Informatics at the University of Oslo (IFI2). Phase: Preproject [Styringsdokument for prosjektet Nybygg for informatikkmiljøene ved UiO, IFI2. Fase: Forprosjekt]. Oslo, Norway: Statsbygg (The Directorate of Public Construction and Property).

Stevens, M. (2002). *Project management pathways.* High Wycombe, UK: Association for Project Management.

Stoker, G. (1998). Governance as theory: Five propositions. *International Social Science Journal*, *50*(155), 17–28.

TerraMar. (2002). Kvalitetssikring av PPG06 Skjold serie [Quality assurance of PPG06 Skjold series]. Oslo, Norway: TerraMar AS.

TerraMar. (2003). Usikkerhetsanalyse av PPG06 Skjold serie [Uncertainty analysis of PPG06 Skjold series]. Oslo, Norway: Terramar AS.

The Defence Study. (2007). Forsvarssjefens forsvarsstudie 2007. Oslo, Norway: The Norwegian Chief of Defence.

Thiry M. (2004). Program management: A strategic decision management process. In, P. W. G. Morris & J. K. Pinto (Eds.). *The Wiley guide to managing projects* (pp. 257–287). New York: Wiley.

Torp, O; Magnussen, O.M.; Olsson, N.O.E. & Klakegg, O.J. (2006) Kostnadsusikkerhet i store statlige investeringsprosjekter (Cost Uncertainty in large Public Investment Projects; Empirical studies based on QA2.) Concept report No. 15.

Turner, J. R. (1999). *The handbook of project-based management: Improving the process for achieving strategic objectives* (2nd ed.). Maidenhead, UK: McGraw-Hill

Turner, J. R. (2006). Towards a theory of project management: The nature of the project governance and project management. International Journal of Project Management, *24*, 93–95.

Turner, J. R., & Keegan, A. (2001). Mechanisms of governance in the project-based organization: Roles of the broker and steward. *European Management Journal*, *19*(3), 254–267.

Turner, J. R., & Simister, S. J. (2000). *Gower handbook of project management.* Aldershot, UK: Gower.

Vedung, E. (2000). *Public policy and program evaluation* (2nd ed.). New Brunswick, NJ: Transaction Publishers.

Warberg, E. N. (2007). Kontrahering i prosjekters tidligfase; Forsvarets anskaffelser. [Procurement in a projects early phases; Defence acquisitions] (In Norwegian with English summary). Concept report no. 16.

Wiener, N. (1948). Cybernetics, or control and communication in the animal and the machine. New York: John Wiley & Sons.

Wikipedia. (2007). Retrieved from http://en.wikipedia.org/wiki/Government.

Williams, T. M. (2005) Assessing and building on project management theory in the light of badly over-run projects. *IEEE Transactions in Engineering Management* 52, 497–508.

Williams, T. M. (2007). Post-project reviews to gain effective lessons learned. Newtown Square, PA: Project Management Institute.

Williamson, O. E. (1979). Transaction-cost economics: The governance of contractual relations. *The Journal of Law and Economics, 22,* 233–261.

Williamson, O. E. (1981). The economics of organization: The transaction cost approach. *American Journal of Sociology, 87,* 548–577.

Williamson, O. E. (1985/1998). *The economic institutions of capitalism.* New York: The Free Press.

Winch, G. M. (2001). Governing the project process: A conceptual framework. *Construction Management and Economics, 19,* 799–808.

Winch, G. M. (2006). The Governance of project coalitions: Towards a research agenda. In D. Lowe & R. Leiringer (Eds.), *Commercial management of complex projects: Defining the discipline* (pp. 324–343). Oxford, UK: Blackwell.

Winston, R. A., & Mallick, P. (2007). *When uncertainties become assumptions in governmental planning.* PM World Today, IX(VII).

World Bank (2007) Strengthening World Bank Group Engagement on Governance and Anticorruption. Joint Ministerial Committee of the Boards of Governors of the Bank and the Fund on the Transfer of Real Resources to Developing Countries, Washington, D.C. [www.worldbank.org/htnil/extdr/comments/governancefeedback/gacpaper.pdf].

Yin, R. K. (1994). Case study research. *Design and methods* (2nd ed.). London: Sage.

Youker, R., & Brown, J. (2001). Defining the hierarchy of project objectives. Paper present at the 14th IPMA World Conference, Ljubljana, Slovenia 1998. Revised 2001.

Young, O. R. (1999). Governance in world affairs. Ithaca: Cornell University Press.

*Unless otherwise specified, the Norwegian government publication entries in the reference list are available in Norwegian only, and the titles have been translated from Norwegian to English by the authors. Norwegian titles are placed in brackets.

Appendix A Questionnaire Frameworks

FRAMEWORKS FOR PUBLIC PROJECT DEVELOPMENT AND ESTIMATION

This document is a list of questions for interviews on governance frameworks for major investment projects. It is part of a research initiative funded by PMI and Concept Research Programme and performed jointly by the University of Southampton and Norwegian University of Science and Technology.

The governance framework of the United Kingdom is often regarded as the established state-of-the-art governance regime, and the Norwegian counterpart is a new and different approach to the same issues. In order to extract more knowledge about governance of major investment projects and the consequences for planning of such projects in early stages (particularly cost and time), the research includes an analysis of these two frameworks. The questionnaire helps us produce comparable descriptions of the frameworks for analysis. This questionnaire is important because it permits us to be able to describe the governance frameworks systematically and to make a meaningful comparison. It includes background and characteristics of the established frameworks in the two countries.

The next step in our research initiative will be analyzing two cases (real projects) in each country that were planned under the mentioned frameworks. In these case studies, we will look into how the frameworks influence cost estimation and time planning.

Our main hypothesis is that the framework under which the investment project is planned and executed is important in determining the effectiveness of cost estimation and reducing the problem of cost overrun.

It is important to have a clear understanding of the frameworks and their characteristics when we look for the underlying causality or influence to explain the effect on project cost and time.

The questionnaire is divided into three parts:

1. The introduction,
2. The framework, and
3. Governance elements and principles

We intend to perform the interview as a semistructured interview following the headlines in this questionnaire. Feel free to address the questions in your own way, but please read through it all before we start.

Thank you for your kind help and the time you spend in giving this information.

Terry Williams   **Ole Jonny Klakegg**
Professor, School of Management   Research Director, Concept Program
University of Southampton   Norwegian University of Science
                                                                          and Technology

1. THE INTRODUCTION

A. Background

This point is important for setting the stage needed to understand and explain the framework's initiation and development. Please explain to us the situation in the period when the current governance framework was established:

- Political setting (Who was in power? democratic system, political traditions)
- Administrative setting (Who was responsible for what? different sectors etc.)
- Social economics (economic situation at the time of initiation, trends)
- Social setting (especially at the time the framework was initiated, trends)
- Judicial setting (constitutional, commercial)
- Traditional market mode of operation (transactions or relations, sectors)
- Triggering incident (What started the development of current framework?)
- Initiators (Who initiated? who made the decisions?)
- What was the espoused aim of the initiators in originally initiating the development?
- Political and administrative anchoring (Who is responsible, and Who are the important stakeholders?)
- Development process (What means have (typically) been used to develop the framework and promote its use?)
- When was the framework officially introduced?

2. THE FRAMEWORK

B. Explicitly Stated Purpose of the Framework

This point identifies the official policy, the statement(s) the framework is funded on.

- Does the framework have a clear objective?
- Any explicit statement of purpose (political) made by the decision makers?

The following two categories give the most concrete descriptions and characteristics of the framework. This is where we will look for causality or influence to explain the effect on cost and time in projects. At all points, answer the question why (if it is not evident from the previous points).

C. Current Status of the Framework (please describe)
- Explicitly stated ends/goals for the framework (and/or responsible party)
- Governance principles (explicitly stated and implicit)
- Framework elements (control measures, arenas for coordination, etc.)
- Framework structure (how elements are put together and interact)
- Vertical integration (level of integration, value chain)
- Horizontal integration (across sectors)
- Extent and control of outside engagement (private sector engagement in governance procedures)

D. Current Process
- What is the policy/strategy of implementation?
- Describe the organization (structure, levels, anchoring within the public administration)
- Roles and parties within the organization supporting/operating the framework
- Users (sectors, levels, etc.)
- How is the framework promoted/informed about available to users?
- Results of the implemented framework (performance measurement, evaluations)
- Any characteristic/important changes in the political or administrative setting during the working period of the framework? What are the consequences?
- Is the effect of the framework assessed to ensure it meets its objectives in a complex world?
- Are regulatory impact assessments carried out?
- What changes occurred in the framework during its working period?

3. GOVERNANCE ELEMENTS AND PRINCIPLES

E. Framework Elements Concerning Cost Estimation and Time Planning
- Are there any explicit statements or framework elements specifically addressing the development of cost and time estimates in the established framework? Which?
- What are the governance principles concerning cost estimation and cost control?
- Has there been any systematic analysis of the effect of these principles under the current framework?

F. Governance Principles in Complexity (optional)
- Does the framework help to establish a common worldview for individuals' action?
- Does the framework help to establish a system to stabilize key players' orientation, expectations, and rules of conduct?
- Does the framework differentiate between projects based on
  - their level of complexity?
  - asset specificity?
  - uncertainty?
  - other?
- Does the framework include any mechanisms (e.g., practices or models) to reduce complexity?
- Are there any methods within the framework for coordinating actions across various social forces?
- What are the principles for distributing risk among participants in projects?
- Does the framework ensure that the contractor cannot exhibit collusive behavior, abuse of dominant position, etc?
- Is there any mechanism to trigger governance processes in response to turbulence in the project environment?
- Does the framework help develop the capacity for dynamic social learning?

Appendix B Questionnaire Case Study

QUESTIONNAIRE FOR FOLLOW-UP INTERVIEW

Prepare to answer these questions and to share documentation of the main points to each answer. The questions are deliberately formed to be quite open to allow room for the respondent's personal experience and opinions to supplement the documented findings.

A. Overview of the Project Process
1. Based on the first round of interviews and other sources, we have made a timeline describing the important events and decisions concerning the project.
    a. Go through the timeline and add your comments before the meeting.
    b. In the meeting, review the timeline for corrections and supplement.
2. What was your role and personal focus at different stages of the development?

B. Framework Specific Questions
3. How did the **external quality assurance**, interact with the project process?
    a. What were the consequences of the interaction?
4. How did the project organization respond/adapt to QA2?
    a. What procedures were established (existing and new) to meet QA2?
    b. What governance principles were established (existing and new)?
    c. What methods and tools were used (existing and new)?
    d. What documents were prepared (existing and new)?
5. Describe interactions and discussions involving the assessment team, the project organization, the government agency and the responsible ministry(ies) during the external assessment.
    a. What was the focus in these discussions?
    b. What were the consequences for the project's cost estimates, time planning or organization?

C. Result Questions

6. What was the impact of the interactions between the project's own planning processes and the QA2 processes?
   a. Did it identify conflicts or deviations?
   b. Did it change working procedures, documents, conclusions?
   c. Did it alter the process or results of the planning process or the final decisions?
   d. Did it set a new focus or identify important or potential risks/improvements?
   e. Did it change the level of confidence within the project or between the parties involved?
7. What is the project's current status?
   a. Are there any specific signs of failure or success at this stage?

D. General Question

8. What is your personal experience with the QA process?
   a. Strengths/weaknesses of the QA scheme?